PATRICK & BEATRICE HAGGERTY LIBRARY
MOUNT MARY COLLEGE
MILWAUKEE, WISCONSIN 53222

Communication, Race, and Family: Exploring Communication in Black, White, and Biracial Families

D1526065

LEA's COMMUNICATION SERIES
Jennings Bryant/Dolf Zillmann, General Editors

For a complete list of other titles in LEA's Communication Series, please contact Lawrence Erlbaum Associates, Publishers.

Communication, Race, and Family: Exploring Communication in Black, White, and Biracial Families

Edited by

Thomas J. Socha
Old Dominion University

Rhunette C. Diggs
University of Louisville

1999

LAWRENCE ERLBAUM ASSOCIATES, PUBLISHERS
Mahwah, New Jersey   London

Copyright © 1999 by Lawrence Erlbaum Associates, Inc.
All rights reserved. No part of this book may be reproduced in any
form, by photostat, microfilm, retrieval system, or any other
means, without prior written permission of the publisher.

Lawrence Erlbaum Associates, Inc., Publishers
10 Industrial Avenue
Mahwah, NJ 07430

Cover design by Kathryn Houghtaling Lacey

Library of Congress Cataloging-in-Publication Data

Communication, race, and family : exploring communication in Black,
White, and biracial families / edited by Thomas J. Socha, Rhunette C.
Diggs.
      p. cm. — (LEA's communication series)
Includes bibliographical references and index.
ISBN 0-8058-2938-5 (cloth : alk. paper) — ISBN 0-8058-2939-3 (pbk. :
alk. paper).
1. Communication in the family—United States—Cross-cultural stud-
ies. I. Socha, Thomas J. II. Diggs, Rhunette C. III. Series.
HQ535.C625   1999
302.2—dc21   98-35641
                                                  CIP

Books published by Lawrence Erlbaum Associates are printed on acid-free
paper, and their bindings are chosen for strength and durability.

Printed in the United States of America
10 9 8 7 6 5 4 3 2 1

302.2
C 734S
1999

Contents

Foreword

Molefi Kete Asante
Temple University

Communication, Race, and Family: Exploring Communication in Black, White, and Biracial Families focuses on the communicative situations that develop in the context of the family, the foundational institution for our racial views and perspectives. Now that communicationists have entered the intellectual discussion on the different kinds of families and their varying communicative and social modalities around the issue of race, the discourse is sure to be richer and deeper. After all, it is through communication that all of our social values and behaviors are initiated and validated. Sociologists have been the primary researchers in this area for several decades and to some observers their work often has been completely linear. No scholarly discipline can monopolize the study of race, as the recent forays into the discussion by political scientists, Afrocentrists, and philosophers have shown. With this volume we have a very real advance into the area of family communication, race relations, and racism.

A few years ago the sociologist John Stanfield decried what he described as a lock on the study of race by the logical positivists. According to Stanfield, there was a lack of critical reflection about methodology in matters dealing with race and ethnicity (Stanfield & Rutledge, 1993). Although his concern was with ideologically determined and biased productions of knowledge, in the end he succumbed to asking authors in his book to lay out the parameters of traditional methods and ways to improve them. What Thomas Socha and Rhunette Diggs have attempted in *Communication, Race, and Family: Exploring Communication in Black, White, and Biracial Families* is to extend and deepen the critical reflection on the communication of race and its methodology. The authors chosen for the volume have made every attempt to advance the idea that communication matters even if race does not in some specific instances matter as much. They are on the cutting edge not simply of the study of race, but also of the study of communication.

This collection of skillfully designed studies addresses the complex social phenomena surrounding raciality and biraciality from several provocative and useful angles. Among the more important discussions in such a collection of intelligently written works is always the question of whether or not race exists. Actually it is a generally accepted practice by most social scientists and hence communicationists to claim race as a social construction. There is nothing wrong with such a claim. However, it does not necessarily change the reality that, in U.S. society, this particular social construction (i.e., race), covers considerable territory in the lives of ordinary people. For this reason, if for no other, Socha and Diggs have endeavored to bring us a volume that speaks to the substance of human interactions around this socially constructed concept.

I have found in these articles an extensive conversation with the best literature and the most enduring studies on race. But what is different in these studies and essays is the fact that the locus of social construction, opinions, beliefs, and attitudes about race is seen to be the family. Exploring the multiple layers of familial interactions in three types of families, Black, White, and biracial, the authors suggest that more importance should be attached to the domestic realm than social scientists have done heretofore. In fact, numerous studies have been made suggesting school and the media as major players in the creation of attitudes about everything from race to politics. Yet we are confronted with a substantial amount of scholarship that demonstrates the role of the family in shaping racial attitudes. This means that the complex of attitudes and behaviors that are central to racist actions may have more than one initiating source. Indeed, now that these scholars have clearly thrown out the idea for others to pick up in this area of research, we are sure to have a veritable trail of other works.

This book, like Eshu in Yoruba mythology, takes us to the crossroads. Because the editors wanted to intersect the areas of race, communication, and families, they have been able to make a giant leap into the discourse on the future of America. Although the convergence of race, communication, and families seems so simple, it was obviously not an easy task to conceptualize, as one can see from the variety of articles that constitute this volume. With expertness and professionalism, the editors have crafted an important work that will enliven the discourse on race for a long time to come.

The ten chapters in this book, as the title suggests, concentrate on communication in Black, White, and biracial families. The scope is wide, but it does not cover families who are biracial by virtue of an African and Asian or Asian and European combination. This is reserved for another volume. Nevertheless, delving into African and European biracial families because of their numbers is a remarkable achievement of communication scholarship. We are granted extended discussions by a number of authors on this rather "hidden" topic in the discourse on race.

The authors of each chapter pursue their own interests, which they demonstrate adds to the racial questions under discussion. The value of this is that many relevant issues of society and history are discussed as necessary. Some authors are more comfortable studying child-rearing practices, others deal with biracial couples and communication, and still others seek to know what White children say about race and culture. I believe that the very heterogeneity and diversity of these case studies suggest the dynamism inherent in such a volume. There is perhaps no standardized way to investigate the problems of race and communication. Hence, Stanfield's concern, expressed in frustration, about the logical positivist method may not succeed here where communicationists are seriously trying every method to explicate the nature of race and culture in the U.S. family. This book, by bringing together outstanding scholars who challenge the crossroads, is a valuable source for theorists, opinion-makers, legislators, and the general public.

REFERENCE

Stanfield, J. H., & Rutledge, D. (Eds.). (1993). *Race and ethnicity in research methods*. Thousand Oaks, CA: Sage.

Preface

Some U.S. institutions have acknowledged their cultural diversity and have taken their first steps on a long and difficult road toward social justice. In education, publishers have "implemented procedures and processes ... to monitor ... and guard against social bias and ethnocentrism" (Macmillan/McGraw-Hill, 1993). In media, researchers have examined television portrayals of African Americans and European Americans (U.S. Commission on Civil Rights, 1977) and scrutinized family comedy–drama series for ethnic portrayal characteristics (Sweeper, 1984). In the social sciences, too, researchers have sought to understand race and children's interpersonal relations (e.g., Holmes, 1995) and have attacked racist perspectives and practices. For example, Greenfield and Cocking (1994), child development researchers, went so far as to say that "the field of developmental psychology is an ethnocentric one dominated by a European-American perspective" (p. ix). Others have developed strategies to uproot racism (e.g., see Katz, 1976, 1978; Katz & Taylor, 1988; Kivel, 1996). Groups of citizens are trying "to convince the Census Bureau and the Office of Management and Budget to add a multiracial category to the existing census form in time for the 2000 Census" (Townsel, 1996, p. 46). And, most recently, President Clinton has been sponsoring town hall meetings as a part of his Presidential Initiative on Race (President's Initiative on Race, 1998).

These encouraging and controversial signs of an emerging concern for diversity are heartening. However, if society desires to continue journeying toward social justice, then participation from all segments of society is necessary. Surprisingly, one societal institution, often mentioned in discussions of race, but understudied in terms of its unique role in race relations, is the family. This is especially surprising because family life is the first and foremost location for forming understandings of self and society (Mead, 1934), and family life continues to impact individuals across the life span (Diggs, 1994, 1996).

Communication in families plays a foundational role in many aspects of society, such as socialization of the young, but the particular focus of this volume is on how communication in families affects understandings of "race" and race relations (see Hecht, Collier, & Ribeau, 1993; Socha, Sanchez-Hucles, Bromley, & Kelly, 1995). Family life is the primary context in which children first learn how to use communication to manage dialectical tensions that are inherent in diverse, multicultural societies, such as integration–segregation and under-standing–bigotry. Also, the content and meanings of family communication about other races that takes place inside families are bound to some under-standing of ourselves and society. No longer can we continue to speculate about the kinds of messages concerning race exchanged among family members at home. Researchers in the social sciences, especially in communication, must recognize that the sanctuary of home may be generating the keys to understand-ing problems concerning diversity. Thus, there is a need for studies of communi-cation at the crossroads of race and family.

All family members are involved in racial matters, but children have emerged as an immediate focus of concern. Young children first learn about race and begin to acquire initial communication strategies for interacting with ra-cially different others from parents and caregivers (Greenfield, 1994). However, not all of the strategies to which they are exposed are prosocial or respectful of diversity. Holmes (1995), for example, in her observations of kindergartners' in-teractions in their classrooms, found that some European-American children made racist remarks about African Americans as they played with Euro-pean-American friends. In the absence of research, we can only speculate about how these children acquired these remarks. However, given the extensive amount of time that young children spend at home, communicating with family members and consuming media would be among the most likely sources.

Exposure to media at home, specifically television, is, of course, another source of information about race that requires scrutiny, especially because the images seen on television may not be serving the cause of diversity (Merritt & Stroman, 1993). It is assumed that television can affect race relations (e.g., by portraying negative stereotypes); however, in remote geographical locations, where populations are often homogenous, television programs might actually represent the only means of interracial contact for family members. If this is the case, then parents' responses to televised images of race (e.g., inattention, ste-reotyping, and/or making racist comments) would be an especially important family communication factor that might affect how children form understand-ings about people who look and behave in ways that are different from them-selves. Black families also spend more money per capita on electronic entertainment, and Black children view more television than do their White counterparts, even after socioeconomic class is considered (see Parks, chap. 4, this volume). This makes studying the interrelationships between and among media, family communication, and race also a prominent concern.

This volume contends that in addition to education, the media, and govern-ment, the map of U.S. race relations needs to depict families and family relation-ships as central to matters of race. Given this, the volume takes a first step toward understanding the role that family communication plays in society's move toward racial justice by reporting explorations that focus on the role of family communication in understanding and managing race relationships in African-American, European-American, and biracial families. Indeed, this volume is the first book in the communication field to explore the crossroads of family communication and ethnic cultural relations from the vantage points of African Americans, European Americans, and biracial Americans. Collectively, the chapters begin to explore how and why race matters in family communication theorizing, family communication research methodology, family communication education, and family communication practice.

This volume also provides an initial forum for African-American, European-American, and biracial communication scholars who are interested in family communication and diversity to report on their work, break new ground, and together set an agenda for the future. The volume seeks to span not only existing boundaries between African-American, European-American, and biracial families, but also those that exist between African-American, European-American, and biracial family communication researchers.

Chapter proposals for the volume were solicited through international (International Communication Association, International Network for the Study of Personal Relationships) and national (National Communication Association) professional association newsletters. An extensive effort was also made to contact prominent African-American and European-American communication scholars whose work was somehow linked to families. This resulted in a volume that is truly an interethnic collaboration between the coeditors, a White, European-American male and a Black, African-American female, who, along with African-American, European-American, and multiethnic researchers, established scholars as well as newcomers, seek to begin, and hopefully continue, this most important dialogue.

ACKNOWLEDGMENTS

This book is the direct result of the high quality work of a number of professionals to whom I owe thanks: my coeditor Rhunette Diggs, with whom I continue to learn about race; Linda Bathgate, acquisitions editor at Lawrence Erlbaum Associates, for seeing the importance of the project, for her support, and for her helpful staff; all the contributors who responded to our deadlines and suggestions; and Gary Edgerton, chair of the Communication and Theatre Arts Department at Old Dominion University for his insights and support. I am grateful for the many conversations about the book with family members and friends, too numerous to list, that inspired and instructed me. In particular, I want to pay tribute and thank my mother, Mary, for teaching me by her words and example to be caring and loving to everyone. And to my brother, Mike, on whom I can always count for penetrating insights and lively dinner conversation, I extend my admiration, my support, and my love. Finally, to my wife, Diana, and children, Stephanie and Paul, who help me keep sight of what really matters, my continued love.

—*Thomas J. Socha*

While I pursued my doctoral degree, Tom Socha expressed scholarly curiosity in my research endeavors. His welcomed, consistent inquiry about my academic well-being has brought us to this place. I am very grateful for his professionalism, excellent scholarship, and mentoring. Other professionals whom I would like to acknowledge include Linda Bathgate, acquisitions editor at Lawrence Erlbaum Associates, for her support on this project; contributors who believed in this work and persevered with us; Gloria Robinson, executive director of P.R.E.V.A.I.L. (a parental education initiative), for our frequent conversations about diverse families; and those colleagues who have provided encouragement. Many thanks to my spiritual family and friends. I owe much gratitude to my early family communication context: My parents, Ophelia and Jasper, maintained a hopeful attitude toward life as they raised nine children in southern Georgia. As my first teacher, my mother instilled in me a respect and concern for God, myself, and others. I appreciate the support of my husband, Larry, who has accompanied me late nights (more times than he cares to remember) to copy centers and postal services; and our children, Angela, Anthony, Aarika, and Alisha, who provide ongoing inspiration for my work.

—*Rhunette C. Diggs*

REFERENCES

Diggs, R. C. (1994). *Perceptions of parent and peer communication, racial esteem, and support among African-American adolescents.* Unpublished doctoral dissertation. The Ohio State University, Columbus, OH.

Diggs, R. C. (1996, March). *Communicating identity: The source of our selves.* Paper presented at the annual meeting of the National Black Family Conference, Louisville, KY.

Greenfield, P. M. (1994). Independence and interdependence as developmental scripts: Implications for theory, research, and practice. In P. M. Greenfield & R. R. Cocking (Eds.), *Cross-cultural roots of minority child development* (pp. 1–37). Hillsdale, NJ: Lawrence Erlbaum Associates.

Greenfield, P. M., & Cocking, R. R. (1994). Preface. In P. M. Greenfield & R. R. Cocking (Eds.), *Cross-cultural roots of minority child development* (pp. ix–xix). Hillsdale, NJ: Lawrence Erlbaum Associates.

Hecht, M., Collier, M. J., & Ribeau, S. A. (1993). *African American communication: Ethnic identity and cultural interpretation.* Newbury Park, CA: Sage.

Holmes, R. M. (1995). *How young children perceive race.* Thousand Oaks, CA: Sage.

Katz, J. H. (1978). *White awareness: Handbook for anti-racism training.* Norman, OK: University of Oklahoma Press.

Katz, P. A. (1976). The acquisition of racial attitudes in children. In P. A. Katz (Ed.), *Towards the elimination of racism* (pp. 125–154). New York: Pergamon Press.

Katz, P. A., & Taylor, D. A. (Eds.). (1988). *Eliminating racism: Profiles in controversy.* New York: Plenum.

Kivel, P. (1996). *Uprooting racism: How White people can work for racial justice.* Philadelphia: New Society Publishers.

MacMillan/McGraw Hill. (1993). *Reflecting diversity: Multicultural guidelines for educational publishing professionals.* New York: Author.

Mead, G. H. (1934). *Mind, self & society: From the standpoint of a behaviorist.* Chicago: University of Chicago Press.

Merritt, B., & Stroman, C. A. (1993). Black family imagery and interactions on television. *Journal of Black Studies, 23,* 492–499.

President's Initiative on Race. (1998). *One America in the 21st century: The president's initiative on race* [Brochure]. Washington, DC: U.S. Government Printing Office.

Socha, T. J., Sanchez-Hucles, J., Bromley, J., & Kelly, B. (1995). Invisible parents and children: African-American parent–child communication. In T. J. Socha & G. H. Stamp (Eds.), *Parents, children and communication: Frontiers of theory and research* (pp. 127–145). Hillsdale, NJ: Lawrence Erlbaum Associates.

Sweeper, G. (1984). The image of the black family and the white family in American prime-time television programming 1970–1980. *Dissertation Abstracts International, 44,* 1964A.

Townsel, L. J. (1996, November). *Ebony Magazine,* pp. 44, 46, 48.

U.S. Commission on Civil Rights. (1977). *Window dressing on the set: Women and minorities on television.* Washington, DC: U.S. Government Printing Office.

1

At the Crossroads of Communication, Race, and Family: Toward Understanding Black, White, and Biracial Family Communication

Thomas J. Socha
Old Dominion University

Rhunette C. Diggs
University of Louisville

> *I prefer to think of a-world-in-which-race-does-not-matter as something other than a theme park, or a failed and always-failing dream, or as a father's house of many rooms. I am thinking of it as home.*
>
> —Morrison (1997, p. 3)

Individuals in the United States continue to talk about "race."[1] During 1997, communities across the United States held public town-hall meetings where thousands of citizens gathered and talked about racial issues and problems.

---

[1]Use of the term *race* (which refers to a biological grouping) is problematic for many reasons that will be considered in the volume. However, because use of the term *race* remains widespread and common, we chose to use it here for ease and consistency. However, our usage of *race* is closer in meaning to the term *ethnic group,* which refers to peoples whose "origins … are constituted through a shared sense of tradition, peoplehood, heritage, orientation to the past religion, language, ancestry … " (Hecht, Collier, Ribeau, 1993, p. 16). The use of quotation marks around the term *race* in the body of this chapter reflects the range of acceptance of the term *race* by the contributors to this volume and by society at large.

These meetings, convened as a part of President Clinton's initiative on "race," intended to "move [us] toward a stronger, more just, and more united America, a country that offers opportunity and fairness to all for all Americans" (President's Initiative on Race, 1998, p. 3).

Historians would remind us that conversations (from monologue to dialogue) about "race" began long before President Clinton's initiative. For example, Takaki (1993) took readers from "before Columbus" to the 1992 Los Angeles racial riots to view the nation's history with a variety of "races." Reimer's (1972) edited volume chronicled the range of social, scientific, political, and economic discussions (including reference to the 1968 President's Advisory Commission on Civil Disorders that was in response to racial violence of the summer of 1967) about racism in the United States. Hidalgo, McDowell, and Siddle's (1990) edited volume examined racism in education. The nation's libraries are filled with similar historical conversations. But what are the implications of the current conversations about "race" that are occurring in our nation?

At school, classroom discussions about "race" seek to raise children's awareness of cultural practices, increase their appreciation for cultural diversity, and improve their intercultural competence. At school, children also read about "race," view instructional media about "race," and celebrate "race" in school-wide festivals. And, the good news is that children's books and instructional media continue to improve, as educational publishers pay greater attention to presenting ethnically diverse images and content (Macmillan/ McGraw-Hill, 1993). Of course, while at school, children also talk informally among themselves about "race." In an example provided by Holmes (1995), Kathy and Anne (African-American kindergartners) try to understand "racial" identity in the context of informal classroom interaction about a biracial student:

> Kathy: There's brown babies and white babies.
> Anne: Ricky has a black mommy. [He nods yes to the group.]
> Kathy: So.
> Anne: And he's white.
> Kathy: And his brother's black. So.
> Anne: He was born like that. His brother's brown. (p. 103)

Television in the United States continues to broadcast documentaries, entertainment shows, news programs, and talk shows that regularly feature "race," "racial" issues, and conversations about "race" (e.g., see Parks, chap. 4, this volume; Sweeper, 1984; U.S. Commission on Civil Rights, 1977). Almost daily, feature articles and editorials in newspapers remind us about "race." Films, such as *Do the Right Thing* (Lee, 1990) and *Jungle Fever* (Lee, 1991), depict dramatic struggles with racism as well as a host of difficulties that occur when people communicate about "race" in restaurants, on street corners, at work, or at home. Fictional films have also sought to raise racial awareness and serve as vehicles for change. The fictional film, *White Man's Burden* (Bender & Makano, 1995), for instance, offers a glimpse of what the world might be like if race roles were reversed, that is, White residents of the United States experiencing discrimination, oppression, and racism at the hands of Black residents of the United States, who, at least in the film, enjoyed privileges often taken for granted by Whites.

Newer forms of computer-mediated communication appear to offer a faceless (but not raceless) opportunity to denigrate other races that are different from the U.S. White form. Surfing the internet leads to sites that express sentiments such as "I'd like all niggers to die" (Personal e-mail message, September 30, 1998). An array of culturally sensitive web-sites and discussion groups also are available to converse, to counter, and to think critically about African-American culture (e.g., Listservs such as H-AFRO-AM; NCA Black Caucus; other NCA culturally sensitive caucus sites: WWW.NATCOM.ORG).

Not everyone is talking about "race," nor relating positive experiences when they do talk. Research shows that when African Americans and European Americans do talk about "race" (or anything else), they often bring to these discussions divergent points of view, differing values, culture-specific experiences, and contrasting communication styles as well as similarities (e.g., see Asante, 1981b; Hecht, Collier & Ribeau, 1993; Kochman, 1981). The kinds of problems that occur during Black–White discussions are illustrated vividly in the film, *Jungle Fever* (Lee, 1991). Producer/writer/director Spike Lee portrayed an African-American male and Italian-American female struggling to develop an intimate relationship (extramarital) amid the clashing viewpoints and divergent communication styles of their families and friends, who equally (and hotly) contested the merits and drawbacks of interracial romantic relationships. The film concluded by a return to the current segregated, racially troubled status quo; the couple ended their relationship, returned to their "homes," faced their devastated families, and continued to talk among themselves while living "separate" lives.

CHAPTER PURPOSE

Ultimately, if discussions by U.S. residents about "race" are to broaden racial awareness, broaden racial understanding, and improve the quality of communication between African Americans and European Americans, or, more generally, improve the status quo, then all facets of society must participate in constructive discussions about race, be open to learning, and keep the focus on the goal of developing values and skills that move us toward living successfully and peacefully in a culturally diverse society. The President's initiative on race is a good start, but much work remains to be done.

This chapter, and the entire volume, argues that the hope for managing the United States' troubles with "race" lies not only in communicating about "race" at public meetings, at school, and in the media, but also, and more fundamentally, with families communicating constructively about "race" at home. Home is where lessons about the merits of diversity and how to navigate diverse environments can be taught and lived. Home is where society's youngest members can be taught how to improve their competency in communicating with an increasingly ethnically diverse world. And, finally, home can and should be "a site clear of racist detritus; a place where race both matters and is rendered impotent" (Morrison, 1997, p. 9).

First, we offer a rationale for studying "race" in the context of family communication. This includes offering brief narratives about our individual, lived experiences that link us, the editors/authors, to this project. Second, we review conceptual and theoretical approaches to studying "race" in the context of family communication. In particular, we highlight the various theoretical approaches represented by the chapters in this volume as well as consider the merits of applying models of intercultural transformation (Kim & Ruben, 1996) and intercultural sensitivity development (Bennett, 1986) to families. We conclude by reviewing selected methodological approaches used to study "race" in the context of family communication and describe various obstacles encountered by the editors and authors in conducting research for chapters appearing in this volume.

RATIONALE FOR STUDYING "RACE" IN FAMILY COMMUNICATION

Families exercise a primary influence on children's ethnic socialization (Aboud, 1977; Daniel & Daniel, chap. 2, this volume; Diggs, chap. 6, this volume; Ferguson, chap. 3, this volume; Goodman, 1964; P. Katz, 1976; Porter, 1971) and this influence extends across the life span (e.g., see Cross, 1981; Diggs, 1994; Mead, 1934; Rosenthal, 1987). *Ethnic socialization* is defined as "the developmental processes by which children acquire the behaviors, perceptions, values, and attitudes of an ethnic group, and come to see themselves and others as members of such groups" (Rotheram & Phinney, 1987, p. 11). However, because family is an element of the "deep structure of culture" (Laubacher Henchy & Samovar, 1995), its impact is often superficially considered when theorizing about societal problems, in general, and society's problems with "race" in particular. According to Burr (1990), "Most people ... agree with the statement that the family is important, but for most people this is merely a glib statement with a cliche rather than a fundamental belief that influences how they think ... The familial factors are thought about so little that they are virtually ignored" (p. 270). This volume, continuing previous work (Diggs, 1995; Socha, Sanchez-Hucles, Bromley, & Kelly, 1995), seeks to begin to remedy this neglect by examining "race" as both an outcome of family communication as well as a factor that influences children's communication development in families.

Second, family communication is a significant context where constructing and managing individuals' ethnic or "racial" identity takes place (Alexander & LeBlanc, chap. 9, this volume; Dainton, chap. 7, this volume; Davilla, chap. 5, this volume; Diggs, chap. 6, this volume; Gopaul-McNicol, 1992; Hecht, Collier, & Ribeau, 1993; Vaughan,1987). According to Boykin and Toms (1985), building on the work of Du Bois (1903/1969), for African Americans, identity management is complex and involves locating identity in "three distinctly different realms of experience ... mainstream, minority, and black cultural" (p. 38), where *mainstream* refers to White culture, *minority* refers to membership in an oppressed group, and *Black culture* refers to values handed down across generations (e.g., see King, 1976; Sudarkasa, 1981, for discussions of African cultural practices among African Americans). The process of constructing and managing ethnic identity is made even more complex in biracial family systems (Orbe, chap. 8, this volume). In addition, families use communication to care for injuries resulting from assaults to its members' personal and racial identities (Daniel & Daniel, chap. 2, this volume; Diggs, chap. 6, this volume; Ferguson, chap. 3, this volume). Personal and racial identity injuries may or may not heal completely and may present long-term complications to racial interaction (see Daniel & Daniel, chap. 2, this volume for a discussion about first, second, and third degree "racial" burns).

Third, family communication is an important source of information about members of ethnic/racial groups other than one's own (Katz, 1978) as well as a context for learning about how to communicate with people of ethnic groups other than one's own (Socha et al., 1995; Ward, 1990). Family members acquire information either directly from each other by asking questions and talking, or indirectly, such as a White child watching how a White parent speaks with a Black store manager. Of course, White children, living in ethnically homogenous environments, may have no contact with African Americans other than through television (Davilla, chap. 5, this volume; Parks, chap. 4, this volume). This is especially troubling given the preponderance of White faces on TV.[2] In addition to talking about race at home, people can take courses in family communication for information about cultural communication practices in families. However, there is work to be done on this front too, as family communication curricula tend to be Eurocentric (Socha & Beigle, chap. 10, this volume).

Fourth, some families build homes troubled by racist foundations, or "windowless prison[s] ... thick-walled, impenetrable container[s] from which no cry can be heard" (Morrison, 1997, p. 4). However, other families "redecorate, re-

---

[2]For an example depicting the reverse of this, see the film, *White Man's Burden* (Bender & Nakano, 1995), where a White child channel surfs through an endless stream of prime-time television shows featuring exclusively Black people as news anchors, game show hosts, and so on.

design, even reconceive the racial house without forfeiting a home [of their own]" (p. 4). All families can "convert a racist house into a race-specific yet nonracist home" (p. 5) by improving their cultural communication understanding and practices (Socha & Beigle, chap. 10, this volume). This process is not easy. "Racist" feelings and racial discomfort may go unspoken, but still be "given off" (Goffman, 1959) by subtle nonverbal cues, such as when a White child sees his or her White mother tighten her grip on her purse upon seeing a Black man join them on an elevator.

Considered together, these reasons provide a preliminary rationale for studying the crossroads of communication, "race," and family and offer starting points from which to begin to explore "race" in the context of family communication. We, too, struggle with "race" and "racial" issues in our own professional and family lives and bring our own personal viewpoints to this project. In this spirit, we offer brief accounts of our relevant, lived experiences concerning "race."

Tom's Story

"Dad, I don't like Tasha's hair," said Stephanie, commenting on one of the children in the Public Broadcasting System (PBS) TV show, *Barney and Friends.* "Oh, really? Why?" I said. "I don't know, it just looks different." Stephanie was three years old when this exchange took place. At that moment, I could only think to say, "Tasha's hair was pretty and there are many kinds of hair and ways to wear hair and they are all equally nice." Later that evening, I brought the exchange to my wife's attention (she's a gifted, first-grade teacher). Together, we decided to follow up on that mornings' teachable moment, which otherwise would have been lost.

The next day, my wife suggested that we shop for a new doll for Stephanie. At the store, we took two Black dolls from the shelf and asked Stephanie which doll she wanted. She chose "Christie," a Black doll dressed in a swim suit, swim fins, mask, and snorkel. Stephanie enjoyed her new doll and proudly showed it to many White people. As she showed her doll, I noticed some of their reactions: "Oh, what an interesting doll." "Oh, Stephanie, you have a Black doll? That's nice." "I bet that your dad bought you that doll" (one of my favorite reactions). "Where did you get the Black doll?" Another common reaction to Christie was a subtle eyebrow raise accompanied by a quick smile before moving to another topic.

These reactions reminded me of Helms' (1990) "contact" stage of racial identity development: a stage characterized by "limited interracial social or occupational interaction with Blacks unless the interaction is initiated by Blacks ... " (p. 57). Furthermore, contact individuals "generally have positive feelings about the 'idea' of Blacks and fair treatment of Blacks ... though state anxiety may be present when actual interactions with Blacks are experienced or anticipated" (p. 57). Considering that contact is Helms' first of six stages of White racial identity development, there is definitely room to grow.

Regarding the effectiveness of our minilesson, a few weeks later we noticed evidence that it had begun to pay off. Stephanie commented, again during *Barney and Friends*, that she now liked Tasha's hair and wanted to wear ribbons like Tasha's.

To some, this may appear to be a very minor lesson. However, my hope is that it might be a first lesson (among many) that lays the foundation to help Stephanie (and her brother Paul) to make progress toward Helms' (1990) last stage of "autonomy," in which they will "actively seek opportunities to learn from other cultural groups ... [and become] ... increasingly aware of how forms of oppression ... are related to racism ... " and act to eliminate them (p. 66).

My children and future grandchildren will live in a global world far more diverse and complex than the world of my childhood or even adulthood. They will encounter, live, work, learn, and form relationships with myriad individuals not all of whom are of their ethnic heritage. Basically, I want them to be competent and effective at communicating with everyone they encounter: to become multicultural people.

As for myself, I am of mostly Irish and Polish heritage and grew up in an inner-city neighborhood in Chicago, populated by blue-collar families of Irish, Mexican, Polish, and Puerto Rican descent. I married Diana, a woman of Mexican and Polish heritage (who also speaks Spanish), which means our children, Stephanie and Paul, are Irish-Mexican-Polish-Americans (ordered alphabetically). My childhood neighborhood afforded me direct contact with European (Irish, Polish) and Hispanic (Mexican, Puerto Rican) cultures, but little or no direct contact with African-American culture.

Of course, indirectly, I was exposed to Black culture (stereotypes and all) by my bedroom posters of Wilt Chamberlin and Kareem Adul Jabbar (then Lew Al Cinder), by watching television shows, such as *Good Times* (often) or *Soul Train* (on occasion), by seeing movies such as *Shaft* (and singing the theme song that includes lyrics like "right on" and "Can ya dig it?"), by glancing through editions of the *Black Panther Review* (often handed to me at the subway), and by playing trumpet, through which I experienced and fell in love with jazz.

When I was in college, I also recall an occasional discussion about "racial" issues during family dinners. I do not remember the details of these talks, but I do recall learning, among other things, the important value, promulgated by my Dad, of creating a home that welcomes open (at times, very heated) debate about even the most controversial topics. I remember family meals and these family discussions fondly.

My most direct and intensive contact with African Americans was during college and graduate school. Through my involvement with jazz (playing trumpet in the university's jazz band and hosting a late-night, jazz radio show), I got to talk with African-American jazz artists and learn from them. I also read many biographies and autobiographies of prominent jazz artists (Dizzy Gillespie's was one of my favorites).

Pursuing my M.A. degree at the University of Illinois Chicago facilitated forming several close relationships with African-American graduate students, some of whom I met in classes about Black communication that were taught by one of my early mentors, Professor Thomas Kochman. It was during this time that I also attended house parties where I experienced what it was like to be the only White person in attendance.

In general, these experiences and education have cultivated my appreciation, understanding, and respect for African-American culture and African culture. I continue to be inspired in my interactions with African-American colleagues, such as Rhunette, whom I have met through this project as well as with my students. In particular, a recent exchange with one of my students stands out for me. During a public speaking class that I was teaching at my university, Javon Hyland, one of my Black undergraduate students, began one of his speeches as follows:

> My hometown, Brooklyn, New York. Not the best neighborhood, but not the worst. I'm six years old. My skin is brown. My hair is black and coarse, just like all my other friends on the block. But, I'm different from them, somehow, some way. Is it because the person who cooks my meals, washes and irons my clothes, runs my bath water, and reads me bedtime stories looks nothing like me? Her skin is pale. Her hair is blond and straight; but yet I call this person my mother. My mother. How can that be? She looks nothing like me. I swear she doesn't. So after listening to my bedtime story I ask, "Mom, why are we so different?" She explains that I was fortunate enough to have a father who is Black and a mother who is White. So, I was considered biracial. I ask, "What does that mean? Am I better than you because I'm darker, or are you better than me because you are lighter?" She begins to explain to the best of her ability to her six-year-old child that no one person is better than the next. We are all considered equal. In the sight of God, there is no color. (Hyland, 1998)

The thesis of Javon's speech was that he was tired of all the negative messages society gives to biracial individuals from both sides of the racial divide. But, he was thankful for the supportive environment created at home, a home filled with his mother's classical and country music and his rap and R & B. As I heard his words, I could not help but hear the echo of Morrison's quote that begins this chapter, and thought to myself, what a wonderful home that must be.

Rhunette's Story

In the summer of 1992 my oldest child, Angela, 12 years old at the time, came home from a volunteer experience at the local library and said to me, "Mom, the Black girl that I volunteer with at the library says that I act gangsta—too Black." To help her deal with this perceived negative evaluation (*gangsta* connotes Black street culture, see Anderson, 1994; it is a term used by inner city and suburban young Blacks, predominantly, to mean a range of behaviors such as expressiveness, Black English, slang, style of dress, and romanticism with violence); we talked about her feelings and how unfortunate it was that we (humans) look at a particular behavior and say that is who a person is. I also penned a poem for my daughter to offset internalization of this perceived negative evaluation.

Two years later, Angela, then 14 years of age, in her first year of high school, came home crying. I captured the experience at the time in an anecdote. Here is a synopsis of that narrative:

> My 14-year-old daughter was hurt badly today. Her special friend, the one who makes her shine, laugh, and somewhat giddy, told her that their friendship must end. No, she's not terminally ill, nor is she leaving the school where they both attend, nor is she concerned about rumors of friendship values, but it is an old, ugly, sharp instrument that leaves gaping wounds that tore into my child's and her friend's hearts. This instrument leaves wounds and sores that even though bandaged and occasionally aired, often erupt full-blown, puffy, and runny. This instrument of pain is called racism.

There were two separate incidents—the first involved two Black girls and the second involved a Black girl and a White girl. The first incident was between acquaintances and the second between friends. My daughter no longer associates with either girl. Perhaps this would have been the case, regardless, but the insertion of prejudice and racism created a distasteful situation for my daughter. I viewed the first incident as prejudice (or prejudging) arising out of the human tendency to implicitly categorize people and behaviors without obtaining sufficient information (J. Katz, 1978). The Black girl used limited information about my daughter (based on her exposure to Black images from a variety of sources, particularly television and music media) to make some statement. During the next few weeks, she and my daughter continued to work together until the program ended without further stereotype incidents reported. I assessed the second incident as racism because the White father explicitly told his daughter that she could not be friends with my daughter because of my daughter's race. Intimacy with the Black race is viewed as intolerable after a certain age. This White father's behavior seemed to reflect J. Katz' (1978) statement about the White community:

> The attitude seems to be that if minorities are not physically present the problem of racism does not exist [the White father and family expressed a religious doctrine]. Whites easily forget—indeed are seldom aware—that they too are part of a group and are subject to ethnocentrism and a unique collective group experience. (p. 4)

I accept that racism is the belief in White supremacy (J. Katz, 1978; Reimers, 1972), and "prejudice plus power" (J. Katz, 1978, p. 51), not prejudice only. In dealing with each incident, my husband and I believed that even though both were painful, the incident of racism suggested an aspect of the U.S. culture that ran very deep and that we needed to teach our children to forever resist the implication that, because of their heritage or their color, Blacks (our children) are less than another race or ethnic group. We eventually agreed that our internal family discussions and management were sufficient to deal with these incidents. However, these incidents and other experiences with race that are captured later point to my personal and scholarly commitment to this present topic of Black and White family communication.

In 1996, I presented three different papers that, in various ways, addressed my ongoing personal and scholarly pursuits(Diggs, 1996a; 1996b; 1996c). The paper that was presented at The National Black Family Conference may be viewed as my initial, formal examination of my perspective on humanity and reflections on my academic pursuits. I referred to this posturing as an evolving-developmental-interactional perspective in which *who I am*—as I claim it or speak it—is a combination of biology and a construction of my past and becomes the central or pivotal framework for my interactions in living or the person *I am becoming* (e.g., see Hernadi, 1995). *Who I am* is stable and has been determined by biology and history (African centered). *Who I am becoming*, however, is being affected subtly and directly by my everyday interactions. As I evolve, certain interactions become chronicled as *recognition* (I take special notice; they demand my attention), which then fuels reflections (looking back on what I am processing), which help to construct the becoming self. I have recognitions of my upbringing, for example, the historical, geographical, and familial contexts; my graduate studies, particularly 1988 to 1994, for this present project; and my entry into academia as a full-time faculty person to offer my lived experiences concerning race. Brief reflections of each recognition is provided below.

As an adult, I realized, even though I was not explicitly taught to use race as a point of identification (by parents and close kin in the 1950s), race was constantly being imposed from external realities, such as racist societal structures. I grew up in a small Southern town—I like to say, "much farther south than Atlanta." The social and political atmosphere of my hometown, Bainbridge, Georgia, in the 1950s to the present, has been aptly described by journalist-author, Atabari Njeri (1990), in her factual book, *Every Good-bye Ain't Gone*. In her book, Njeri has visited Bainbridge to investigate covertly the death of her grandfather, a Black physician (who, she discovers, was politically active). She writes:

> Black people in Bainbridge had told me my grandfather was buried in Pineview Cemetery. "It's the black cemetery in the white part of town".... "The white cemetery is in the black part of town." ... Bainbridge, Georgia's "first inland port," population 12,714 then. (pp. 12–13)

During an interview, a Bainbridge White doctor (Njeri introduced herself as a newspaper reporter focusing on small-town doctors), who often had helped Njeri's grandfather with surgery, spoke of Njeri's grandfather this way: "He was a bad man ... Blacks didn't like him either. He tried to bring the NAACP in here ... He just didn't fit in ... We were all glad when he was gone" (p. 16). What

Njeri discovered about my hometown and the Black people in it was that there was little political involvement because institutional constraints created impossible choices for the poor laborers and the intellectual community. For example, one retired school teacher (interviewee) reported, "We couldn't openly contribute to the NAACP and keep our jobs." In the Black sphere of sociopolitical influence, in which the Black intellectuals often lead social change, the wheels turned very slowly in this southern town (see West, 1993, chap. 5; Asante, 1988, on the Black intellectual). Even though the Supreme Court ruled that separate was not equal in 1954, Njeri noted that it was not until 1970, after much "pleading the cause" (p. 18) that the only city-owned swimming facility was integrated. This was my home for 18 years.

In 1986, my interest in communication seemed to crystallize as I cared for children in my home child-care business. I wondered aloud about my influence on the lives of the children in my care. At that time, and for some years thereafter, I thought that the answer to such a concern could simply be found in a careful scientific examination of the variables and people involved in the immediate setting. I even thought that it was important to study African-American families to prove that African-American families are more like Whites than unlike them. So the agenda of deficit (the Black family is a different family form in a negative sense) and cultural equivalent models (the Black family is functional the closer it parallels the White family) were entrenched in my head even though I had not formally studied this topic (on Black family theory, see Allen, 1978; Nobles, 1978). I believe that my existence as an African American in a racist society helped to shape my search for similarity between these races. By adopting this goal, I was accepting that a White United States was indeed the standard.

Over time, my consciousness was transformed by my experiences (on Black identity development, see Asante, 1988, chap. 3; Cross, 1991, chap. 6). My Black identity is salient to me along with other salient identities as I continue to become. I have come to think of race as an important variable to consider as a potential source of identification because of (a) the evolving/changing times (e.g, for a thorough overview of identity bases, see Cross, 1991; Leibkind, 1992); (b) my overall development (what I know and how I think now versus what I knew and how I thought then) that indicates that African Americans need a range of behaviors and sources of self-esteem to be successful in the array of environments; and (c) the varied interactions that a pluralistic society requires that we engage in and which require a range of knowledge and behaviors/skills that help define the roles we like, the selves we like, and the actions/behaviors that we discover beneficial to our self-feelings.

Presently, and finally, as a full-time faculty member, I recognize that through my interactions with others I have the potential for *becoming* but the meanings that I embrace for me must be consistent with the *who I am* identity. The recognition of the hiring of minority faculty at my present institution has helped me to enter my classroom and specifically engage every class at some level in provocative issues around stereotypes, race, and equity issues. I find it personally satisfying and intellectually stimulating to be teaching interpersonal and family communication courses that often address the "absolute present" (see Wilson, Hantz & Hanna, 1995) in order to teach skills that require mindfulness (motivations, context) about their applications. I view communication faculty in strategic positions to lead and follow in this endeavor, whether in predominantly Black, White, or racially balanced or imbalanced settings.

By the way, Angela is now 18 years of age, a freshman at Kentucky State University, and has an ample supply of friends, mostly Black and some White.

APPROACHING THE CROSSROADS: AN OVERVIEW OF THEORIES AND METHODS

In this section, we review approaches to studying the crossroads of communication, race, and family from theoretical and methodological vantage points and, where relevant, highlight work of the other chapters in the volume.

Concepts and Theories

The literature that informs the study of "race" in the context of family communication combines the work of scholars in intercultural communication and family communication. Space limitations do not allow for a comprehensive review of the major theories of these two well-established areas of the communication discipline, so instead, we highlight those theories and concepts that we see as being particularly useful to future theorizing and research. In particular, we examine the Afrocentric perspective, the cultural variability perspective, and what we label as the transformation perspective.

Afrocentric Perspective. An Afrocentric approach (see Asante, 1980, 1981a, 1988, 1990) is grounded in an African-American frame of reference and centers upon experiences on the African continent. The unique values and beliefs stemming from lived experiences of Africans and African Americans (whose ancestors were forcibly removed from Africa as slaves) are assumed to shape how theories are developed, including how basic terms are defined. For example, according to Sudarkasa (1981), differential reliance on consanguinality (African heritage) and conjugality (European heritage) in defining what constitutes "family" suggests differential emphases on family-defining qualities such as the extended family, polygamy, and openness (African heritage), contrasted with the nuclear family, monogamy, and closedness (European heritage). Asante (1990) summarized the upshot of Afrocentrism for contemporary theorizing: "Thus, if one concentrates on studying Africans in the inner cities of the Northeast United States ... it must be done with the idea in the back of the mind that one is studying African people, not 'made-in-America Negroes' without historical depth" (p. 15).

In this vein, Dainton (chap. 7, this volume) examined the terms that African-American, European-American, and African/European married couples' used to define *marriage*. Her data suggest that there might be more similarities than differences among these three groups in the terms used to define marriage. However, she also identified a few differences that are consistent with an Afrocentric perspective and in need of further inquiry. For example, her African-American couples viewed marriage in more spiritual terms, placed less emphasis on the companionate aspects of marriage, and held more consanguine views than her European and biracial couples. Her biracial couples' meanings for marriage seemed to differ from same-race couples. In particular, her biracial couples placed greater emphasis on marriage as "work" and as an "enduring emotional connection" when defining marriage (contrasted with same-race couples who emphasized the romantic side of marriage).

Dainton's exploration, which finds more similarities than differences (attributable to sharing U.S. culture), points out a problem that Asante (1990) called the "complex issue of 'bleeding cultures' … [which refers to] overlaps in social and cultural definitions, explanations, and solutions … For example, something might be the result … in African American patterns from the South or from Jamaica" (p. 9). In response, some Afrocentric theorists, following Asante's lead, have attempted to develop frameworks built around the unique qualities that they argue comprise an Afrocentric perspective. For example, Covin (1990) featured five constructs in his "Afrocentric" framework: (a) common experience, struggle, origin in Africa; (b) resistance to the assault upon traditional values by Europeans; (c) traditional African values of harmony with nature, humaneness, and rhythm; (d) development of a theory of an African way of knowing; and (e) some form of communalism. Similarly, Baldwin and Bell (1990) developed a 42-item, Afrocentric measure of the dimensions of Black personality, or what they labeled, "African Self-Consciousness" (ASC). Four assumptions make up their framework:

1. Awareness of Black identity (a sense of collective consciousness) and African cultural heritage and sees value in the pursuit of knowledge of self;
2. Recognizes Black survival priorities and the necessity for institutions … which affirm Black life;
3. Actively participates in the survival, liberation, and pro-active development of Black people and defends their dignity, worth, and integrity; and
4. Recognizes the opposition of racial oppression … to the development and survival of Black people, and actively resists it by any appropriate means. (p. 144)

The ASC scale uses a Likert-type format and its items are worded to cover "education, family, religion, cultural activities, interpersonal relations, and political orientation" (Baldwin & Bell, 1990, p. 145). Examples of ASC family items are "It is good for Black husbands and wives to help each other develop racial consciousness and cultural awareness in themselves and their children" (p. 148) and "If I saw Black children fighting, I would leave them to settle it alone" (p. 148). The latter item is reversed-scored, that is, a person scoring higher in African self-consciousness would step in and oversee the children whether they belonged to their family or not (assumed to reflect the cultural value of communalism). Baldwin and Bell's (1990) preliminary tests of the ASC scale found adequate validity and reliability; however, the scale has yet to be used in communication studies.

Not everyone thinks it is possible or necessary to discover the unique features of African culture and then examine how those features play out in the lives of African Americans. In an essay, Smith (1997) raised two questions: First, "Who are Black people?" He answered:

> Black people can have white skin, blue eyes, and naturally straight hair; they can be half, three-quarters, seven-eighths or more white; they can deny or not know they are black... (p. 180)

And, second, "What is Black culture?" He answered:

> Black culture is not a fixed, single thing 'out there' in the empirical world. It is ... a complex and ambiguous set of processes and interactions, facts and fantasies, assertions and inquiries, passionately held and passionately contested ... intangible ... yet its effects are powerfully immediate. (p. 193)

Smith's essay also raised questions concerning methodology that are taken up later in the chapter.

From the vantage point of family-communication theorizing, a family's ethnic-cultural orientation is an important feature to consider. However, following an Afrocentric perspective, family communication theorists must first begin to understand the complexities of a family's orientation to their ethnic cultural heritage in their own terms (e.g, Diggs, 1996b; 1996c). In particular, within a given cultural group, a family may hold differing orientations to different dimensions of ethnic culture (however they are described) that might affect the content and patterns of their own communication as well as the content and patterns of communication with families of cultures other than their own. Because research examining "race" and family communication is just beginning to emerge (this is the first volume to examine the topic), at this point it is best to be aware particularly of sensitizing constructs developed from an Afrocentric approach in order to improve the level of cultural sensitivity of this research as well as remain open to the complexities and variability of findings.

Cultural Variability Perspective. "A cultural variability perspective refers to how cultures vary on a continuum of variations in accordance with some basic dimensions or core value characteristics" (Ting-Toomey, 1994, p. 360). For example, Hofstede's (1980; 1981) four key value dimensions that appear across most all the cultures of the world have been widely studied: individualism–collectivism; power distance (valuing equality or valuing hierarchy); uncertainty avoidance (related to the need for security/predictability); and gender (masculinity—task-oriented; femininity—relationship oriented). According to Hofstede (1980), the culture of the United States, for example, is individualistic, displays small power distance, shows weak uncertainty avoidance, and leans toward masculine qualities. African culture is collectivistic, displays large power distance, shows weak uncertainty avoidance, and leans toward more feminine qualities.

Laubacher Henchy and Samovar (1995) illustrated the utility of examining family communication from the vantage point of cultural variability using Hofstede's work. Regarding individualism–collectivism, for example, Laubacher Henchy and Samovar noted, "Within each family a child will begin to develop habits regarding how much emotional support to expect from other people. In other words, within the context of the family the child learns where to turn for needed emotional support and who will provide that support" (p. 11). In a collectivistic family, children learn that they can expect and receive support from a wide bandwidth of people (e.g., extended family, distant friends, acquaintances, possibly strangers) whereas in individualistic families, children learn that support comes from very few people, often only those members of the immediate family who reside with them. Because African culture is categorized as collectivistic, to the extent that an African-American family internalizes this particular African cultural value, members might display behaviors consistent with collectivism (as opposed to individualism). Dainton (chap. 7, this volume), for example, observed this in the terms used by her participants to define marriage.

Another example of research exploring Black and White communication from a cultural variability perspective is the work of Kochman (1976, 1981, 1983, 1987), who, among other topics, studied communication style differences that mark boundaries between Blacks and Whites, and that are grounded in a framework of the ethnography of communication.

According to Kochman (1987), among the basic questions ethnographers ask are "What's going on? And from whose point of view? And what are the organizing schemes that give rise to the kinds of productions and understandings that individuals from various sociocultural realms generate in their everyday interactions?" (p. 221). In one study, Kochman (1987) used this approach to examine the racial terms that Blacks and Whites use to label themselves and each other. His results show that most all the terms used by both Whites and Blacks about each other were negative. However, Blacks did label Whites whom they perceived as not prejudiced and/or who interacted with them as equals as "half-an-halfs" or "straight." According to Kochman, because "Whites have no identification of themselves as a racial group" (p. 226), there are few, if any, raced-based terms that they use for themselves (e.g., one such term is "nigger-lover," a White person who does not hate Blacks). And, the negative terms that Whites use for Blacks focus "almost entirely on Black physical features ... burr head, shine ... " (p. 225) and so forth. Kochman interprets that Whites use these negative racial terms as a means of socially self-interested, status classification. In an edited volume (Johnson, 1972), Kochman noted, in a discussion of the vocabulary of race, that racial-identity labels that Blacks (from Chicago) have for White people can be negative (e.g., blue-eyed devils, the man, honky, peckerwood, cracker), neutral (e.g., republican, whitey), or positive (e.g., blue-eyed soul or real brother, golden girl). Such terms are viewed as grounded in experience and reflect the antagonistic contact with the White culture, particularly White males.

Kochman's work is highly relevant to the project of examining the crossroads of communication, race, and family, insofar as we need to understand better how families' produce and understand the racial labels they use to define themselves and others. Beyond that, we need also to understand better family stories about "race" so that we might gain a fuller picture of their implicit theories concerning race and race relations and the mechanisms by which these understandings are communicated to younger generations.

Toward this end, Alexander and LeBlanc (chap. 9, this volume) begin to examine "race" and family stories in the context of growing up in southern Louisiana. An underlying metaphor they use to illustrate the similarities between Blacks and Whites living in this part of the country is participation in the shared ritual of "cooking gumbo." Other chapters in this volume, including Daniel and Daniel (chap. 2; racism and care giver-child communication where they use a hot stove metaphor for racism), Ferguson (chap. 3; communication and Black parents' responses to episodes of racism), Diggs (chap. 6; adolescents' self-esteem), Parks (chap. 4; race and watching TV), and Davilla (chap. 5; White children's understanding of the term "race" and how they acquired meanings for these terms) adopt approaches that are similar to Kochman's ethnography of communication approach.

Among the drawbacks of the cultural variability perspective is the problem of how to reliably assess the degree to which a particular cultural value is present in a given family and then link these variations to variations in communication behaviors. Given that socioeconomic status, education, and myriad other factors come into play, the prospect of linking specific cultural variables to family communication behavioral differences seems daunting. However, because Ting-Toomey (1994) has shown that cultural variability differences do affect communication behaviors, and because data from large-scale studies of families remain to be collected, the cultural variability perspective continues to be a viable vantage point from which to consider communication, race, and family.

Transformation Perspective.   How family communication is learned in the homes of Blacks and Whites (e.g., see Daniel & Daniel, chap. 2, this volume; Davilla, chap. 5, this volume; Parks, chap. 4, this volume) as well as in family communication classes (Socha & Beigle, chap. 10, this volume) is important to consider when approaching the crossroads of communication, race, and family. For example, the content of lessons learned about "race" in the homes of Blacks and Whites differ; that is, Black children seem to be exposed regularly to "racial lessons" (Daniel & Daniel, chap. 2, this volume) whereas White children are not (Davilla, chap. 5, this volume). And, with a few important exceptions (i.e., Galvin & Brommel, 1996; Turner & West, 1998), students (both Black and White) in family communication classes are learning a predominantly European-American perspective of family communication (Diggs, 1996c; Socha, 1995; Socha et al., 1995).

Messages that comprise lessons about race have the potential to transform the ways that family systems and individual members in those systems produce and interpret messages both within "race" and across the "racial" divide. Families can develop ways of interacting that facilitate or inhibit the internalization of multiculturalism. Relevant to this point are Kim and Ruben's (1996) systems theory of the process of intercultural transformation and Bennett's (1986) developmental theory of intercultural sensitivity (see also Helms, 1990).

Kim and Ruben (1996) proposed a theory that seeks to account for why and how transformations take place inside individuals as they participate in intercultural communication. "In this process of internal change, the individual's cognitive, affective, and behavioral patterns are viewed to develop beyond their original, culturally conditioned psychological parameters" (p. 299). Although intended to apply to individuals, it would seem that their theory could profitably be extended to explain the transformation of families' cognitive, affective, and behavioral patterns in response to interactions with people whose ethnic culture is different from their own.

Kim and Ruben's (1996) systems theory of intercultural transformation is based on seven assumptions and five axioms that lead to seven testable propositions. Because space limits preclude extensive details, we discuss the theory in general terms, link it to family communication, and refer the reader to Kim and Ruben for particulars.

Kim and Ruben's (1996) theory is predicated on what they label the cyclical process of experiencing "stress" in response to intercultural encounters, followed by "adaptation," and then "growth." Applying Kim and Ruben's model to families, we find that families, as open communication systems, interact with the world and desire to maintain homeostasis (internal balance). However, if balance "is disturbed when the … [family]-environment symmetry is broken" (p. 308), the family experiences stress, which can be reduced by adapting the system to its changed environment. According to Kim and Ruben, stress and growth are inseparable. Furthermore the growth of the family facilitates their ability to adapt to new and changing environments.

Kim and Ruben argue that stress motivates a person's adaptation. Further-more at least in theory, the more a person encounters stress, the more likely that intercultural transformations will occur with simultaneous increases in intercultural abilities, including the capacity to be behaviorally, emotionally, and cognitively flexible as they communicate with dissimilar others, which, in turn reduces their stress. Diggs's (chap. 6, this volume) research findings suggest a hypothesis for communication influences on adolescent self-esteem using aspects of Kim and Ruben's theory.

Although the theory awaits testing, the general idea is interesting when it is applied to studies of "race" and families. It is clear from the chapters that follow as well as our own experiences that communication between Blacks and Whites, both inside and outside of families, is stressful. Also, families can manage this stress in adaptive or maladaptive ways. To us, adaptive ways include what Kim and Ruben proposed, such as an increased capacity to "learn and in-tegrate new experiences, altered perceptions, and flashes of insights" (p. 318), or, in general, to be more effective communicators across the racial divide. However, there are also maladaptive ways to cope with stress prompted by inter-racial encounters (e.g., families can choose to minimize contact with dissimilar others, thereby avoiding the stress, and support this choice with racist reasons). It is also possible to facilitate change in positive and less stressful ways by show-ing how adding features of another culture to one's family can be enriching and even fun.

It would be heartening (utopian) to report that talk about "race" in the United States is wearing down voluntary segregation and prompting wide-spread reexamination of maladaptive strategies in managing relationships with dissimilar others. However, according to Cose (1993), there still remains "a per-ceptual chasm separating so many blacks and whites. [In particular,] the prob-lem is not only that we are afraid to talk to one another, it is also that we are disinclined to listen" (p. 13). Cose offers numerous and vivid examples of highly educated, nationally known, and economically successful African Americans confronting day-to-day racism such as:

> a Harvard-educated [African American] lawyer [who] learned to carry a Bally bag when going to certain shops. Like a sorceress warding off evil with a wand, she would hold the bag in front of her to rebuff racial assumptions, in the hope that the clerk would take it as proof that she could be trusted to enter. (p. 42)

Also, "one of the nation's most successful [African-American] lawyers," ex-pressing his frustration with continued racism, framed the problem of living with discrimination in terms of "home": "You educate your kids with the hope they will be given a fair shot ... [Unfortunately,] the kids are going to have to fight this again ... [and] I don't want my kids to have to go through this shit" (Cose, 1993, p. 18).

If education to combat racism is to be effective, it needs to happen on both sides of the racial divide, occur through societal institutions, especially home, and, in particular, focus on ways to increase intercultural sensitivity. Relevant to this point is Bennett's (1986) model of the development of intercultural sensitivity.

Bennett (1986) began with the assumption that "Intercultural sensitivity is not natural ... [and that] cross-cultural contact usually has been accompanied by blood-shed, oppression, or genocide" (p. 1). Defined "in terms of stages of personal growth ... the model [of intercultural sensitivity] posits a continuum of increasing sophistication in dealing with cultural difference, moving from ethnocentrism through stages of greater recognition and acceptance of difference ... termed ethnorelativism" (p. 2). Bennett's model includes three ethnocentric stages, that is (a) "Denial" of differences, (b) "Defense" (e.g., superiority), and (c) "Minimization" (of differences) and three ethnorelative stages, that is (a) "Acceptance" (which includes respect for differences in values and behaviors), (b) "Adaptation" (including empathy and commitment of pluralism) and (c) "Integration" (as personified by Adler's, 1976, "multicultural person").

Although Bennett's model applies to individuals, we see merit in extending the model to families. Families hold collective attitudes and collective values about many things, including other cultures. Some families hold values that create homes where communication practices and rituals reflect ethnorelative and culturally plural values whereas other families hold ethnocentric and segregated ones. An important point made by Bennett (also by Helms, 1990) is that not all teaching/learning strategies (concerning culture) will work equally well with all families (nor individuals in those families) because of differences in the family's stage of intercultural sensitivity development. For example, teaching that communication style differences exist between Blacks and Whites (with no elaboration) will appear simplistic to families at more ethnorelative stages.

Thus, in addition to considering Afrocentric and cultural relativism perspectives, future work should begin to explore family communication and intercultural transformation by examining intercultural sensitivity. Currently, communication researchers who have had a successful interethnic relationship are rethinking the assumption of difference in explaining intercultural relationship development (see Clark & Diggs, 1996). The messages that families use when they seek to transform their ways of communicating in order to move themselves closer toward multiculturalism should become a prominent focus in family communication theorizing.

Methods

In this final section, we consider the import of "race" on methods in communication research in general (Orbe, 1995) and family communication research in particular (Dilworth-Anderson & Burton, 1996).

Among the various kinds of threats to the internal validity of a study are those attributable to the researcher. For example, Black families might perceive a White researcher collecting data about "family life" as potentially threatening, which, in turn, could threaten a study's internal validity (Socha, 1995). Given Black families' experiences with racism, it makes sense that they might be reluctant to open up and provide information to White, male researchers about personal topics such as how they parent or participate in marriage, especially if they are aware of past examples of data provided by Black families leading to misinformation and harm (e.g., see Moynihan, 1967). This problem would seem to be especially salient when interviewing is used to collect data, but it comes into play with surveys also.

There are various strategies that can help to minimize potential threats attributable to a researcher to a study's validity. For example, a research team that includes African-American and European-American scholars can be used when gathering data (see Socha et al., 1995 for one example, and Bantz, 1993, for a discussion of cross-cultural team research). Further, European-American scholars should seek out African Americans (and vice versa) to coauthor/coedit when writing across racial lines. This will help to ensure that, at minimum, both insider and outsider perspectives are considered in designing survey items, interpreting findings, making claims, and writing up the final results. This is not to say that White and Black scholars cannot do an adequate job of studying each other's families. However, they should, at least, be educated about the relevant culture (Black scholars are typically exposed to White scholarship, but the reverse may not always be the case). For example, White scholars' education about Africa and African Americans should include reading the work of African-American authors and scholars and having experience working with African Americans. It makes good sense when approaching an unfamiliar crossroad, to have an indigenous person(s) there to help guide and direct you.

There can be problems, however, with a biracial research team approach. For example, coscholars who are low in intercultural sensitivity might have a difficult time developing a working relationship (but the growth potential is definitely there!). This can be managed by open dialogue about issues and problems that the researchers' own views about race might be bringing to the project. Certainly, in our own discussions about this book, we have not always seen eye-to-eye, but at base, there is a two-way respect that helps to keep the dialogue open and continuing.

"Race" also can influence the external validity of research about family communication, in particular, by the failure of studies to include African Americans in subject pools, or not breaking down analyses of data by cultural group. Socha et al. (1995) also found very few studies in family communication that specifically incorporated ethnic culture and even fewer that specifically focused on African-American families. We admit that external validity problems can be tricky to handle. Researchers often rely on students in their classes to be participants, and because the percentage of African-American students might not rise above 10% to 12% at some schools, this means that scholars need to take extra measures to insure that African Americans are adequately represented in the sample of any given study. This, of course, increases the costs of a study, and perhaps, takes more time.

Assumptions underlying particular methods, such as the experiment, may also run counter to the assumptions derived from an Afrocentric perspective (see Orbe, 1995). For example, the cultural value of wholeness (African heritage) is antithetical to the exercise of reducing complex phenomena into discrete categories (scientific heritage). Thus, there needs to be further reflection and examination of method when studying the communication of families of different cultural heritages as well as when studying family communication and intercultural relations. Methods used by the authors of chapters in this volume emphasize survey, interview, ethnography, and autoethnography, (chap. 7, this volume) which render data that are primarily qualitative, although Dainton (chap. 7, this volume), Diggs (chap. 6, this volume; also uses qualitative), Ferguson (chap. 3, this volume), and Socha and Beigle (chap. 10, this volume) gathered quantitative data using surveys. According to Asante (1990), Afrocentric methods share some of the assumptions of ethnomethodology, but go further by arguing that the same methods used to study others should also apply to studying the role that self plays in the creation of knowledge.

CONCLUSION

As indicated by the title of this book, the chapters contained in it represent initial explorations of the crossroads of communication, race, and family, and collectively, are intended to open a dialogue about race within the context of family communication. Indeed, this is just the beginning and clearly much more needs to be done.

The volume also marks the opening of important and unprecedented dialogue between Black and White family communication scholars. It is ironic that the family communication literature, which has shown great sensitivity in its efforts to define the term *family*, has spent so many years neglecting ethnic culture, and, in the context of this book, neglecting African Americans. It is now time that we begin to enrich the study of family communication and truly begin to explore all families.

REFERENCES

Aboud, F. E. (1977). Interest in ethnic information: A cross-cultural developmental study. *Canadian Journal of Behavioral Science, 9,* 134–146.
Adler, P. (1976). Beyond cultural identity: Reflections upon cultural and multicultural man. In L. A. Samovar & R. E. Porter (Eds.), *Intercultural communication: A reader* (pp. 362–380). Belmont, CA: Wadsworth.

Allen, W. R. (1978). The search for applicable theories of Black family life. *Journal of Marriage and the Family, 40*(1), 117–129.

Anderson, E. (1994, May). The code of the streets. *The Atlantic Monthly, 273,* 80–94.

Asante, M. K. (1980). *Afrocentricity: The theory of social change.* Buffalo, NY: Amulefi.

Asante, M. K. (1981a). Black male and female relationships: An Afrocentric context. In L. Gary (Ed.), *Black men* (pp. 75–82). Thousand Oaks, CA: Sage.

Asante, M. K. (1981b). Intercultural communication: An inquiry into research directions. In D. Nimmo (Ed.), *Communication Yearbook 4* (pp. 401–410). New Brunswick, NJ: Transaction Books.

Asante, M. K. (1988). *Afrocentricity* (7th ed.). Trenton, NJ: Africa World Press.

Asante, M. K. (1990). *Kemet, Afrocentricity, and knowledge.* Trenton, NJ: African World Press.

Baldwin, J. A., & Bell, Y. R. (1990). The African self-consciousness scale: An Afrocentric personality questionnaire. In T. Anderson (Ed.), *Black studies: Theory, method, and cultural perspectives* (pp. 142–150). Pullman, WA: Washington State University Press.

Bantz, C. R. (1993). Cultural diversity and group cross-cultural team research. *Journal of Applied Communication, 21,* 1–20.

Bender, L. (Producer), & Nakano, D. (Director). (1995). *White man's burden* [Film]. (Available from HBO Home Video).

Bennett, M. J. (1986). Towards ethnorelativism: A developmental model of intercultural sensitivity. In R. M. Paige (Ed.), *Cross-cultural orientation: New conceptualizations and applications* (pp. 26–51). New York: University Press of America.

Boykin, A. W., & Toms, F. D. (1985). Black child socialization: A conceptual framework. In H. P. McAdoo & J. L. McAdoo (Eds.), *Black children: Social, educational, and parental environments* (pp. 33–51). Beverly Hills, CA: Sage.

Burr, W. R. (1990). Beyond I-statements in family communication. *Family Relations, 39,* 266–273.

Clark, K. D., & Diggs, R. C. (1998). *Connected or separated?: Towards a dialectical view of interethnic relationships.* Manuscript submitted for publication.

Cose, E. (1993). *The rage of a privileged class.* New York: HarperCollins.

Covin, D. (1990). Afrocentricity in O Movimento Negro Unificado. *Journal of Black Studies, 21,* 126–146.

Cross, W. (1981). Black families and black identity development. *Journal of Comparative Family Studies, 12,* 19–50.

Cross, W. E., Jr. (1991). *Shades of black: Diversity in African-American identity.* Philadelphia: Temple University Press.

Diggs, R. C. (1994). *Perceptions of parent and peer communication, racial esteem, and support among African American Adolescents.* Unpublished doctoral dissertation, The Ohio State University, Columbus, OH.

Diggs, R. C. (1995, June). *Black family communication: A course proposal.* Paper presented at the annual meeting of the Speech Communication Black Caucus Summer Conference, Frankfort, KY.

Diggs, R. C. (1996a, November). *African American faculty on a White campus: Considering self-identification, recognitions, and reflections.* Panel presented at the annual meeting of the Speech Communication Association, San Diego, CA.

Diggs, R. C. (1996b, March). *Communicating identity: The sources of our selves.* Paper presented at the annual meeting of the National Black Family Conference, Louisville, KY.

Diggs, R. C. (1996c, June). *Pursuing an Afrocentric methodology in studying African-American communication.* Paper presented at the annual meeting of the Black Caucus Division of the Speech Communication Association Summer Conference, Frankfort, KY.

Dilworth-Anderson, P., & Burton, L. M. (1996). Rethinking family development: Critical conceptual issues in the study of diverse groups. *Journal of Social and Personal Relationships, 13,* 325–334.

Du Bois, W. E. B. (1903/1969). *The souls of Black folk.* New York: American Library.

Galvin, K., & Brommel, B. (1996). *Family communication: Cohesion and change* (4th ed.). New York: HarperCollins.

Goffman, E. (1959). *The presentation of self in everyday life.* Garden City, NY: Doubleday.

Goodman, M. E. (1964). *Race awareness in young children* (Rev. ed.). New York: Collier.

Gopaul-McNicol, S. A. (1992). Racial identification and racial preference of Black preschool children in New York and Trinidad. In A. Hoard Burlew, W. C. Banks, H. P. McAdoo, & D. A. ya Azibo (Eds.), *African American psychology: Theory, research, and practice* (pp. 190–193). Thousand Oaks, CA: Sage.

Hecht, M., Collier, M. J., & Ribeau, S. A. (1993). *African American communication: Ethnic identity and cultural interpretation*. Newbury Park, CA: Sage.

Helms, J. E. (1990). Toward a model of white racial identity development. In J. E. Helms (Ed.), *Black and white racial identity* (pp. 49–66). Westport, CT: Greenwood.

Hernadi, P. (1995). *Cultural transactions*. Ithaca, NY: Cornell University Press.

Hidalgo, N. M., McDowell, C. L., & Siddle, E. V. (Eds.). (1990). *Facing racism in education*. Cambridge, MA: Harvard Educational Review.

Hofstede, G. (1980). *Culture's consequences: International differences in work-related values*. Beverly Hills, CA: Sage.

Hofstede, G. (1981). *Cultures and organizations: Software of the mind*. London: McGraw-Hill.

Holmes, R. M. (1995). *How young children perceive race*. Thousand Oaks, CA: Sage.

Hyland, J. (1998, August). Speech given in Public Speaking at Old Dominion University, Norfolk, VA.

Johnson, K. (1972). The vocabulary of race. In T. Kochman (Ed.), *Rappin' and stylin out: Communication in urban Black America* (pp. 140–151). Chicago: University of Illinois Press.

Katz, J. H. (1976). The acquisition of racial attitudes in children. In P. A. Katz (Ed.), *Towards the elimination of racism* (pp. 125–154). New York: Pergamon.

Katz, J. H. (1978). *White awareness: Handbook for anti-racism training*. Norman: University of Oklahoma Press.

Kim, Y. Y., & Ruben, B. D. (1996). Intercultural transformation: A systems theory. In Y. Y. Kim & W. B. Gudykunst (Eds.), *Theories in intercultural communication* (pp. 299–321). Newbury Park, CA: Sage.

King, J. R. (1976). African survivals in the Black-American family. *Journal of Afro-American Issues, 4*, 153–167.

Kochman, T. (1976). Perceptions along the power axis: A cognitive residue of inter-racial encounters. *Anthropological Linguistics, 18*, 261–274.

Kochman, T. (1981). *Black and white styles in conflict*. Chicago: University of Chicago Press.

Kochman, T. (1983). The boundary between play and nonplay in Black verbal dueling. *Language in Society, 12*, 239–337.

Kochman, T. (1987). The ethnic component in Black language and culture. In J. S. Phinney & M. J. Rotheram (Eds.), *Children's ethnic socialization: Pluralism and development* (pp. 219–238). Newbury Park, CA: Sage.

Laubacher Henchy, V., & Samovar, L. A. (1995, February). *The deep structure of culture: An exploration into the family*. Paper presented at the meeting of the Western States Communication Association, Portland, OR.

Lee, S. (Producer, Writer, and Director). (1990). *Do the right thing* [Film]. (Available from MCA Universal Home Video).

Lee, S. (Producer, Writer, and Director). (1991). *Jungle fever* [Film]. (Available from MCA Home Video).

Liebkind, K. (1992). Ethnic identity—Challenging the boundaries of social psychology. In G. M. Breakwell (Ed.), *Social psychology of identity and the self concept* (pp. 147–185). New York: Surrey University Press.

Macmillan/McGraw-Hill. (1993). *Reflecting diversity: Multicultural guidelines for educational publishing professionals*. New York: Author.

Mead, G. H. (1934). *Mind, self & society: From the standpoint of a behaviorist*. Chicago: University of Chicago Press.

Morrison, T. (1997). Home. In W. Lubiano (Ed.), *The house that race built* (pp. 3–12). New York: Random House.

Moynihan, D. P. (1967). The Negro family: A case for national action. In L. Rainwater & W. L. Yancey (Eds.), *The Moynihan report and the politics of controversy* (pp. 41–124). Cambridge, MA: MIT Press.

Njeri, A. (1990). *Every good-bye ain't gone: Family portraits and personal escapades* (5th ed.). New York: First Vintage Books.

Nobles, W. W. (1978). Toward an empirical and theoretical framework for defining Black families. *Journal of Marriage and the Family, 40*(4), 479–688.

Orbe, M. P. (1995). African American communication research: Toward a deeper understanding of interethnic communication. *Western Journal of Communication, 59*, 61–78.

Porter, J. D. R. (1971). *Black child, white child: The development of racial attitudes*. Cambridge, MA: Harvard University Press.

President's Initiative on Race. (1998). *One America in the 21st century: The president's initiative on race* [Brochure]. Washington, DC: U.S. Government Printing Office.

Reimers, D. M. (Ed.). (1972). *Racism in the United States: An American dilemma?* New York: Holt, Rinehart & Winston.

Rosenthal, D. A. (1987). Ethnic identity development in adolescents. In J. S. Phinney & M. J. Rotheram (Eds.), *Children's ethnic socialization: Pluralism and development* (pp. 156–179). Newbury Park, CA: Sage.

Rotheram, M. J., & Phinney, J. S. (1987). Introduction: Definitions and perspectives in the study of children's ethnic socialization. In J. S. Phinney & M. J. Rotheram (Eds.), *Children's ethnic socialization: Pluralism and development* (pp. 10–28). Newbury Park, CA: Sage.

Smith, D. L. (1997). What is Black culture? In W. Lubiano (Ed.), *The house that race built* (pp. 178–194). New York: Random House.

Socha, T. J. (1995, November). *Family communication education and African American families: A selected primer.* A paper presented at the Family Communication Pre-Conference at the annual meeting of the Speech Communication Association, San Antonio, Texas.

Socha, T. J., Sanchez-Hucles, J., Bromley, J., & Kelly, B. (1995). Invisible parents and children: African-American parent–child communication. In T. J. Socha, & G. H. Stamp (Eds.), *Parents, children and communication: Frontiers of theory and research* (pp. 127–145). Hillsdale, NJ: Lawrence Erlbaum Associates.

Sudarkasa, N. (1981). Interpreting the African heritage in Afro-American family organization. In H. P. McAdoo (Ed.), *Black families* (pp. 37–53). Thousand Oaks, CA: Sage.

Sweeper, G. (1984). The image of the black family and the white family in American prime-time television programming 1970–1980. *Dissertation Abstracts International, 44,* 1964A.

Takaki, R. (1993). *A different mirror: A history of multicultural America.* Boston: Little Brown.

Ting-Toomey, S. A. (1994). Managing intercultural conflicts effectively. In L. Samovar & R. Porter (Eds.), *Intercultural communication* (7th ed., pp. 360–372). Belmont, CA: Wadsworth.

Turner, L. H., & West, R. (1998). *Perspectives on family communication.* Mountain View, CA: Mayfield.

U.S. Commission on Civil Rights. (1977). *Window dressing on the set: Women and minorities on television.* Washington, DC: U.S. Government Printing Office.

Vaughan, G. M. (1987). A social psychological model of ethnic identity development. In J. S. Phinney & M. J. Rotheram (Eds.), *Children's ethnic socialization: Pluralism and development* (pp. 73–91). Newbury Park, CA: Sage.

Ward, J. V. (1990). Racial identity formation and transformation. In C. Gilligan, N. P. Lyons, & T. J. Hanner (Eds.), *Making connections: The relational worlds of adolescent girls at Emma Willard School* (pp. 215–232). London: Harvard University Press.

West, C. (1993). *Keeping the faith: Philosophy and race in America.* New York: Routledge.

Wilson, G. L., Hantz, A. M., & Hanna, M. S. (1995). *Interpersonal growth through communication* (4th ed.). Madison, WI: Brown & Benchmark.

2

African-American Childrearing: The Context of a Hot Stove

Jack L. Daniel
Jerlean E. Daniel
University of Pittsburgh

RACISM AS A SOCIALIZATION VARIABLE

In the presence of a kitchen stove, even when it is turned off, parents exclaim "No!" as their toddlers inch toward the stove. Because the stove represents significant potential and actual danger that the toddler is unable to discern, the negative imperative is a developmentally appropriate caregiving response. In everyday life, racism functions as a hot stove for African-American children. Herein, racism refers to its occurrence institutionally (e.g., employment and housing discrimination) as well as to everyday interpersonal occurrences, such as the telling of racial jokes and the assumption that one needs to lock one's car because an African-American male teenager is standing on the corner. Given the pervasiveness of racism throughout one's life span, a major caregiving function is to provide early childhood developmental experiences that enable African-American children to make appropriate responses to this hot stove. Because parents and other surrogate primary caregivers lack sufficient control over the hot stove and African-American children often experience the hot stove's harmful effects when they are least expected, characteristics such as resiliency (healthy growth and development in spite of adversity), adaptability (code switching), and healthy self-esteem (feeling positively about oneself in spite of oppression) are critical early childhood outcomes for African-American children. The hot stove burns relentlessly from birth through death, and therefore, it is a fundamental part of the context related to understanding African-American caregivers' early childhood communication with their children. "Burns" may range from "first-degree" occurrences, such as feelings associated with stares in response to one's color, to "third-degree" occurrences, such as a college student's inferiority complex resulting from years of reinforced underachievement.

In what follows, the "hot stove" is used interchangeably with "racism" as a pervasive factor that must be addressed when discussing African-American child socialization processes across social classes. Moreover, the hot stove dynamic is made more complex according to children's gender. For example, when addressing African-American females' perceptions of how the hot stove affects the socialization of African-American male children, Joyce Ladner wrote, "Every generation of black women has experienced tremendous anxiety about keeping their men alive" (Golden, 1995, p. 11).

Regarding the socialization of African-American females, Hopson and Hopson (1990) wrote:

> Another young lady said that her mother had always felt that if one of her (the mother's) children were to have been darker than the other, she would have preferred that her son be dark and her daughter be light. This mother was expressing an understanding of a situation that has been true throughout the history of Black people in America: American society has always held the White woman as the highest standard of beauty, goodness, and desirability. (p. 85)

One can further understand the seriousness of the hot stove dynamic for African-American males by considering the unfortunate Johnny-Gammage-type experience that other African Americans have had with police officers. Johnny Gammage was stopped in Brentwood, Pennsylvania, for a traffic violation. Several police cars responded from various communities. By the time the scuffle was over, Johnny Gammage was dead from asphyxiation. Given how dangerous the hot stove can be when it is represented by a police officer, an African-American mother shared with us that she consistently warned her teenage son, when he left home alone with the family car, "Be careful, Son. Just remember, you're everything they are looking for" (M. Echols, personal communication, November, 1997).

In addition to the hot stove manifesting itself through individuals, there is a plethora of media "carriers of culture" (Milner, 1983, p. 76) that make real the damaging effects of the hot stove, including racism in children's literature, comics, television, and movies. These mass distributors are often reinforced by "everyday racism," which, according to Essed (1991), is systematic and recurrent (p. 3). When discussing the impact of everyday racism, Page (1996) offered the following anecdotal illustration:

> When our son was four years old he arrived home from his day care center to announce to his mother, "I want to be a white policeman." ... She was incapable of re-

sponding to his announcement other than to ask "Why?" … He simply thought it would be "cool," the kids' universal stamp of approval. (p. 8)

Everyday racism is so ever present that African-American caregivers can be the unintentional sources of the hot stove's burns. As Poussiant wrote in the forward to Hopson and Hopson (1990),

Black parents who read traditional fairy tales and folklore to their children send them messages very early on that kings, queens, princes, and princesses are White and that the world is controlled and run by White people. In addition, important cultural symbols and the fantasy heroes who exercise dominant power over children are White, among them Superman, Batman, He-Man, Master of the Universe, and even Captain Midnight. (p. xiv)

Matters are made worse when the caregivers themselves have internalized racist viewpoints and deliver daily doses to their children (see Socha & Beigle, chap. 10, this volume, concerning family communication educators). For example, in a self-report, Santos (1996) wrote,

My mother taught me that my blackness and my femaleness were two strikes against me. She convinced me these two "flaws" were somehow of my own making. She taught me I would get or not get what I deserved based on these two flaws, that I was to be thankful for whatever I did get and that I had to accept the limitations placed on me.

These teachings did not involve structured lessons on her part or conscious learning on mine. Rather, they were taught through the everyday interactions of our lives. Whether she was scrubbing my knees with a scouring pad, or scolding me for my "achiness" or admonishing me to stay out of the summer sun so as not to get "even darker," the message was the same—my blackness was an embarrassing defect. (p. 23)

From their color contributing to them not being selected as child-care playmates to being subjected to ridicule by the television images of "Stymie" and "Buckwheat" from reruns of The Little Rascals show, African-American young children experience the hot stove's ongoing assaults on their developing selves. Later, as teenagers, everyday racism continues a relentless war on the internal and external beings of African Americans (Diggs, chap. 6, this volume). For example, in her discussion of efforts to contain African-American rap music as an extension of the general racist desire to contain African Americans spatially and otherwise, Rose (1994) indicated.

However, informal, yet trenchant forms of institutional discrimination still exist in full force. Underwriting these defacto forms of social containment is the understanding that black people are a threat to the social order. Inside of this, black urban teenagers are the most profound symbolic referent for internal threats to social order … The public school system, the police, and the popular media perceive and construct young African Americans as a dangerous internal element in urban America; an element that, if allowed to roam freely, will threaten the social order; an element that must be policed. (pp. 125–126)

To understand how and why the hot stove continues its presence in African-American adult life, it is helpful to consider the following remarks James Baldwin made to his nephew on the 100th anniversary of Africans' emancipation in the United States. Specifically, Baldwin wrote,

> Any upheaval in the universe is terrifying because it so profoundly attacks one's sense of one's reality. Well, the Black man has functioned in the White man's world as a fixed star, as an immovable pillar; and as he moves out of his place, heaven and earth are shaken to their foundations. (1963, p. 20)

The essence of Baldwin's statements was demonstrated by the following true incident involving the father of this chapter's coauthor, J. E. Daniel. Nathaniel S. Colley, Sr., graduated from Yale Law School and became a renowned trial lawyer as well as a devoted servant of the National Association for the Advancement of Colored People (NAACP). At the time of the following incident, he was also a retired Army captain, part-time law faculty member, and had consulted, at their requests, with Presidents Kennedy, Carter, and Reagan. For recreation, he became the proud owner of thoroughbred race horses. Eventually, he served as Chairman of the California Horse Racing Board. During his chairmanship, he was invited to a posh New York event for thoroughbred owners. Colley, proud of his accomplishments, appeared dressed in his finest black tie attire. When he took his designated seat on the dias, a White female inquired of him, "For whom do you groom?"

Regardless of his degrees earned, social services rendered, and legal distinctions deserved, Colley was still a "fixed star" in this particular White woman's constellation of "African-American men associated with horses." It was of no consequence that Colley had overcome childhood as well as adult experiences with severe poverty and racism. Having embedded in her psyche a comprehensive set of negative presumptions against African-American men and with Colley being a fixed as well as dim star, the White woman recalled the appropriate negative presumption, and asked Colley, "For whom do you groom?" See also Cose (1994) for other similar anecdotes.

Whereas Colley had a tremendous amount of internal and external validation of his worth as a human being, Colley still felt deeply the burn from the hot stove. Notwithstanding what Kim and Ruben (1988) and other scholars have written regarding "humans' uniquely adaptive capacity" (p. 307), some nonadaptive racists make the hot stove a birth-through-death phenomenon in the lives of African Americans (see Socha & Diggs, chap. 1, this volume, for a discussion of openness to transformation). Thus, this socialization context must be understood thoroughly in order to understand better African-American caregivers' communication with their children and what constitutes healthy adaptation to exposure to racism (see Ferguson, chap. 3, this volume). The purpose of this chapter is to explore elements of the complex nature of racism in the United States that shape certain African-American familial modes of communication.

THE AFRICAN-AMERICAN CHILD
SOCIALIZATION EXIGENCY

Between birth and age 8, American children make transitions through life phases commonly referred to as "early childhood education." A healthy early childhood start includes caregivers providing effective transitional experiences (J. E. Daniel, 1993, 1995; J. E. Daniel & Shapiro, 1996) that develop children's individual and collective identity, social competencies, and cognitive skills. In general, early childhood is a time period in which children are integrated effectively into the prevailing culture(s). For all children, especially African-American children in light of the hot stove, it is imperative that early childhood be a time when preparation begins for them to become effective as intercultural beings (Alejandro-Wright, 1985; Diggs & Robinson, 1994).

Just as Kim and Ruben (1988) indicated that success as business managers, diplomats, and teachers demands a high degree of "interculturalness" (p. 299), African-American children's mental and physical health depend on African-American parents and/or their surrogates helping their children develop a high degree of interculturalness, given the hot stove's presence. Specifically, their early childhood education caregiving roles include providing

> specific messages and practices that are relevant to and provide information concerning the nature of race status as it relates to: (1) personal and group identity, (2) intergroup and interindividual relationships, and (3) position in the social hierarchy. (Thornton, Chatters, Taylor, & Allen, 1990, pp. 401–402)

In addition, Greens (1990) described the African-American child racial socialization dynamic process as follows:

> A special task and added stressor confronting Black parents involves finding ways of warning Black children about racial dangers and disappointments without overwhelming them or being overly protective. Either extreme will facilitate the development of defensive styles which leave a child inadequately prepared to negotiate the world with a realistic perspective. (p. 209)

As Greens indicated, other scholars (Boyd-Franklin, 1989; Collins, 1987; Ferguson-Peters, 1985; Pinderhughes, 1989) have discussed how African-American families' childrearing practices are a function of responses to a hostile cultural environment and, in particular, the need to buffer their children (Greens, 1990) from what is deemed herein as the hot stove.

A similar explanation of the hot stove exigency was described by Miller and Miller (1990) who indicated that, by six years old, most African-American children are aware of their color and the negative responses made by racists. Consequently, Miller and Miller (1990) contended;

> The primary tasks of an African-American parent are to (1) negate dominant cultural messages which undermine self-esteem and efficacy, (2) validate uniqueness, (3)

teach strategies for emotional and physical survival in the face of racism, and (4) foster the development of coping mechanisms for dealing with legal and defacto discriminatory experiences. (p. 170)

Given the baseline importance of physical and emotional survival, these variables furnished the focus for our discussion of African-American caregivers' communication strategies with their children. A variety of strategies for living with the hot stove, such as validating uniqueness, are considered.

SURVIVAL NEEDS AND THE IMPERATIVE COMMUNICATION MODE

At first glance, many lower socioeconomic class African-American caregivers might appear to be overly harsh and directive when communicating with their children (Socha, Sanchez-Hucles, Bromley, & Kelly, 1995). However, childrearing viewed across cultures must take into consideration the context of the racial, ethnic, and class-based experiences of the particular culture and the adjustments necessary for physical and mental health survival in order to fulfill the hope of productive contributions to society (Jackson, 1993; Julian, McKenry, & McKelvey, 1994; McLoyd, 1990). This point was made clear by Collins (1994) in her discussion of mothering by women of color. Specifically, Collins indicated,

> Motherhood occurs in specific historical situations framed by interlocking structures of race, class, and gender, where the sons and daughters of white mothers have "every opportunity and protection," and the "colored" daughters and sons of racial ethnic mothers "know not their fate." (p. 45)

According to Adams (1993), many African-American children grow up in an environment where "too many ... have their childhood snatched away from them because they die young or grow up too fast." For many, "childhood" itself is a "broken symbol" (p. 2). Collins (1994) also noted,

> African-American children face an infant mortality rate twice that for white infants; and approximately one-third of Hispanic children and one-half of African-American children who survive infancy live in poverty. In addition racial ethnic children often live in harsh urban environments where drugs, crime, industrial pollutants, and violence threaten their survival. (p. 49)

Although there is clear value in providing young children with detailed and rational explanations, when a child is in imminent danger of physical harm or of breaking a significant taboo, such as disrespect of parental authority, generally a caregiver responds with urgent commands or "restricted" as opposed to "elaborate" codes (Bernstein, 1986). Note that imminent danger refers also to episodes that can do long-term physical and/or emotional damage. Regarding language, Bernstein indicated that the "imperative mode" of control reduces the role discretion accorded to the regulated (child).... The imperative mode is realized through a restricted code (lexicon prediction): "Shut up," "Leave it alone," "get out," or extra verbally through physical coercion. (p. 485)

The imperative mode of social control is often accompanied by harsh tones, which are intended to catch the child's immediate attention and to exert immediate control over the child's behavior. As described by McLoyd (1998):

Parenting that is strict and highly directive (i.e., well-defined house rules, clear sanctions for breaking rules, close supervision), combined with high levels of warmth, helps poor, inner-city children resist forces in their extra-familial environments that in ordinary circumstances contribute to low levels of achievement (e.g., peer pressure against achievement and poor-quality schooling). These parenting behaviors distinguish poor, inner-city children exhibiting high academic achievement from their low-achieving counterparts exposed to similar stressors. (p. 194)

Further corroboration of the effectiveness of this parenting style comes from the research of Hrabowski, Maton, and Greif (1998) who studied the childrearing practices of parents of academically successful African-American males. The study included single and two-parent families from a range of economic and educational backgrounds. Hrabowski et al. found that strong limit setting, child-focused love, high expectations, consistent open communication, positive racial and male identity, and active use of community resources were critical to the success of African-American male college high achievers. The Burleson, Delia, and Applegate (1995) description of elaborate coding as person-centered (developmental, contextual, and increasing in complexity) adds insight and relieves the dichotomous tension between authoritative parenting (position-centered/restricted codes) and authoritarian parenting (person-centered). The parents studied by Hrabowski et al. were not just strict disciplinarians. They used highly contextual, person-centered strategies. It is our contention here that effective parenting by African Americans asserts the position of parenthood. Simultaneously, within the confines of that protective authority, African Americans contextualize thinking, problem-solving, and decision-making opportunities for children.

Additionally, Masten and Coatsworth (1998) further delineated the contextual nature of person-centered communication when they indicated the following:

In extremely dangerous environments, effective parents are likely to be more strict but remain warm and caring. When a parent like this is not available in a child's life, competence is often linked to a surrogate caregiving figure who serves a mentoring role. When adversity is high and no effective adult is connected to a child, risk for maladaptation is high. The development of competence requires the involvement of caring, competent adults in a child's life; ensuring that every child has this fundamental protective system is a policy imperative. (p. 215)

One of the authors observed children in her role as an administrator in child-care settings over an 18-year period and was afforded numerous opportunities to observe African-American caregivers' use of the imperative mode. One dominant communication tactic was "the look," and if necessary, "the look" was followed by physical contact (i.e., pressure applied to the child's arms to turn the child toward the adult for immediate eye contact, or one or more hits applied to the child's rear end). Consider the following scenarios drawn from a composite of real-life situations:

Three-year-old Suliman's mother was talking with his teacher about Suliman's cold medication. Suliman was standing at a table, banging wooden blocks and singing loudly a stream of nonsense syllables, "Yah, yah, yah, tha, tha, tha, tha." In the middle of a sentence, Suliman's mother stopped talking. When Suliman turned toward her, his mother looked intently, and, for a few seconds, stared into Suliman's eyes. Suliman lowered his voice, and, in slow motion, pretended to be banging the blocks together.

In another instance, Suliman's mother came to pick him up about 15 minutes behind her normal schedule. She said to Suliman, "Let's go," and as he ran away from her, he bumped into another child. When Suliman fell on the floor, he looked back at his mother, and she gave him "the look." Suliman turned his head away from his mother, stood, and began to run. With several quick strides, Suliman's mother caught Suliman, grabbed him by one arm, and smacked his bottom. The mother said nothing, and Suliman did not cry. Rather, he laid his head on his mother's shoulder as she sat tying his shoe. As they left the room, Suliman's mother asked him, "So, what did you do interesting today, Handsome?"

There are numerous everyday situations in which African-American children need to be especially attentive to imperatives. In the classroom, failure to comply with the teacher's imperative mode could combine with the hot stove to cause serious problems. Consider the following illustration:

Three-year-old Jamal (African American) was sitting at a table in his preschool classroom, playing a picture lotto game (cardboard pictures of umbrellas, balloons, dogs, firefighters, flowers, etc., must be matched with the same pictures on the board by setting the piece on top of its corresponding portraiture on the board). Each time Jamal made a match he smiled to himself. After pursuing the task for approximately 15 minutes, Billy (3-year-old White male) dashed to the table and stood by Jamal's side. After watching Jamal for a few seconds, Billy used his right hand to scatter the matched pieces. Jamal yelled loudly, "No, that's mine!" The White teacher, standing across the room with her back to the boys, said without looking at them, "Jamal, I have told you before, no loud voices in this room. Use your inside voice." As she was speaking, again Billy scattered the pieces of the game. Immediately, Jamal punched Billy on the arm, and Billy yelled, "You hurt me!" as he began to cry. The teacher turned toward the boys and directed Jamal to go sit in the time-out chair. Next, the teacher walked over to the crying Billy, looked at his arm, rubbed it gently, and said,

"Oh, I am so sorry." She looked over at Jamal in the time-out chair and said, "I mean it Jamal, no hitting." Later that day, she discussed with Jamal's mother the need to "work with" Jamal to get his hitting under control before he became a "major disciplinary problem."

By not heeding the teacher's initial imperative, Jamal got burned even though he was initially the victim. The burn, represented in the form of his further victimization by the teacher, resulted in immediate punishment and later a discussion with his mother in which he was chastised on the way home. Jamal's mother asked him, "Why on earth were you hitting? I have told you absolutely no hitting anyone." In addition, a "second-degree" burn could result in Jamal being classified by his teacher as a "problem child, prone to using violence to resolve conflicts."

In another situation, just before Easter, a White teacher concluded a lesson on primary and secondary colors by asking the 5-year-old children to undertake the following assignment: The children were to use the primary colors to make two other colors, and then use the two resulting colors to paint a picture. About 20 minutes later, Emily (White) called to the teacher to show her picture. Emily had painted and cut out a green and orange egg. "Oh, how clever," the teacher exclaimed, and then added, "Look children, Emily made a beautiful green and orange egg and then took the time to cut it out."

Next, Jasmine (African-American) said to the teacher, "I've made a rabbit," and she held up her green-eyed purple rabbit. When she held up the picture, the teacher noticed that Jasmine had glued a cotton tail and cotton ears to the rabbit, and she had used sparkles to make a multicolored mustache. Immediately, the teacher said, "Oh no, that is not what you were supposed to do. That cotton is for tomorrow's project, and a few minutes ago I noticed that someone had ruined many of the sparkles by dripping glue into them." With a frown on her face, the teacher continued, "Jasmine, because you didn't follow instructions, your picture can not go up on the wall with the rest of the pictures. You will have to take it home." Jasmine quietly laid her picture on the floor, and began to suck her bottom lip.

Again, by not heeding the imperative mode, Jasmine got burned by a stove that was hot before Jasmine painted her picture. Emily was praised for her "creativity," but Jasmine was punished for her "failure to follow instructions." In addition to the immediate punishment of having her picture banished, Jasmine was scolded by her father, when, at pick-up time, he learned that Jasmine had "ruined" some of the teacher's supplies.

Another illustration of the importance of the imperative mode was provided by the authors' son, Omari. Safety concerns were the reason Omari had been told many times, by both parents, to simply get on the school bus, sit down, never get out of his seat, and not to play on the bus. One afternoon, the White, female, elementary school principal called Omari's mother at work to report that Omari was not permitted to ride the school bus for a week. The reason given was that, on the bus that day, Omari had threatened a White female student with a pen knife. Further probing revealed that the girl's mother (a neighbor of ours) had called to report the knife threat. This latter information was of considerable concern because both of Omari's parents believed they had excellent relationships with the neighbor and her children. Indeed, our daughter, Marijata, had befriended our neighbor's older daughter who was having difficulties with other neighborhood children. In this instance, the authors were mistaken in their belief that the stove was turned off when our children were in the presence of our neighbors.

When the authors discussed the matter at home, the first fact that was established was that Omari neither owned nor had obtained a pen knife. Instead, on a key chain, he had a miniature knife, with a blade length of less than a quarter-inch and about an eighth-of-an-inch in width. Omari had indeed gotten out of his seat and joked about the knife on his key chain, playfully indicating, "I'm going to get you" after the girl asked to see the miniature knife. Omari's failure to adhere to the imperative meant that we had to underscore the critical nature of the imperative by severely critiquing his actions and the ensuing series of events, including the role of racism. It should be noted that the inclusion of racism in the discussion on our part ran counter to research by Spencer (1985), which found that many African-American parents did not discuss race as part of their socialization strategies. The theme of this conversation was, "Look what you brought on yourself." As a punishment, he was not allowed to watch television, an activity he enjoyed, for a specified period of time.

Our parenting style at the time of this incident is best described as a blend of authoritative and authoritarian. Parental authority was asserted when Omari was punished for ignoring the imperative. He received a protective parental embrace when we gave him the blunt, "grown-up" perspective (We will tell you what others will not). And finally, our dialogue was person-centered as he was prodded to accept responsibility and problem solve about how not to put himself into similar situations. Omari needed to understand that this particular, externally imposed imperative had more than the obvious rationale that was appropriate for his developmental level at the time that it had first been issued. He had to be made to feel and understand the burn of the hot stove in very direct terminology so that he would eventually be able to construct his own internal imperatives.

The authors subsequently talked with the neighbor and the child and confirmed that no genuine threat had been made. The neighbor offered no explanation when she was asked by Omari's mother, "Given our relationship, why didn't you call me if you had a problem with Omari, and why did you call the principal before carefully checking your daughter's story?" In lieu of the girl's mother offering an explanation, the authors concluded that Omari had been burned by a hot stove, similar to the one that burned his grandfather, Nathaniel S. Colley, Sr. This time, instead of the specter of a lowly Black groom, there was an even greater menace of a Black man with a knife, encountering a White woman.

As stated earlier, the use of imperatives, harsh tones, yelling, and spanking, might appear to be inappropriate childrearing practices, especially if viewed through middle-class White-in-the-United-States lenses. However, as Ogbu (1985) indicated, these tactics have considerable value across the developmental spectrum in a hostile environment as experienced by most African-American children and from which they need protection. It is critical that observers comprehend the context of the hot stove and include in their judgments the full range of those same parents' childrearing practices that in healthy relationships also include plenty of warmth and nurturance. In support of this view, Ogbu stated that "the use of physical punishment discourages emotional dependency while simultaneously encouraging early independence and self-reliance bordering on 'defiance'" (p. 59). And Ogbu continued:

> Purposive training in early independence and self-reliance makes black children independent and self-reliant much earlier than white middle-class children and thus shortens the duration of effective parental control of black children. (p. 60)

Finally, Ogbu stated:

> Emphasis on aggression in early play and parental insistence that the child fight back when attacked by peers encourage children to accept physical actions as a legitimate technique for solving problems. (p. 60)

In fact, Jamal had no one to protect his interests when Billy destroyed his lotto game. He took it upon himself to resolve his dilemma. When his mother finally heard the whole story, she realized that her son had not been given a fair hearing. When she talked to the teacher the next day, she told the teacher that she wanted Jamal to stand up to bullies and defend himself at all costs. "My no hitting rule," she told the teacher, "means don't start anything, don't be a trouble maker. Jamal, however, does get in trouble with me if he does not defend himself." Jamal's mother was teaching him a complex series of lessons that on the surface may appear to be contradictory. If Jamal is to survive encounters with the hot stove, he will have to fuse paradoxes into lessons to live by.

Survival Messages

In order to prepare African-American children to adapt, be resilient, and maintain self-esteem when they encounter the recurring situations emanating throughout their lives from the hot stove, many African-American caregivers have transmitted what have been termed "survival messages," lessons to live by that have specific characteristics. Of cultural importance to these survival messages is not only their responsiveness to African-American children's current social circumstances, but also the fact that the messages are often encoded in ways associated with the African diasporic tradition of proverbial use for childrearing practices (J. L. Daniel & Effinger, 1996).

Use of the simultaneously abstract and concrete proverbial form permits children to make more use of the survival messages as they acquire higher levels of understanding and experience. For example, a 7-year-old African-American girl burned a finger while playing with matches. Using characteristic sarcasm as well as the proverbial form her mother said, "Good, go play with matches again and burn your whole hand off. Bought 'wit' is better than told" (Anonymous, personal communication, 1977). As an adult, the child might find effective application of the proverb when she consciously raises her children by letting them experience artifacts related to sex education, as opposed to simply telling her children about them. In this instance, she might present and explain to her teenage daughter condoms, diaphragms, and birth control pills, knowing the realities of teenage sex and life-threatening sexual diseases.

In an earlier study of African-American intergenerational survival messages, J. L. Daniel and Effinger (1996) concluded as follows:

> The primary caregivers, mostly mothers, stressed the importance of getting a good education, engaging in hard work, and behaving in morally sound ways. Racism and poverty were the perceived major obstacles to success, and women had a heavier burden as a consequence of the combined effects of racism and sexism. Based on the respondents' reports, these bosom biscuits [words of advice] have truly nurtured them through childhood in an effective manner, and they continue to be of tremendous value as guides for living. (p. 199)

J. L. Daniel and Effinger found that to make sure that African-American children understood that racist responses to their color would require extra of them, some of the "hard work survival messages" passed to them were as follows:

1. It's not what you are, but being the best. If you are a street sweeper, then be the best street sweeper there is.
2. You will always have to work harder and try harder than other people, especially White people, to be successful.
3. You have to go through the thorns to get to the roses. (1996, p. 195)

To address matters related to developing healthy self-esteem, African-American children were advised as follows:

1. Pretty is as pretty does, and it is what you do that counts.
2. Always remember that you are (primary caregiver's) daughter. [You are a person born to somebody, a person of worth by virtue of to whom you were born.]
3. It is always best to ask forgiveness rather than permission. [You subjugate yourself when you ask permission. Just do it, and if it is wrong, then ask forgiveness.] (J. L. Daniel & Effinger, 1996, p. 193)

Given the precarious nature of African-American families due to their often unstable economic circumstances and the prevalence of sexism and racism, African-American female children in particular were advised, "Be independent, get an education, and with the education you will be able to take care of yourself" (J. L. Daniel & Effinger, 1996, p. 198). In general, African-American children were advised strongly to get a "good education," given its utility for overcoming their negative social, economic, and political circumstances.

A final illustration captures the proverbial wisdom of "If you don't listen, you will feel." This true story also demonstrates a complex combination of seemingly harsh childrearing in a safe, protected environment, delivered by adults who clearly loved the child, in a situation where the child did not obey the imperative communication mode. Evelynn Ellis, a college professor, told the following story from her childhood.

When Evelynn was 4 years old, she was in the family kitchen with several female members of her extended African-American family. While her mother, aunts, and great grandmother enjoyed their conversation, Evelynn was mesmerized by the beautiful glow emanating from the potbelly, wood-burning stove. She repeatedly tried to get close enough to touch the stove. Each time, her mother and other relatives stopped her by either warning her verbally to stay away from the stove or by physically pulling her back. Evelynn remained enchanted by the stove, seeing only its beauty. Finally, one of her mother's sisters, Ethel, said, "Let her go. Let her touch it. She's not going to let it rest until she finds out for herself." Evelynn's mother looked horrified, but the other family members held her mother and told Evelynn to go ahead and touch the stove. Evelynn remembers thinking that she should probably be leery of this opportunity, but she dismissed the thought because she really wanted to know more about the fascinating glow of the hot stove.

As her mother, who was still being held back, turned away, and the others watched close by, Evelynn moved in awe toward the stove. Very slowly Evelynn raised her hand and touched the hot stove with her finger tips. The pain was excruciating! In those brief seconds, the pain seemed to consume her whole body. One of the women snatched her back from the hot stove. No one had ever again to tell Evelynn about the dangers of the potbelly stove. It was a lesson she has never forgotten. "I am grateful to my family for allowing me to learn an important lesson about something very dangerous in the safety of their company. They knew it was very dangerous, but they had no intention of letting anything really terrible happen to me" (personal communication, May, 1998).

Ellis' literal experience vividly demonstrates the paradoxical context of African-American childrearing practices in a society in which racism is an ever-present danger. The imminency of the danger to the African-American child's physical, emotional, social, and cognitive growth and development requires the imperatives of a survival modality. The health and well-being of the African-American child requires that their caregivers create a safe haven in which to simultaneously expose the child to the hot stove of racism and shield the African-American child from the hot stove's damage.

Negating Cultural Messages That Undermine Self-Esteem

In 1990, Collins noted that, "racial ethnic children must first be taught to survive systems that oppress them. Moreover, this survival must not come at the expense of self esteem" (Collins, 1994, p. 57). Thus, it is not mere rhetoric when Jesse Jackson chants, "I am," and some African-American auditors respond with "somebody." There are so many opportunities for African-American children to be told that they are "nobody" that their very existence is at stake when it comes to their self-esteem. As noted by Curry (1996), "Our children's encounters with racism make the fostering of self-esteem an 'ongoing process'" (p. 137). This fact was made clear when Curry's 17-year-old African-American son was followed by the police who called his home because they thought he had stolen the "nice" jeep he was driving (p. 147).

Regarding the assault on women of color's self-esteem, Collins (1994) wrote,

> Negative controlling images infuse the worlds of male and female children of color....
> Native American girls are encouraged to see themselves as "Pocahontases" or
> "squaws"; Asian-American girls as "geisha girls" or "Suzy Wongs"; Hispanic girls as
> "Madonnas" or "hot-blooded whores"; and African-American girls as "mammies,"
> "matriarchs" and "prostitutes." (p. 57)

In a related study, *The Wisdom of Sixth Mount Zion*, J. L. Daniel (1979) interviewed elderly African-American Baptist church members. Among the resulting extensive collection of intergenerational proverbial messages were those that were consistent with what has been presented regarding the imperative mode and stern parenting. "Spare the rod and spoil the child" and "A child should be seen and not heard" were cited as sound childrearing principles. Others emphasized the need for adaptability, flexibility, and creativity, as children were told, "Stumbling blocks can be carved into stepping stones." When dinner consisted of yesterday's red beans and rice with a side helping of collard greens, the complaining child was told, "Enough is as good as a feast."

Many of the intergenerational proverbial messages were designed to enhance African-American children's self-esteem. To make it clear to the children that they had intrinsic value, notwithstanding their low economic status, African Americans taught children, "The price of the hat ain't the measure of the brain." When children were taunted about their dark skin color, the adults taught that "the blacker the berry, the sweeter the juice." If a child complained about not being able to do something as well as other children, he or she might be told, "If you can't be the bell cow, then gallop in the crowd." "He who steals my purse steals trash, but he who steals my good name steals all that I have" introduces another significant factor related to building self-esteem.

One key dimension of African-American children's self-esteem is related to their personal names. Although from birth through death, skin color serves as a triggering mechanism for racist responses, in time other correlates obtain a similar salience. One of the most important additional stimuli for racist responses is also a stimulus of profound importance for self and collective identity: one's personal name. The authors' research (J. E. Daniel & J. L. Daniel, 1998) indicated that by 4 and 5 years of age, African-American and White children make significantly different behavioral and character attributions as a function of names such as "Megan" and "Cody" when compared to "Tanisha" and "Malik" (see also Holmes, 1995).

J. E. Daniel and J. L. Daniel (1998) interviewed 182 4- and 5-year-old Head Start children (102 African Americans and 80 European-Americans). The authors interviewed the children by asking them to respond to various questions, such as:

> In your new neighborhood, at lunch time, you went to the bathroom. While you were in the bathroom, another child took a bite out of your sandwich. Guess who bit the sandwich, (a) Adam or (b) Jamal? If someone else bit the sandwich, guess who did it (a) Emily or (b) Jasmine? Or, In your new neighborhood, guess who is the smartest person in school, (a) Kyle or (b) Malik? In your new neighborhood, guess who is the smartest, (a) Sarah or (b) Shaniqua? (pp. 478–479)

The statistically significant factor of most importance was obtained in response to the children selecting the name of the person who looked most like them, that is, "In your new neighborhood, guess who looks the most like you, (a) Shante or (b) Samantha? (For males: (a) Maurice or (b) Cody?)" At the .001 level of confidence, it was found consistently for boys and girls, that 86% of the European-American children chose European-American personal names, and 58% of the African-American Children chose European-American personal names. The summarized significance of these findings for the current discussion follows:

> Children as young as 2½ years of age "are learning the appropriate use of gender labels (girl, boy) and learning color names, which they begin to apply to skin color" (Derman-Sparks, 1989, p. 2). Derman-Sparks (1989) also noted that 4- and 5-year-old children have offered racial reasons for not interacting with children (p. 2). Hence, we believe it is a reasonable expectation that everyday stimuli of race-related personal names, along with the many sources of racist information, constitute part of the integrative learning process that children experience with regard to the development of racial stereotyping. (J. E. Daniel & J. L. Daniel, 1998, pp. 488–489)

Thus, it is recommended that African-American children's names be selected with extreme care, that names be selected to truly reflect positive images grounded in such things as African-American culture and family traditions. African-American children's caregivers will need constantly to educate African-American children regarding the uniqueness associated with their personal names as a means of further enhancing self-esteem. For example, we named our son Omari. A number of times during his early childhood, we explained that Omari was a powerful ancient African king and that for some time he persecuted people for their religious faith. Later in life, he changed his mind and became a convert. We explained that we named him Omari both because of ancient African royalty as well as the importance of powerful people being reasonable, being willing to understand others, and if appropriate, modifying their own behavior as opposed to modifying the behavior of those with less power.

Names are just one facet of the self-esteem issues related to skin color. Thus, racism can be so destructive (Erikson, 1963; Grier & Cobbs, 1992) that caregivers must be prepared to address the hot stove on a number of fronts. For example, early language experiences, such as reading to children and conversing with them, not only offer opportunities to share African-American culture and images, but also build school readiness skills that keep children from falling behind and staying behind academically (Hart & Risley, 1995; see also Davilla, chap.5, this volume). The parents of academically successful African-American males supplemented the assigned school work (Hrabowski et al., 1998). The authors regularly gave their son and daughter additional reading to do. By the end of high school, they were familiar with a variety of books that might have been used in a college-level introductory African-American literature course.

Media images of African Americans are another example of the hot stove (Parks, chap. 4, this volume). All forms of the media are notorious for presenting images of African Americans in far less than flattering light. African-American children can better disregard and combat the racist images if they are media literate. The role of adults is critical in deciphering truth from fiction, whether it appears in a story line or an advertisement. A number of strategies for addressing the self-esteem of African-American young children can be found in the recommendations of other authors listed in the "Resources for Parents About Raising African-American Children" (Appendix; and see also Parks, chap. 4, this volume).

SUMMARY AND CONCLUSION

Progress in research related to parent–child interactions requires that scholars recognize the importance of studying child development practices in the context of the children's dominant cultural milieu. For African Americans, the hot stove of racism is a constant dangerous part of their life experiences and contributes to childrearing practices that often assume the imperative mode, a mode easily misinterpreted through White, middle-class cultural lenses. With rules applied disproportionately against them and having to pay the severest of penalties for breaking rules, African-American children's healthy growth and development depend considerably on their ability to function within a rule-governed social system permeated with racism. Recognizing the need to also enhance their children's self-esteem, many African-American caregivers use strict and simultaneously warm approaches that assist the children in becoming resilient and socially and academically competent (Hrabowski et al., 1998; Masten & Coatsworth, 1998; McLoyd, 1998; Ogbu, 1985).

Notwithstanding the omnipresent nature of the hot stove phenomenon, future research should help eliminate the oversimplification of parenting styles, giving greater analysis to the complex task of parenting African-American children across the developmental spectrum of socioemotional, cognitive, and physical growth, albeit in the context of the hot stove. There is a need to understand better how African-American children, at different developmental levels and in view of their personal experiences with the hot stove, receive and make meaning of the imperatives coming from their caregivers. It would also be useful to reassess (Cross, 1985; Spencer, 1985) the frequency and complexity of racial dialogue African-American caregivers engage in with children at various developmental levels, but particularly the early childhood years.

Ultimately, what is needed is valid and reliable information that assists African-American caregivers to parent in ways that aid their children in becoming strong at their "centers of being," that is, sufficiently prepared affectively and cognitively to self-correct, regain their balance, or regenerate when exposed to the harmful effects of the hot stove.

APPENDIX: RESOURCES FOR PARENTS ABOUT RAISING AFRICAN-AMERICAN CHILDREN

Comer, J. P., & Poussaint, A. F. (1992). *Raising Black children*. New York: Plume.
Edelman, M. W. (1992). *The measure of our success: A letter to my children and yours*. Boston: Beacon.
Golden, M. (1995). *Saving our sons: Raising Black children in a turbulent world*. New York: Doubleday.
Hale, J. E. (1982). *Black children: Their roots, culture, and learning styles*. Provo, UT: Brigham Young University Press.
Hale, J. E. (1994). *Unbank the fire: Visions for the education of African American children*. Baltimore, MD: Johns Hopkins University Press.
Hopson, D. P., & Hopson, D. (1990). *Different and wonderful: Raising Black children in a race-conscious society*. New York: Prentice-Hall.
Hrabowski, F. A., Maton, K. I., & Greif, G. L. (1998). *Beating the odds: Raising academically successful African American males*. New York: Oxford University Press.

REFERENCES

Adams, J. H. (1993). Leadership in an era of broken symbols. In A. S. Hoots (Ed.), *Prophetic voices: Black preachers speak on behalf of children* (pp. 1–3). Washington, DC: Children's Defense Fund.
Alejandro-Wright, M. N. (1985). The child's conception of racial classification: A socio-cognitive developmental model. In M. B. Spencer, G. K. Brookins, & W. R. Allen (Eds.), *Beginnings: The social and affective development of Black children* (pp. 185–200). Hillsdale, NJ: Lawrence Erlbaum Associates.
Baldwin, J. (1963). *The fire next time*. New York: Dial Press.

Bernstein, B. (1986). A sociolinguistic approach to socialization with some reference to educability. In J. J. Gumprez & D. Hymes (Eds.), *Directions in sociolinguistics: The ethnography of communication* (pp. 465–497). Oxford, England: Blackwell.

Boyd-Franklin, N. (1989). *Black families in therapy: A multisystems approach.* New York: Guilford.

Burleson, B. R., Delia, J. G., & Applegate, J. L. (1995). The socialization of person-centered communication: Parents' contribution to their children's social-cognitive and communication skills. In M. A. Fitzpatrick & A. L. Vangelisti (Eds.), *Explaining family interactions* (pp. 34–76). Thousand Oaks, CA: Sage.

Collins, P. H. (1987). The meaning of motherhood in Black culture and Black mother–daughter relationships. *Sage: A Scholarly Journal of Black Women, 4,* 3–10.

Collins, P. H. (1994). Shifting the center: Race, class, and feminist theorizing about motherhood. In E. N. Glenn, G. Chang, & L. R. Forcey (Eds.), *Mothering: Ideology, experience, and agency* (pp. 45–65). New York: Routledge.

Cose, E. (1994). *Rage of a privileged class.* New York: HarperCollins.

Cross, W. E. (1985). Black identity: Rediscovering the distinction between personal identity and reference group orientation. In M. B. Spencer, G. K. Brookins, & W. R. Allen (Eds.), *Beginnings: The social and affective development of Black children* (pp. 155–171). Hillsdale, NJ: Lawrence Erlbaum Associates.

Curry, B. R. (1996). Mothers confronting racism. In M. T. Reddy (Ed.), *Everyday acts against racism: Raising children in a multiracial world* (pp. 132–143). Seattle, WA: Seale.

Daniel, J. E. (1993). Infants to toddlers: Qualities of effective transitions. *Young Children, 48*(6), 16–21.

Daniel, J. E. (1995). New beginnings: Transitions for difficult children. *Young Children, 50*(3), 17–23.

Daniel, J. E., & Daniel J. L. (1998). Preschool children's responses to race-related personal names. *Journal of Black Studies, 28,* 471–490.

Daniel, J. E., & Shapiro, J. (1996). Infant transitions from home to center-based care. *Child and Youth Care Forum, 25*(2), 111–123.

Daniel, J. L. (1979). *The wisdom of Sixth Mt. Zion.* Pittsburgh, PA: Author.

Daniel, J. L., & Effinger, M. J. (1996). Bosom biscuits: A study of African American intergenerational communication. *Journal of Black Studies, 27,* 183–200.

Derman-Sparks, L. (1989). *Anti-bias curriculum: Tools for empowering young children.* Washington, DC: National Association for the Education of Young Children.

Diggs, R., & Robinson, G. (1994, November). *Exploring family communication's valuing and respecting in two African-American families by prevail: Parent role empowerment through values, acceptance, interaction and love.* Paper presented at the meeting of the Speech Communication Association, New Orleans, LA.

Erikson, E. (1963). *Childhood and society* (2nd ed.). New York: Norton.

Essed, P. (1991). *Understanding everyday racism: An interdisciplinary theory.* Newberry Park, CA.: Sage.

Ferguson-Peters, M. (1985). Racial socialization of young Black children. In H. McAdoo & J. McAdoo (Eds.), *Black children* (pp. 159–173). Beverly Hills, CA: Sage.

Golden, M. (1995). *Saving our sons: Raising Black children in a turbulent world.* New York: Doubleday.

Greens, B. (1990). Sturdy bridges: The role of African-American mothers in the socialization of African American children. *Women and Therapy, 10*(1–2), 205–225.

Grier, W. H., & Cobbs, P. M. (1992). *Black rage* (2nd ed.) New York: Basic Books.

Hart, B., & Risley, T. R. (1995). *Meaningful differences in the everyday lives of young American children.* Baltimore: Brookes Publishing.

Holmes, R. M. (1995). *How young children perceive race.* Thousand Oaks, CA: Sage.

Hopson, D. P., & Hopson, D. (1990). *Different and wonderful: Raising Black children in a race-conscious society.* New York: Prentice-Hall.

Hrabowski, F. A., Maton, K. I., & Greif, G. L. (1998). *Beating the odds: Raising academically successful African American males.* New York: Oxford University Press.

Jackson, J. F. (1993). Multiple caregiving among African Americans and infant attachment: The need for an emic approach. *Human Development, 36,* 87–102.

Julian, T. W., McKenry, P. C., & McKelvey, M. W. (1994). Cultural variations in parenting: Perceptions of Caucasian, African-American, Hispanic, and Asian-American parents. *Family Relations, 43,* 30–37.

Kim, Y. Y., & Ruben, B. D. (1988). Intercultural transformation: A systems theory. In Y. Y. Kim & W. B. Gudykunst (Eds.), *Theories in intercultural communication* (pp. 299–321). Thousand Oaks, CA: Sage.

Masten, A. S., & Coatsworth, J. D. (1998). The development of competence in favorable and unfavorable environments: Lessons from research on successful children. *American Psychologist, 53*(2), 205–220.

McLoyd, V. C. (1990). The impact of economic hardship on black families and children: Psychological distress, parenting, and socioemotional development. *Child Development, 61*, 311–346.

McLoyd, V. C. (1998). Socioeconomic disadvantage and child development. *American Psychologist, 53*(2), 185–204.

Miller, R. L., & Miller, B. (1990). Mothering the biracial child: Bridging the gaps between African-American and White parenting styles, *Women and Therapy, 10*(1–2), 169–179.

Milner, D. (1983). *Children and race.* Beverly Hills, CA: Sage.

Ogbu, J. (1985). A cultural ecology of competence among inner city Blacks. In M. B. Spencer, G. K. Brookins, & W. R. Allen (Eds.), *Beginnings: The social and affective development of Black children* (pp. 45–66). Hillsdale, NJ: Lawrence Erlbaum Associates.

Page, C. (1996). *Showing my color: Impolite essays on race and identity.* New York: HarperCollins.

Pinderhughes, E. (1989). *Understanding race, ethnicity and power: The key of efficacy in clinical practice.* New York: The Free Press.

Rose, T. (1994). *Black noise: Rap music and Black culture in contemporary America.* Hanover, NH: Wesleyan University Press.

Santos, P. A. (1996). A mother's birth. In M. T. Reddy (Ed.), *Everyday acts against racism: Raising children in a multicultural world* (pp. 20–30). Seattle, WA: Seale.

Socha, T. J., Sanchez-Hucles, J., Bromley, J., & Kelly, B. (1995). Invisible parents and children: Exploring African-American parent–child communication. In T. J. Socha & G. H. Stamp (Eds.), *Parents, children, and communication: Frontiers of theory and research* (pp. 127–145). Hillsdale, NJ: Lawrence Erlbaum Associates.

Spencer, M. B. (1985). Cultural cognition and social cognition as identity correlates of Black children's personal-social development. In M. B. Spencer, G. K. Brookins, & W. R. Allen (Eds.), *Beginnings: The social and affective development of Black children* (pp. 215–230). Hillsdale, NJ: Lawrence Erlbaum Associates.

Thornton, M. C., Chatters, L. M., Taylor, R. J., & Allen, W. R. (1990). Sociodemographic and environmental correlates of racial socialization by Black parents, *Child Development, 61*, 401–409.

❦ 3 ❦

African-American Parent–Child Communication About Racial Derogation

Isabel B. Ferguson
University of Pennsylvania

This chapter examines communication between African-American parents and children about racially negative interpersonal encounters. In particular, the focus is on episodes of *racial derogation*—a term used here to include expressions of disparagement, depreciation, or low opinion directed at an individual because of membership in a racial group. Group derogation may express overt enmity, or it may casually relay a message to members of the group that they are disrespected. Racial derogation, as with any form of group derogation, is potentially harmful to its individual and group targets. As a communication problem, derogation disrupts interactions in the immediate environment and undermines relationships in the larger society. When preventive efforts fail and if incidents of derogatory communication are not addressed, their negative messages may be internalized by anyone who is exposed to them—the targeted person, the derogator, or witnesses to the occasion. Although researchers disagree about the age range for children's internalization of racial stereotypes (Holmes, 1995; Spencer, 1982), children may imitate the derogating behavior they observe, especially when it is unchallenged. For that reason, racial derogation is an issue that should be addressed by parents of all races.

This investigation considers how African-American parents approach the problem of racial insults and what conditions might account for differences in their family communication about the issue. The study is concerned with incidents that respondents perceive as racial derogation or racial insults regardless of the speaker's intent. The primary goal of the study is to generate insights to assist African-American parents in preparing their children to maintain feelings of personal integrity and self-control in the face of these negative experiences (see also Daniel & Daniel, chap. 2, this volume). A secondary aim of the analysis is to contribute to understanding the potential effects of parent–child communication about race in all U.S. families.

RATIONALE

The problem of preparing African-American children to meet, survive, and overcome the negative treatment anticipated for them as devalued members of U.S. society has been addressed from various perspectives. Preventive and remedial efforts to protect children from negative racial interactions have been incorporated in collective action by U.S. individuals of all races. For example, the semiannual magazine, *Teaching Tolerance* (see Bullard, 1994), was developed to teach children to accept and value cultural differences. The magazine is distributed free to educators through contributions of private donors. Numerous colleges have established policy regulations, applicable to their employees and students, that define, prohibit, and describe mechanisms for addressing racial harassment. Legal scholars struggle to frame these rules in a way that overcomes the objections raised on constitutional grounds (Bussian, 1995).

In addition, many African-American parents have recognized the importance of "racially socializing" their children, that is, preparing them to cope with the racial environment (Daniel & Daniel, chap. 2, this volume; Greene, 1990; McAdoo, 1985). Parents employ a variety of modeling and communication approaches in their attempts to accomplish this task (Thornton, Chatters, Taylor, & Allen, 1990), and most parents find this responsibility an awesome challenge. Yet, prior research has not adequately examined what parents do to fulfill that commitment (see Socha, Sanchez-Hucles, Bromley, & Kelly, 1995).

The research reported in this chapter selects one type of negative interracial episode, racial derogation, and considers how African-American parents teach children to cope with this experience. An hypothesis underlying this study is that parents' conceptualization of racial derogation influences which approaches they adopt to combat it personally and to teach to their children. In determining the range of possible methods an African-American parent considers, one crucial factor may be whether he or she construes racial derogation as primarily an insult or defines the racial component as the critical element in the event. When race predominates in the conceptualization, the insult represents the social and political history of race in the United States, an impossibly complex conundrum for the child or the parent to confront. When racial insults are analogized to other kinds of group derogation in children's experience (gender, age, or weight, for example), myriad psychosocial behaviors are imaginable to address the problem.

In particular, the present study seeks to identify factors that may influence how racial derogation is construed and considers the role that parents' direct communication can play in preparing children to respond to racial derogation. The motivating hypothesis here is that, through purposive communication, parents can define efficacious, resilient behavior for children to perform in anticipated circumstances. Dissonance theory (Festinger, Riecken, & Schachter, 1956) provides a basis for understanding some of the potential effects of derogation on targeted children. Particularly relevant is the construct of the dissonant communications environment in which direct verbal attacks express racial, religious, or ethnic hostility and carry messages to children about how much they and their group are disliked (Rosenberg, 1977). Self-efficacy research (Bandura, 1991, 1993) and resilience research (Luthar, 1993) offer theories about African-American parents' socializing practices that address problems of race. General systems theory provides an holistic perspective of derogation as an interactive communications phenomenon in which participants have a potential for modifying the dynamic (e.g., see Kim & Ruben, 1988). And finally, immunization theory and research present a methodology by which anticipatory communication can promote resistance to the predictable challenges contained in derogatory messages (McGuire & Papageorgis, 1961).

REVIEW OF BACKGROUND STUDIES

Considerations about race and public policy have engaged the attention of social scientists throughout U.S. history. For example, about 100 years ago, DuBois (1899) investigated the social and economic conditions of African Americans and made policy recommendations for improving their relations with White fellow citizens. In the late 1940s and 1950s, researchers studied segregation and desegregation in the armed services, examining the effects on Black and White service members and on local communities and considering policy implications for the country's future (Bogart, 1969). After World War II, several studies of race investigated the effects of legally enforced segregation on African Americans. This helped lead to the Supreme Court conclusion in *Brown v. Board of Education* (1954) that intangible factors in legally mandated separation of educational facilities tended to retard the educational and mental development of African-American children. Subsequently, social scientists have increased their efforts to improve their conceptualizations of the intangible effects of race.

   In the decades following court-mandated desegregation (i.e., after 1954), researchers repeatedly investigated hypotheses about associations between the racial environment and psychodynamic characteristics of African Americans. These studies frequently have been framed in terms of the relation between race and self-esteem (Diggs, chap. 6, this volume). Coopersmith (1967) defined self-esteem as the relatively enduring evaluation that an individual makes regarding his or her own capabilities, significance, and worth. He noted that low self-esteem implies subjective feelings of inadequacy, unworthiness, anxiety, guilt, and shame. Coopersmith described self-esteem as socially determined; thus, derogation and demeaning actions by others can lead to low self-esteem.

A number of studies set in desegregated schools of the 1970s, using a variety of self-esteem measures, overwhelmingly found lower global self-esteem among African-American children than other children in the schools (Rosenberg, 1977). However, some researchers argue against the inference that damage to self-esteem is because of minority status, and question whether the notion of a unitary self-concept is appropriate for accounting for children's conflicting and ambivalent attitudes about various dimensions of themselves (Martinez & Dukes, 1991; McAdoo, 1985). Studies using global measures of self-esteem may tend to erroneously attribute some damage to the fact of minority status, whereas proper consideration of the effective interpersonal environment would reveal that the vehicle for damage is hostile treatment (Rosenberg, 1977).

Reviewing the 1970s' self-esteem research in terms of contextual dissonance provides insight into the dynamic of derogation for African-American children. The term *contextual dissonance* (Aronson, 1992) characterizes environments in which there is discrepancy between an individual's social characteristics and those in the surrounding population. When an individual's self-concept is implicated in such an environment, he or she will be highly motivated to reduce dissonance (Aronson, 1992).

Dissonant experiences fall into three categories, which derive from (a) communication, (b) culture, or (c) comparison reference group differences (Rosenberg, 1977). The dissonant communication environment features widespread direct verbal attacks expressing racial, religious, or ethnic hostility. These negative communication episodes contain messages targeted to children not only about how much they themselves are disliked, but also about how much their group is disliked. Children in these environments have a more negative (and more accurate) perception of the status of their group in the overall culture (Aronson, 1992). Cultural dissonance occurs if people find that the prevalent group norms in an environment differ from the norms of their culture or subculture. Limited research has demonstrated that higher status minority individuals also experience cultural dissonance, with the effect of lowering self-esteem (Rosenberg, 1977). The practical consequences for children in this setting may be to not fit in, be rejected, be ridiculed, or be despised. Cultural dissonance is more subtle than other forms, and it may be difficult to distinguish some effects of cultural dissonance from effects of the hostile verbal and nonverbal messages that comprise communication dissonance. The notion of "dissonant comparison reference groups" is based on the theory of social comparison processes (Festinger, Riecken, & Schachter, 1956). The theory postulates that people make positive, neutral, or negative self-evaluations through a process of comparing themselves to standards set by others and that the others—comprising a comparison reference group—are usually those in their immediate environment. Negative racial experience can be a mechanism by which racism results in relatively enduring lower self-esteem for African Americans. However, racial derogation is more certain to risk a transitory disruption of the child's subjective feeling of well-being, which amounts to dissonance. Some studies suggest that, among White students, lower economic level or social status in the school context also generates dissonance and has negative consequences for self-esteem (Rosenberg, 1977).

Taken as a whole, this research suggests the following dynamic of racial derogation and potential responses to it. Dissonance is created as African Americans' belief in their self-worth is confronted by the conflicting belief communicated by derogators that African Americans are not valued. Maximum dissonance results when the lower evaluation is attributable to an individual's comparison reference group. When the reference group is composed of those in the immediate environment (as is usually the case), and the derogator is seen as representative of the reference group, individuals, in order to reduce dissonance, tend to abandon their belief in their own worth in favor of a lowered self-evaluation. However, if individuals maintain a group other than those in a particular environment as their comparison reference group or if a derogator is seen as not representative of the immediately surrounding group, then dissonance may be resolved by discrediting the derogator, and self-esteem can be maintained. Note that witnesses to derogation may unwittingly support the derogator's standing as representative of the relevant comparison reference group.

A general systems perspective offers further understanding of the phenomenon of racial derogation (e.g., Kim & Ruben, 1988) and suggests the potential benefit for African-American children if they learn strategic responses for such incidents. Intentional racial derogation can be viewed as a system in which the derogator, the target, and witnesses, if any, are interdependent participants in the continual give-and-take process of communication between races. Derogation disrupts the target's existing internal order, and he or she experiences disequilibrium and stress (dissonance in Aronson's terms as discussed earlier). When targeted persons respond adaptively to derogation, they might transform their internal conditions and affect other elements of the system. Thus, the stress of derogation, accompanied by an adaptive response, may result in an internally stronger individual, better prepared to cope with analogous environmental challenges in the future.

Although environments in which racial derogation occurs may often have an intercultural dimension, I argue that racial derogation is essentially an intracultural rather than an intercultural event. That is, racial derogation relies on shared cultural knowledge of a social status hierarchy regarding race in order to have meaning for the interdependent parties in the system. Without that shared knowledge, the racially derogatory expression, or any group derogation, would lack impact. The importance of shared knowledge is most easily recognized in nonverbal derogation. An example was provided by a respondent in this study who reported a public display of a rope tied in the shape of a noose in a predominantly White high school. One consequence of that distinction is that the particular stress-reducing activities undertaken by the targeted person in an intracultural systems event must differ in kind from those theorized as adaptive in the intercultural context. Thus, for example, it should not be inferred that internal growth would result if African-American children were to adopt a positive orientation toward the particular environmental system where they have been derogated. On the contrary, I propose that there is advantage for derogated children in not accepting the phenomenon of derogation as an immutable characteristic of any given environment.

Prior research has found that minority-group children may not necessarily internalize stereotypes about their race—especially before age 7, the concrete operational stage of cognitive development (Spencer, 1982). This research suggests that internalization of negative messages and concomitant damage to self-esteem might be forestalled if preparation for defending against racist communication begins early, before children reach age 7. As an expression of communication dissonance or disequilibrium, racial derogation's effects might be reduced through reinterpretation of one of the inconsistent elements in the experience, for example, by cognitive, strategic responses that resolve dissonance in favor of a positive self-concept. Although researchers disagree about the age range for children's internalization of racial stereotypes and about the relation between those stereotypes and cognitive development (Hirschfeld, 1995; Holmes, 1995), the harmonious interracial relations commonly observed among young children may be associated with their relatively limited cognitive ability to form hierarchical categories (Holmes, 1995).

Responses to Derogation

An individual's affective and behavioral responses to experiences of derogation may be varied and complex. Affective responses may include anger, shame, guilt, and feelings of personal powerlessness. Fear may also be part of the reaction, for example, when the communication is perceived as a precursor of physical attack. Behavioral responses may involve appealing to an authority to control the derogator, turning to a supportive person or community for comfort, attempting to ignore the problem by hiding signs of emotional injury, expressing a verbal rebuttal, or retaliating with physical aggression.

Although it is sometimes argued that the history and duration of racial hostility in U.S. national culture result in derogation experiences for African Americans that are distinguishable in kind as well as degree from those of other groups, analysis of behaviors practiced by other socially targeted groups may be applicable in an interracial context. This approach is suggested by the holistic perspective of general systems theory, which encourages us to construct the intracultural phenomenon of group derogation (whether related to race or any other stratified, stereotyped, social designation) as an interactive system and to examine it without reference to the specific content of the communicated messages (e.g., Kim & Ruben, 1988).

Sexual harassment provides a useful analogy. That is, those instances of sexual harassment that consist of expressions of disparagement and low opinion directed at an individual because of gender amount to group derogation as the term is used in this chapter. Responses to sexual harassment have been characterized as falling into three general categories: sociostructural (political or economic change), organizational (altered policies, procedures, or programs), and interpersonal. Sociostructural and organizational remedies for group derogation, such as legislation and regulations designed to deter or punish perpetrators, typically acknowledge that group derogation poses a risk of psychological damage to members of the derogated group and threatens the well-being of society. These approaches attempt to control the derogator's ability to initiate and direct action. That is, they implicitly acknowledge agency in the person who derogates. With respect to sexual harassment as with racial derogation, researchers have paid little attention to interpersonal responses, such as directly and verbally confronting the harasser (Bingham & Burleson, 1989). This chapter argues for supplementing sociostructural and organizational remedies with interpersonal strategies where derogated children also behave as agents, assuming some control over their own well-being.

Racial Socialization

Building such coping skills in children is one aspect of their socialization: the process of preparing them to assume the roles and responsibilities of adults in their society. Many children in the United States experience cultural dissonance from time to time, and some parents are aware of the need to socialize them to incorporate norms that conflict with those of their cultural group. However, researchers have generally recognized that U.S. society makes it necessary for African-American parents to "racially socialize" their children, that is, to teach them how to live in the frequently hostile U.S. environment (Boykin & Toms, 1985; Daniel & Daniel, chap. 2, this volume; Ferguson-Peters, 1985). The distinctive developmental task for these children is to incorporate dominant societal values that insidiously devalue their group (McAdoo, 1985). Furthermore, Black children frequently operate in a context of arbitrary responses to their behavior, unable to either predict whether certain actions will be approved, disapproved, or ignored or to determine when they will be permitted to openly express hurt and anger (Greene, 1990).

Many African-American parents recognize that racial matters contribute to stress in their lives and in their young children's lives and perceive themselves as investing special effort in preparing their children for coping with racism. Yet, Black parents are concerned that they avoid overwhelming or overprotecting their children as they impart the essential warnings about racial dangers and disappointments. In a study of the rearing of African-American toddlers, parents reported feeling that they had not been adequately prepared by their own parents for dealing with the negative racial interactions they had experienced. Although most of these parents believed that their children (ages 2½ to 3 years) had not yet experienced racial incidents, about one half of them had already told their children that they were Black (Ferguson-Peters, 1985).

Racial socialization and Black cultural expression in general may reflect traditional West African cultural ethos as modified by the U.S. experience (see Socha & Diggs, chap. 1, this volume), which includes racism and oppression. Communalism in African-American culture, that is, the notion that group interests and interdependence of people have priority over individual endeavors, has been identified as a significant theme in African-American family life and culture (Boykin & Toms, 1985; Dainton, chap. 7, this volume; Jagers & Mock, 1993; Socha & Diggs, chap. 1, this volume). Because cultural experiences affect the priorities given to various beliefs, values, and behaviors, when African cultural prioritization dominates, it may foster group interdependence at the expense of individual empowerment. That is, parents might perceive that teaching children to practice cognitive strategies encourages self-contained individualism and threatens the cultural tradition of communal responses to racism (Allen & Boykin, 1992; Franklin & Boyd-Franklin, 1985). A research question addressed by the present study is whether parents tend to perceive the two approaches (individual and communal) as competing options.

Skills Training, Self-Efficacy, and Resilience

Children assessed as having higher levels of actual and self-perceived competence in a domain are more likely to have parents who perceive the childrearing tasks in that area as less difficult, and parents' perception of higher levels of difficulty is generally associated with lower actual competence in that domain (Ladd & Price, 1986). Research findings in Ladd and Price's study were ambiguous as to causal direction of this association, and the authors hypothesized a bidirectional relationship, where (a) parents might perceive their tasks as easy because their children display the skills, or (b) parents might perceive their own mastery of skills in the domain and easily provide a model of self-confidence that their children imitate through self-perception and actual performance. Self-efficacy theory argues that perceived capabilities affect or control one's level of performance of tasks—including one's own thought processes, affective states, and social interactions (Bandura, 1991, 1993). Some investigators challenged the theory and related research supporting the causal attributes of self-belief (Corcoran, 1991; Powers, 1991). However, this chapter argues that African-American children can avoid some negative effects of derogation if they hold self-efficacious beliefs and learned skills for responding to derogation.

For any individual child, making a self-efficacious verbal response to racial derogation may represent totally novel behavior or may reflect a skill he or she exercises in certain other contexts. Children who already possess the necessary verbal and social skills may require training to manage anxiety caused by the negative interracial context. This prompts the hypothesis that parents' perceived self-efficacy in dealing with problems of racial derogation may affect their level of engagement in teaching related skills to their children and may present the additional task of overcoming their own anxieties about assertive responses.

The term *resilience*, in general, refers to the ability of individuals to display competence in a domain (for example, academic, social, or emotional areas) despite the high risk associated with their circumstances. Three aspects of resilience identified in prior studies—overcoming unfavorable odds, functioning competently in a chronically stressful environment, and recovering from trauma (Nettles, 1992)—are all relevant to African-American children's ability to combat racist communication. One useful model for building resilience in children is coaching, that is, teaching skills through demonstration of performance, with the learner bearing responsibility for learning (Nettles & Pleck, 1993). Teaching resilience should also incorporate proactive problem solving and strategy development as means for managing various adverse experiences, including racial derogation. Strategy development will be most effective when children actively participate in the process (Luthar, 1993; Rosenthal & Zimmerman, 1978). Fictional and personal narratives as models of resilience and triumph are also socializing mechanisms that can limit the negative impact of racial messages (Joseph, 1994). Because self-perception of social skill in itself may be effective in reducing stress (Luthar, Doernberger, & Zigler, 1993), another research question to be answered here is whether parents and children who have a reserve of socially efficacious strategies experience less stress when insults occur—even if the strategy is not exercised.

Anticipatory Protective Communication: The Immunization Model

Early persuasion research suggests guidelines for designing communication strategies to protect children from the effects of insults. Empirical studies, prompted by defections of U.S. prisoners of war during the 1950s, investigated preemptive protection against persuasive communication. The experimental design used in the studies was conceptualized according to the medical model for immunization against physical disease. Pre-treatments were accordingly termed *inoculation*. Subjects were exposed to messages composed of potentially damaging communication in order to build resistance against later encounters with more potent challenges to beliefs.

Two general categories of inoculation were found to differ in effectiveness. Messages supporting original beliefs had very little protective effect, whereas messages refuting speculated arguments against the original beliefs provided protection against subsequent challenge. Pretreatments that addressed generalized challenges to a belief seemed to provide protection without anticipating the specific content of the challenging arguments (McGuire & Papageorgis, 1961; Papageorgis & McGuire, 1961).

Benefits from preemptive communication strategies have also been demonstrated in situations in which supporters of political candidates gained protection against attack messages from the opposition (Pfau & Kenski, 1990). The effect of inoculation increased as the level of party identification strengthened, and the authors argued that stronger party identification generates greater motivation for supporters to defend their existing attitudes. This finding suggests that African-American children with stronger racial identities will benefit most from learning verbal response strategies. Other research has shown that adolescent attitudes against smoking initiation can be strengthened through inoculation (Pfau, Van Bockern, & Kang, 1992). Inoculation pretreatments appeared to confer greater resistance among adolescents with low self-esteem. The authors suggested that adolescent susceptibility to peer pressures played a role in the relationship between self-esteem and effective inoculation.

Because racial insults contradict African-American children's beliefs in their own self-worth, inoculation pretreatments offer the means to reduce dissonance by defending against the challenging message. Self-concept is implicated with derogation, therefore, children should have strong motivation to actually employ defenses and reduce dissonance (Aronson, 1992). In general, my review of past research suggests various additional hypotheses: (a) Participation by children in developing the strategies will increase effectiveness, (b) defensive strategies need not be addressed to the specific content of derogation, and (c) supportive messages (e.g., simply reassuring a derogated child that she or he is worthwhile) will probably have only minimal effect.

PRELIMINARY STUDY

A preliminary study[1] featured 17 exploratory interviews conducted during spring and fall of 1994. These interviews attempted to answer the following questions: (a) Under what circumstances do African-American parents and children talk about racial derogation? (b) Do parents have an interest in teaching children specific skills for coping with derogation? (c) How do parents explain derogatory experiences to children? The general purpose of the interviews was to help formulate questions for a subsequent survey.

Participants

The sample included 5 personal friends and 7 acquaintances of the interviewer, and 5 persons recruited from a community organization meeting or referred by

---

[1]These studies were conducted for a Master's thesis at the Annenberg School for Communication, University of Pennsylvania (1995). A preliminary analysis of the study was presented at the 1996 Mid-Atlantic Graduate Communication Conference, sponsored by Temple University, Mass Media and Communication Program.

other participants. Sampling among friends and acquaintances attempted to identify respondents who were articulate, known to reflect on their childrearing goals and practices, and representative of diverse educational backgrounds and ages. Recruits not previously known to the interviewer were self-selected. The attempt to recruit an equal number of fathers and mothers from any source was markedly unsuccessful.[2]

Respondents included 3 fathers and 14 mothers. Ages were either known or estimated to be as follows: 8 parents in their 30s; 2 parents in their 40s; and 7 parents in their 50s. Information about educational status for some respondents was as follows: 2 had undergraduate degrees; 2 had graduate degrees; 3 were college students; and 4 parents were high school graduates. No information was gathered regarding the educational status of the other 6 respondents or about the economic status of any respondents.

Procedures

Eight interviews were conducted in person and 9 respondents were interviewed by telephone. (Taping was not requested for the initial interview, and one respondent refused to be taped. All other interviews were taped but not transcribed.) The interviews consisted of loosely framed questions about racial derogation: the experiences of respondents' children, memories of incidents in their own childhood, and stories respondents had heard. Interviews conducted in the fall presented respondents with one or both of the following vignettes, which depict previously reported encounters of children with racial insults.

Vignette 1

An African-American family lives in a racially mixed neighborhood with other African-American, European-American, Indian-American, and Asian-American families. Their 8-year-old son's class in school has a similar mix of children. One evening the boy told his father, "I'm so mad at Sarah! I hate her!" The father asked what had happened, and this is what the son told him.

"At recess today I was playing with the other boys. We were chasing each other around. Sarah (who is White) came over to where I was and said, 'Black people are mean.' I didn't pay any attention to her. I just kept on playing. She kept following me and saying that. 'Black people are mean.' 'Black people are mean.' After a while I got so mad, I pushed her! Then she said, 'You see there? My Mom and Dad told me Black people are mean!"

Vignette 2

An African-American teenager was working in a fast-food restaurant after school and on weekends. One day he overheard his White supervisor say to the cook, an Afri-

---

[2]In general, greater effort was required to engage fathers as compared to mothers in responding to the survey. Future studies should consider whether male interviewers might improve participation by fathers or whether some other factor may account for the observed difference between genders.

can-American young man, "Do all Black people work the way you do? If so, it's no wonder that Black people don't have jobs."

The primary purpose of the vignettes was to help keep interviews focused on racial derogation as opposed to the broader topic of race relations. A secondary objective was to gauge parents' willingness to develop strategies when presented with a new instance of derogation. Interviews were subjectively interpreted and used to guide subsequent stages of the research.

Results and Discussion

The interviews tended to support prior findings of researchers, who concluded that many African-American parents are concerned with racially socializing their children to protect them from the emotional harm of racial discrimination (Greene, 1990; McAdoo, 1985). Parents in the sample perceived that communication about race is problematic in general and especially difficult when talking with their children. Many of them struggled with questions about whether and when to warn children about problems concerning race relations and what the content of the warnings should be.

The variation in these parents' attitudes concerning communication with their children about racial insults was very wide, and there was a notable contrast between men and women in regard to their anticipatory instructions to children. All 3 male respondents indicated a clear commitment to talk to their children about race relations before incidents occurred. Only 1 of the 14 female respondents specifically warned her child about racial problems. Two mothers explicitly rejected the notion of teaching their sons strategic responses to racial derogation.

One father reported that he had instructed his grade-school children to use class discussions on historical European accomplishments as opportunities to introduce analogous information about African history. Another father reported that he used newspaper text and photographs to demonstrate to his 8-year-old son that portrayals of African Americans in the news media are often false or misleading. The third father reported that he had given his children warnings about potential racial problems, but he believed that actual occurrences carry different impact, specifically, "a dramatic awakening to the real world. It makes real what has been told about how the world is organized. The child would listen differently after that."

One mother's report of her communication with her son about derogation addressed his distress and included an explanation of the interpersonal dynamic involved in the incidents. Her son had been repeatedly insulted by children at school when he was between the ages of 10 and 12. When incidents arose, she explained them in the following terms:

> I tried to encourage him—make sure that he understood that what was said is not reality itself. They said that because of ignorance, and trying to hurt. It has nothing to do

with who he is … People who have their own faults and weaknesses do this to cover up their own problems.

This mother characterized her son as "basically passive." "He felt overwhelmed," she said. "We prayed about it a lot."

Ambivalence about initiating discussion of race can be inferred from one respondent's report of a conversation with her daughter. The daughter, who was then attending a predominantly Black school, was expected to attend a racially mixed school the following year. After the mother informed her daughter of the impending change in her school environment, the following conversation took place:

> Mother: "Do you have any problems with that?"
>
> Daughter: "Why should I have problems?"
>
> Mother: "The school will be mixed."
>
> Daughter: "I don't have a problem with that."
>
> Mother: "Is there anything you want to know?"
>
> Daughter: "No."

The exchange shows the mother's interest in allowing for communication with her daughter about race. At the same time, the mother appeared to have her daughter's complicity in actually avoiding substantive discussion. Exploration of conversations such as the preceding one from a family systems perspective might provide better understanding of this dynamic (e.g., see Alexander & LeBlanc, chap. 9, this volume). However, that analysis was beyond the scope of this research.

Other respondents were less ambiguous in reporting their avoidance of communication about race. One mother had decided never to introduce the topic of race when talking to her pre adolescent son for the reason that "I don't want to be the culprit, if it's not in his mind." Another mother implied that anticipatory communication about race cannot be effective. She related that her son often experienced racial insults as a 5-year-old child when he visited the market with her. The incidents did not surprise him, and they made him repeatedly angry. The mother reported that she did not warn her son about incidents such as these because "Nothing can be told." The interviewer understood this remark to mean that words can not effectively address a situation of this kind.

SURVEY STUDY

Research questions

The survey asked the following specific questions regarding communication about race (a) Do parents talk to their children about race? (b) What opportunities do parents utilize for talking about race? (c) What social influences do

2

parents recognize as conveying messages to children about how to respond to racial derogation? (d) Do parents instruct children in strategies for responding to racial insults? (e) Are racial insults by adults managed differently from insults by other children?

Participants

Parents were recruited from several sites in a large metropolitan area: a recreation center, social service agency, university, mixed-race preschool, state office for unemployment, and other sources. Fifty-five parents voluntarily completed the questionnaire. Seven surveys from respondents who were not African Americans or who were parents of older children were eliminated. The resulting sample, 48 African-American parents of children ages 3 to 24, consisted of persons from widely disparate economic circumstances, with estimated family income ranging from poverty level to $84,000 per year. Thus, these findings must be viewed in the context of the small, self-selected sample on which they are based, and results are not generalizable to the African-American population. Nevertheless, the results are striking and merit further study with larger representative samples.

Survey Description

Most questions were presented in a true-false format that was convenient for respondents, yet allowed the constructed categories to provide substantive information about communication behavior. Selected survey items are shown in Table 3.1.

Gender and age of parents and children defined subpopulations that were considered as potentially associated with different patterns of communication. The gender factor was posited on the following subjective observations and reasoning. U.S. society appears to treat African-American boys and men more harshly than girls and women. If this is actually the case, then fathers, having experienced more negative racial experiences during their lives, might anticipate more problems than mothers and might socialize children differently. Similarly, if the notion of gender differences in racial experiences is common wisdom for African Americans, associations might be found between children's gender and the instructions they receive.

It was presumed that a child's age might influence the full range of parent–child communication practices investigated in the study. Respondent's age was considered in order to determine whether differences in parents' practices might be associated with historical changes in interracial relations during the parents' formative years.

One of the survey's purposes was to inquire about respondents' perceptions of their children's racial environment. Children's experiences of racial deroga-

TABLE 3.1
Sample Items From Survey of Family Racial Communication

6.	Have you ever talked with your child about race relations? (If no, please skip to question #7.)	Yes	No
6a.	When do you talk with your child about race relations? (Please circle all answers that apply.)		
	While talking about other things?	Yes	No
	When he or she asks questions?	Yes	No
	While talking about a problem they have?	Yes	No
	When you hear about a positive racial incident in the news?	Yes	No
	When you hear about a negative racial incident in the news?	Yes	No
	When he or she goes to an interracial environment?	Yes	No
	When you think unpleasant incidents might happen?	Yes	No
	When you expect a pleasant interracial environment?	Yes	No
	Other occasion? (Please specify):		
8.	Have you ever told your child what to do about racial insults from children? (If no, please skip to question #9.)	Yes	No
8a.	What have you told your child to do? (Please circle all that apply.)		
	Ignore the person.	Yes	No
	Forget the incident.	Yes	No
	Try to avoid the person in the future.	Yes	No
	Tell the teacher (or adult in charge) about it.	Yes	No
	Tell a family member about the incident.	Yes	No
	Say something to the person who insulted you?	Yes	No
	Say nothing to the person who insulted you.	Yes	No
	Insult the person who insulted you.	Yes	No
	Hit the person who insulted you.	Yes	No
	Other (Please specify):		

tion were considered from three temporal perspectives: past occurrences, present exposure to interracial environments (where incidents could occur), and future expectations. Some questions distinguished between insults from other children as opposed to insults from adults. An alpha level of .05 was used for all statistical tests.

Results

Forty-four percent of the respondents reported that their children had experienced racial insults. It is surprising that the percentages of children reported to have been insulted by other children was only slightly higher than the percentage insulted by adults. However, it seems likely that occurrences of derogation, as with other experiences of varying significance to children, may not always be reported to parents. (Thus, any estimate of the rate of underreporting would be speculative at this time.) The majority of parents (83%) expected that their children would encounter racial derogation at some time in their youth.

Talking About Race.   Almost all parents of children between ages 9 and 17 (95%) reported talking to their children about race. (For age groups less than 5 years old, 5 through 8, 9 through 12, 13 through 17, and more than 17, the percentages were 33%, 77%, 92%, 100%, and 80%, respectively.) An inference drawn from the limited data is that parents usually initiated communication about race when children reached age 6 or 7. This age coincides with the developmental stage when, according to Spencer (1982), there is increasing risk of internalization of negative messages. However, it is not clear how much of the reported dialogue about race concerns racial derogation or whether this communication typically begins before children experience racial derogation.

Circumstances for Socialization.   Parents were asked to react to nine brief descriptions of circumstances in which they might talk to children about race, and space was allocated for respondents to name opportunities they used that were not included in the list. Because this study addressed anticipatory communication and its potential effectiveness in managing racial derogation, circumstances parents used for talking about race relations in general were categorized as either proactive (anticipatory) or reactive (nonanticipatory) communication. For example, "While talking about other things" was designated as proactive; "When he or she asks questions" was designated as reactive.

For reactive communication, parents of children who had been racially insulted ($M = .86, SD = .36$) reported using more nonanticipatory occasions than did other parents ($M = .52, SD = .51, t = 6.69, p = .01$). For proactive communication, there was no significant difference between reports of anticipatory communication by parents of children who had experienced insults ($M = .52, SD = .51$) and other participants ($M = .33, SD = .48, t = 1.75, p = .19$). These results suggest that past incidents of derogation prime parents to utilize more reactive occasions for talking about race, but may not influence them to engage in more proactive communication.

Influences on Children's Socialization.   Because family socialization must compete with many other influences, such as content in mass communication (see Parks, chap. 4, this volume) and models implicit in the behavior of others, several potential sources of socializing messages were examined, and parents were asked to indicate which they perceived as consequential. This list included overlapping categories of personal communication, mass communication, entertainment, narratives, and personal experiences. Nearly all parents (99%) acknowledged influence from stories (oral, written, and visual presentations), from children's own experiences, and from friends (see Davilla, chap. 5, this volume for a similar discussion about White children). Almost as many respondents (95%) also indicated that advice from parents and relatives had an effect.

Parents' Instructions for Responding to Racial Insults.   Several generic instructions that parents might give children were described on the survey. Respondents were asked to indicate all instructions they sometimes gave in their communication about race. The majority of parents (65%) instructed children on responding to other children; less than one half of parents (46%) gave directions for responding to offending adults. The group of parents whose children had experienced racial insults ($M = .95, SD = .22$) reported including more instructions for responding to offenses by children than did other participants ($M = .48, SD = .46, t = 15.49, p = <.01$). The most frequently reported instructions were for children to tell someone, such as a family member or an adult in charge, when incidents occurred. One half of the respondents instructed children to reply verbally to offending children. Significantly more fathers ($M = .75, SD = .44$) recommended that action than did mothers ($M = .32, SD = .48, t = 10.0, p < .01$). Notably, only one parent (4%) recommended countering with an insult to the offender.

Follow-Up Interviews and Discussion

Following a review of survey results, a subset of survey respondents were then interviewed at greater length to provide further understanding about information reported on their questionnaires. One mother had used survey space allocated for comments to describe instructions for her 10-year-old daughter concerning how to respond to an insult. The circumstances of the derogation and the strategic instruction were introduced by the interviewer for discussion in subsequent interviews. In the reported incident the perceived racial derogation was a teacher's repeated assertion, "I can't tell you apart" in regard to her daughter and another African-American girl. The mother recommended that the daughter select an unattractive comparative for the teacher and reply with a similar assertion: "I understand just how you feel, Miss A. I can't tell you and Miss B apart either."

The interviewer related the girl's age, reports of the teacher's repeated comment, and the mother's advice for the daughter's response to the seven other parents interviewed. Parents were then asked what they thought of the mother's advice. The seven parents presented with this scenario displayed predictable discomfort as the researcher related the child's problem, and they appeared to be additionally disquieted by the mother's instruction. All interviewees disapproved of the suggested reply; however, most listeners reacted by laughing or smiling. Two criteria for evaluating the instruction seem to have influenced the parents' responses: (a) social norms for African-American children's behavior, and (b) the risk of retaliation by the teacher. All of the reviewing parents indicated that the countering comparative reply would be inappropriate within the relationship between child and teacher or between child and adult. Parents expressed the view that a child should not "talk back" regardless of the provocation. These parents had not been given details about the context to aid them in evaluating the risk of retaliation to the child in this situation, and only one half of them cited risk as a reason for disapproving the advice.

The particular context of the aforementioned incident partially explains this mother's estimation of a relatively low risk if her child responded as advised, and these circumstances may also account for her implicitly different perspective on appropriate behavior for children. The family lives in a predominantly White, suburban, working-class community where they are not experiencing overt racial hostility. The daughter is a well-mannered and self-confident child whose academic performance is exceptional. The child's sense of offense was apparently due to being confused with an average student who also differed in physical appearance. The mother had advised the child how to perform the response and explained the rationale: "Just say it nicely. And that way, it starts her thinking. She doesn't know ... 'How should I take this? Was she being "smart," or was she being honest?'"

According to the mother's report, her daughter's reaction to the advice was strikingly similar to the reactions of interviewed parents. The child was unwilling to make this reply, but hearing it and referring to it later made her laugh. The scenario suggests how parent–child communication about responding to derogation might be profitably understood in terms of dissonance and skills training theory. The occasion of racial derogation (and its retelling) evoked dissonance that appeared to be reduced by strategic communication about how to respond. Having a rebuttal ready, if the insult recurred, appeared to be self-assuring for the child even though she did not use the strategy. The mother's instruction conformed to the guidelines suggested by skills training theory: the child participates in designing the strategy by choosing the comparative teacher.

This report demonstrates the potentially difficult task for parents of discovering and understanding their children's perspectives. Parent–child views may differ in regard to whether or why an incident should be characterized as racial derogation or whether a problem exists at all. These uncertainties may seriously affect the approach African-American parents adopt in talking to children about race. However, exploration of children's perspectives on their experiences was beyond the scope of this study.

Parents' Views.   Approximately two-thirds (66%) of parents responding to surveys reported that they gave children instructions for responding to racial insults. However, the only specific strategy reported was the instruction described earlier (the daughter's response to the teacher). Some interview comments suggested that the apparent absence of strategy formulation might be because of the general burden of talking about race: "Racial issues are difficult. And I don't care how many times you handle [them] … they're still painful. And I don't necessarily like to go through that aspect to get to where I have to go."

Some interviewees reported that television prompted them to proactively talk with their children about race:

> Watching television, something would come up … [and I would] say what was being implied by the message … I think at that point it was more of a game to her … because she would see if she could see what I was trying to say … and I don't think it had so much meaning to her outside of that … She'd say, "Yes, I see that Daddy, but would you be quiet, because I want to hear what Mr. Rogers is saying."

The reported comments of another parent to her children seemed quite vague: "And so through time—or through something that we'll see on television, or something that will happen I will say that … you know, 'This may not be so unusual.' Or 'Sometimes you will see this happening when other people don't understand.'"

One father generalized his advice to his children on responding to racial problems and insults as follows:

> I … tell them, "You really don't understand what's going on. You have to not only be sharp, but you have to have manners, so that you can flow through the maze. You also have to be man enough to know when to react and when not to react. Because you can get into trouble. And no one's really concerned about who's right or wrong. You're just in trouble." So … I explain from that end.

Parents' efforts to build children's self-efficacy were sometimes tempered by circumstances that could not be specifically defined, and parents' intervention when their children experienced racial problems may be a negotiated decision between them. For example:

> Some things—she'll say, "Mom I don't want you to [intervene]." I'll say, "Well maybe I should go talk to the teacher." And she'll say, "No, that isn't necessary." But she wouldn't—I don't think she would anyway—respond [to a teacher] without talking [to me first] … But if she came home and she was upset—you know—and I detected she was upset, then … I would be the one to make the decision to go … I would let her know … I was going to talk to the teacher.

Similarly, another mother responded that discussion with her young children about recurring racial problems in their summer camp ended with her asking, "Would you like me to talk to the counselor?" and their answering, "No, we don't want you to talk to the counselor."

One aim of the interviews was to investigate whether tension between values of self-efficacy and communalism, prominent African-American values (Boykin & Toms, 1985), might also account for some parents not teaching children strategic responses to racial affronts. One father's description of an incident implied a dichotomy of approaches. He reported an occasion when a teacher's racial insult, addressed to an adolescent student, sparked a concerted student response. The father supported his daughter's participation in the group action that followed:

> The student [as] I recall vaguely … didn't want to do anything about it. Her friends said, "No, we shouldn't take this." And they pushed it along … [A] group of them approached the principal and told her they were going to walk out.

When asked whether an immediate verbal response by the student would have been inconsistent with the group response, the respondent repeatedly reiterated a preference for group action without addressing the issue of exclusivity. Later, he answered:

> That's why it very often doesn't go any further than that … [On a] personal level it's kind of like resolved. "I told him, I put him or her in his place. They won't do that with *me* again anyway. They might do it with someone else, but they won't do it with *me* again."

The inference was that, when one person prevails against a derogator, the burden for the remainder of the group is increased.

In contrast, another father explained the relation between individual action and welfare of the group in terms implying an appreciation for teaching children self-efficacy:

> Well, I think you run into a thought process deficit if you don't include the child … in the resolution, whatever the problem is. You help them; you don't do it all for them. You sort of help them come up with [solutions] … Otherwise you'll have to do it all the time, and they haven't gained anything from that experience. Because … my vision of what you want out of this is for your child to be stronger and to be able to help other children who may … go through that same type of situation.

In this father's view, the self-efficacious child who benefits from making a strategic verbal reply to derogation provides other African-American children with a model of success.

CONCLUSION

This chapter has focused on the instructive practices used by African-American parents to socialize their children for coping with racial derogation. The studies reported are based on a conceptualization of derogation as a communication phenomenon that is potentially manageable by social skills. The survey method used here allowed respondents to contemplate the phenomenon of derogation while keeping many of the more complex and confounding issues of racism somewhat in the background. Interviews show that African-American parent–child communication about racial derogation is often consistent with theories regarding experiences of dissonant communications, benefits of self-efficacy, objectives of racial socialization, and effectiveness of preemptive protective communication.

This research demonstrates that, among the variety of strategies parents employ, some African Americans advise children to respond to racial derogation with a direct verbal reply. The survey's presentation of real-life derogation scenarios to interviewees elicited evidence that, although only one half of respondents instructed children to make verbal responses, parents could be prompted to devise verbal replies for children to use. This study discouraged the concern that an emphasis on interdependence within African-American culture might limit parents' willingness to teach children self-efficacious behavior.

The sample of African-American parents included some who held sophisticated views about the interpersonal dynamics of racial derogation. Some taught their children to recognize racial affronts as attempts by others to manipulate and control their behavior. The example of a verbal response (the mother's instruction for her daughter's reply to a teacher) and the reactions of the child and other parents to that reply provide evidence of the emotional benefit that sometimes derives from a prepared reply, regardless of whether it is actually used. However, encouraging parents to prepare children with strategic replies to derogation may meet with varying levels of resistance.

Several important questions raised by these studies urge further investigation. For example, the interview prestudy revealed that standards for appropriate children's behavior play an important role in proscribing the responses parents advise. Neither children's perspectives on their experiences of derogation nor parents' estimation of the risks to a child in a derogating environment and their evaluation of the risks of retaliation associated with a child's verbal response were explored. Additionally, the family's usual patterns of communication and the number and relative ages of members of the family are likely to affect parent–child communication about derogation. The small sample in this study also limited inferences concerning the effects of variables such as the child's age and the socioeconomic status of the family. Nevertheless, this research demonstrates that an empirical approach can help generate data about how African-American families teach children to cope with racial derogation. Future research must examine a larger, representative sample of parents so that complex relationships between various factors can be statistically explored.

For many African-American children, racial derogation is their first palpable encounter with racism. For other U.S. children, witnessing a racial insult may be an introductory, casual encounter with racist behavior. Thus, parent–child communication about racial derogation is an issue to be considered by all U.S. families. This research has provided empirical support for the recommendation that parent–child communication be included among the important methods of addressing racial derogation.

ACKNOWLEDGMENTS

I express my appreciation to my thesis advisor, Professor Joseph N. Cappella, for his guidance in the conceptualization and development of this research. I also thank the editors of this volume for their contribution of new perspectives and their patient assistance during preparation of this chapter. I offer my special thanks to Professor Jeanne B. Robinson of the University of Chicago, School of Social Service Administration, who provided critical commentary, insights, and personal support throughout the progress of this research.

REFERENCES

Allen, B. A., & Boykin, A. W. (1992). African-American children and the educational process: Alleviating cultural discontinuity through prescriptive pedagogy. *School Psychology Review, 21*, 586–596.

Aronson, E. (1992). The return of the repressed: Dissonance theory makes a comeback. *Psychological Inquiry, 3*, 303–311.

Bandura, A. (1991). Human agency: The rhetoric and the reality. *American Psychologist, 46*, 157–161.

Bandura, A. (1993). Perceived self-efficacy in cognitive development and functioning. *Educational Psychologist, 28*, 117–148.

Bingham, S. G., & Burleson, B. R. (1989). Multiple effects of messages with multiple goals: Some perceived outcomes of responses to sexual harassment. *Human Communication Research, 16*, 184–216.

Bogart, L. (1969). Introduction. In L. Bogart (Ed.), *Social research and the desegregation of the U.S. army: Two original 1951 field reports* (pp. 1–42). Chicago: Markham.

Boykin, A. W., & Toms, F. D. (1985). Black child socialization: A conceptual framework. In H. P. McAdoo & J. L. McAdoo (Eds.), *Black children: Social, educational, and parental environments* (pp. 33–51). Beverly Hills, CA: Sage.

Brown v. Board of Educ., 347 U.S. 483 (1954).

Bullard, S. (Ed.). (1994, Fall). *Teaching tolerance*. (Available from Editor, Teaching Tolerance, 400 Washington Ave., Montgomery, AL 36104).

Bussian, J. R. (1995). Anatomy of the campus speech code: An examination of prevailing regulations. *South Texas Law Review, 36*, 153–189.

Coopersmith, S. (1967). *The antecedents of self-esteem.* San Francisco: Freeman.

Corcoran, K. J. (1991). Efficacy, "skills," reinforcement, and choice behavior. *American Psychologist, 46*, 155–157.

DuBois, W. E. B. (1899). *The Philadelphia Negro: A social study.* New York: Schocken Books.

Ferguson-Peters, M. (1985). A racial socialization of young black children. In H. P. McAdoo & J. L. McAdoo (Eds.), *Black children: Social, educational, and parental environments* (pp. 159–173). Beverly Hills, CA: Sage.

Festinger, L., Riecken, H. W., & Schachter, S. (1956). *When prophecy fails.* Minneapolis, MN: Lund.

Franklin, A. & Boyd-Franklin, N. (1985). A psychoeducational perspective on black parenting. In H. P. McAdoo & J. L. McAdoo (Eds.), *Black children: Social, educational, and parental environments* (pp. 194–210). Beverly Hills, CA: Sage.

Greene, B. (1990). Sturdy bridges: The role of African-American mothers in the socialization of African-American children [Special Issue: Motherhood: A feminist perspective]. *Women & Therapy, 10*, 205–225.

Hirschfeld, L. A. (1995). Do children have a theory of race? *Cognition, 54*, 209–252.

Holmes, R. M. (1995). *How young children perceive race.* London: Sage.

Jagers, R. J., & Mock, L. O. (1993). Culture and social outcomes among inner-city African American children: An Afrographic exploration. *Journal of Black Psychology, 19,* 391– 405.

Joseph, J. M. (1994). *The resilient child: Preparing today's youth for tomorrow's world.* New York: Plenum Press.

Kim, Y. Y., & Ruben, B. D. (1988). Intercultural transformation: A systems theory. In Y. Y. Kim & W. B. Gudykunst (Eds.), *Theories in intercultural communication* (pp. 299–321). Thousand Oaks, CA: Sage.

Ladd, G. W., & Price, J. M. (1986). Promoting children's cognitive and social competence: The relation between parents' perceptions of task difficulty and children's perceived and actual competence. *Child Development, 57,* 446–470.

Luthar, S. S. (1993). Annotation: Methodological and conceptual issues in research on childhood resilience. *Journal of Child Psychology, 34,* 441–453.

Luthar, S. S., Doernberger, C. H., & Zigler, E. (1993). Resilience is not a unidimensional construct: Insights from a prospective study of inner-city adolescents. *Development & Psychopathology, 56,* 703–717.

Martinez, R., & Dukes, R. L. (1991). Ethnic and gender differences in self-esteem. *Youth & Society, 22,* 318–338.

McAdoo, H. P. (1985). Racial attitude and self-concept of young black children over time. In H. P. McAdoo & J. L. McAdoo (Eds.), *Black children: Social, educational, and parental environments* (pp. 213–242). Beverly Hills, CA: Sage.

McGuire, W. J., & Papageorgis, D. (1961). The relative efficacy of various types of prior belief-defense in producing immunity against persuasion. *Journal of Abnormal and Social Psychology, 62,* 327–337.

Nettles, S. M. (1992). *Coaching in communities: A review* (Rep. No. 9). Baltimore: Johns Hopkins University, Center for Families, Communities, Schools & Children's Learning.

Nettles, S. M., & Pleck, J. H. (1993). *Risk, resilience, and development: The multiple ecologies of black adolescents* (Rep. No. 44). Baltimore: Johns Hopkins University, Center for Research on Effective Schooling for Disadvantaged Students.

Papageorgis, D., & McGuire, W. J. (1961). The generality of immunity to persuasion produced by pre-exposure to weakened counterarguments. *Journal of Abnormal and Social Psychology, 62,* 475–481.

Pfau, M., & Kenski, H. C. (1990). *Attack politics: Strategy and defense.* New York: Praeger.

Pfau, M., Van Bockern, S., & Kang, J. G. (1992). Use of inoculation to promote resistance to smoking initiation among adolescents. *Communication Monographs, 59,* 213–230.

Powers, W. T. (1991). Commentary on Bandura's "Human agency." *American Psychologist, 46,* 151–153.

Rosenberg M. (1977). Contextual dissonance effects: Nature and causes. *Psychiatry, 40,* 205–217.

Rosenthal, L., & Zimmerman, B. (1978). *Social learning and cognition.* New York: Academic Press.

Socha, T. J., Sanchez-Hucles, J., Bromley, J., & Kelly, B. (1995). Invisible parents and children: Exploring African-American parent–child communication. In T. J. Socha & G. H. Stamp (Eds.), *Parents, children, and communication: Frontiers of theory and research* (pp. 127–145). Hillsdale, NJ: Lawrence Erlbaum Associates.

Spencer, M. B. (1982). Preschool children's social cognition and cultural cognition: A cognitive developmental interpretation of race dissonance findings. *Journal of Psychology, 112,* 275–286.

Thornton, M. C., Chatters, L. M., Taylor, R. J., & Allen, W. R. (1990). Sociodemographic and environmental correlates of racial socialization by black parents. *Child Development, 61,* 401–409.

4

Race and Electronic Media in the Lives of Four Families: An Ethnographic Study

Sheri L. Parks
University of Maryland, College Park

The collective aesthetic life of a family may be one of the more telling components of family life. An examination of the time spent together in leisure and in aesthetic pleasure may highlight consistent but otherwise muted family behavior and meaning patterns. Although the selection and interpretation of aesthetic pieces, as with many aspects of family life, appear to be informed by systemic patterns and mythology, which in turn are informed by culture of origin, that which a family does together and in a ritualistic fashion may make systemic patterns clearer than more fragmented activities and that which the family defines as "play" may display more undisguised subjective information than other behavioral aspects of daily life.

The mass media, particularly the electronic media of television and radio, are the linchpins of the collective and individual everyday aesthetic lives of the vast majority of families in the United States. Television, more than any other form, is now an intimate part of U.S. family life. More families have televisions than have telephones or running water (Economics and Statistics Administration, 1997, pp. 566, 723). Almost every family has at least one television set that is typically operated from 4 to 7 hours a day. The majority of families have more than one television, cable, and at least one VCR (Andreasen, 1994). The phenomena of television content and the ways in which families integrate the form and content in their daily lives and meaning systems become central concerns for the study of everyday family life (see Alexander, 1994, for an overview).

The media in general and television in particular are publicly generated forms of communication, which are then consumed primarily in the intimacy of the home. Because of this, the media appear regularly to transgress traditional boundaries that families maintain to regulate the influence of other outside systems, such as the state and the church (see Kantor & Lehr, 1975; Socha, in press). The media can also partially replace other systems with which families traditionally interact, such as the school, the church, or even interaction with other families. The mass media have also become the chief representatives of the state for many families (see Garbarino & Abramowitz, 1992, for an overview of families and traditional intersystem interaction). Once mass media are entered into the home, consumption may be the primary leisure activity for the youngest and oldest members of the family and may be one of the few activities for which the family members ritualistically come together. Even in multiset households, families appear to often regularly gather around the "best set" (Andreasen, 1994). What do active family systems do with their particular media forms and content? Where do they fit among other factors—culture of origin, family structure, socioeconomic status, and age—which may strongly influence the family system? Because media's content is information, what is the interaction of that information and the mythology of the family?

Although media usages are influenced by their somewhat unique forms and content, they also enter into a family as system and are contextualized by the other rhythms and meaning systems, or mythology, of the family. I am using the term *family myth* in a way similar to Cronen, Pearce, and Tomm's (1985) usage, as a high order conceptualization of the interrelation of family members into the family system and the interrelation of the family into the larger world. These conceptions often appear to be passed down from previous generations and modified or intensified in the new nuclear family. Race is an important variable among many in the family's interaction with media. In particular, African Americans use television differently, that is, they spend a larger percentage of family income on electronic media generally and more time watching television specifically (an average of 10 hours per day compared to the 4 to 10 hours cited for all U.S. viewers; Andreasen, 1994; Economics and Statistics Administration, 1997; Nielsen Media Research, 1994). They also watch almost completely different content, suggesting a different relationship to the medium. Ratings surveys that examine the top shows watched by African-American and all U.S. viewers have revealed that very few shows are to be found on both lists. The only program that has remained consistently popular with both groups has been *Monday Night Football* (Nielsen Media Research, 1991, 1994, 1997).

For instance, *Seinfeld* was the top-rated program in 1998 for all U.S. viewers but was rated 50th for African Americans, up from 1997 when the program did not even appear in the top 100 shows watched by African Americans. In 1998, the top three programs among Black audiences were Fox's *Between Brothers, 413 Hope Street,* and *Living Single,* all subsequently canceled by the network because of low overall viewership. In 1994, *Home Improvement* was the most-watched program for all U.S. viewers but was 30th among African Americans. The top show for African Americans that year was *Living Single*, which was 69th for all U.S. viewers (Braxton, 1998; Farhi 1994a).

Racial differences in viewing have emerged relatively recently. In the 1985 season, 15 of the 20 shows that were most popular with African Americans were also in the top 20 for all viewers. By 1993, only 3 programs were in the top 20 for both Black and all viewers: ABC's *Monday Night Football,* NBC's *Monday Night Movies,* and NBC's *The Fresh Prince of Bel Air.* In other words, during the years in which there was almost no Black-oriented television, Black audiences watched what everyone else did. When the network programmers realized that the longer viewing hours of African Americans meant that the available television audiences were disproportionately Black, networks sought to raise their ratings by presenting more Black-oriented programming and African Americans began to watch those shows. In 1991, there were 16 programs on four networks that were created for, by, or about Black people. By 1993, there were 25. In 1991, 7 of those 16 were in the top 10 shows for Black audiences. None of these shows were in the top 10 for all U.S. viewers. A survey by BBDO advertising agency found that Black audiences prefer programs that star African Americans and portray them positively. For instance, *Designing Women* had a costarring Black character but he was a former inmate; the program rated 50th for Black audiences while rating 5th for all audiences in 1991 (Braxton, 1998; *Business Report,* 1992; Farhi, 1994a, 1994b).

If African Americans appear to use different media content and to use it differently, or at least in different amounts, then perhaps the media take on different roles in their family systems. This question is more complex than it may at first seem. The ratings-by-race reports on African-American media usage cited earlier are composites, stripped of all the complexity that real people and real families manifest. What happens when racially self-identified families choose to bring mediated content into their homes? Directly related literature is scant. Studies on African Americans and media have concentrated on content-analyses of media content. Studies on real audiences and media content historically have concentrated on individuals, primarily children. In the more recent cases of family-media studies, the emphases have not been on African-American families.

A STUDY OF FAMILY AND MEDIA

Selecting Participants: Issues and Concerns

In this study, four nonclinical families, two Black and two White, were interviewed. It is difficult to isolate the role of race because it appears to interact with so many other variables, such as social class and family patterns, but nonetheless, other factors were held as constant as was practical by selecting families with similar life situations. All four families were middle class by education and occupation; all four lived in the middle-class suburbs in the Baltimore–Washington, DC corridor. Two families, one Black and one White, were composed of two parents and two adolescent children. The other two families, one Black and one White, were composed of a single mother and one male adolescent child. The parents of all four families defined themselves as child centered, or as positioning the children as the primary focus of family life, with careers and other activities secondary and supportive to the welfare of the children. All of the parents had full-time careers. It should be noted that all four families defined their political positions as moderate to liberal and that the daily lives of the White families reflected a high level of concern for class and race diversity through chosen professions and political, civic, and social activities.

In order to center the discussion around race, only middle-class families were examined. This approach has been criticized as racist by Nobles (1997) because it appears to disregard the level of economic disparity between Black and White families. Although no one would disagree with the argument that slavery and deprivation are very important cultural legacies for all African Americans, it would be difficult to ignore the growing, Black middle class. Arguments such as that of Nobles seem to be based on the assumption that African-American people are primarily impoverished, which is no longer the case. There are now about as many middle-class African Americans as there are impoverished African Americans. In 1994, 31.3% of African-American families had incomes below the poverty line, whereas 30.6% had incomes above $35,000, placing them solidly in the middle class. Approximately 38% had family incomes that placed them above poverty but not squarely in the middle class (Economic and Statistics Administration, 1995, p. 48).

More to the point, the Black middle-class families behave differently than the middle classes of other groups and appear to have much in common with impoverished Black families. Black culture is very conservative, holding on to historically based traditions and practices. Middle-class, Black families appear to retain the old cultural and familial practices and to carry the legacies with them into the middle class. Numerous findings (see Staples & Johnson, 1993, for an overview) have found a number of family practices that are similar across economic class. In the specific area of media consumption, the sharp class and education differences that appear in White audiences (the more affluent and more educated Whites are, the less they watch television) do not appear in Black audiences (Bower, 1973).

Because of their relative affluence, middle-class, Black families may be able to retain cultural practices more easily than impoverished families. After providing evidence that middle-class Black fathers are especially nurturant toward daughters as well as sons (supportive of the traditional egalitarianism of Black families), McAdoo (1997) called for the field of African-American family research to move beyond its emphasis upon "the most economically devastated" families. I compared middle-class Black and White families, in effect holding class constant, to see more clearly the role of race on media patterns. The only way to "strain" out, as much as possible, the effects of race versus class was to study the practices that remained after the immediate effects of economic deprivation were removed; thus, I could compare them to White families in similar economic circumstances. Yet, with all their similarities, these still were different families and were examined at the level of the individual unit, and so each emerged as a unique system.

Questions

Although each family interview was customized to investigate the patterns and themes identified through the family's individual survey, each family was asked a tailored version of these questions:

> *Introduction*: "Would you describe yourself as a child-centered home?" "How did that come about?"
>
> *Family media behavior patterns and power*: "What is the family's weekday media routine?" "What is the family's weekend media routine?" "Who initiates the what?" "Who does what with which media forms?"
>
> *Parental roles and authority*: "Who worries the most about what the children watch/listen to/read/play?" "Are there guiding principles for what is allowed?" "What can't they see/hear/play?" "Has that changed with age?" "What do parents see for themselves?"
>
> *Multigenerational patterns*: "How different is your family from your parents' families?"
>
> *Family myth*: "What is the most important trait or value that you are trying to teach your children?"

These questions were used only to open up lines of conversation between family members; most of the interview was about specific behaviors of the family members, who were encouraged to talk among themselves and to delineate the behavior of other family members. Interspersed throughout these questions were questions designed to further examine patterns that were suggested by the individual family's survey. This method of questioning, although appearing indirect, allowed the families to lead quickly and deeply into the family system and to grasp the role that media play in the whole life of the family. Most important to this study, the roles of race or media emerged not as isolated elements but as part of a complex family system. Attitudes and behaviors about race appeared in the context that informed them. As the family discussion moved from the general to the specific, I was able to discern patterns and themes, which were presented to the family for their critique. I said, "Let me tell you what I am working on, why I asked that last question." Then, the family would comment upon the themes and patterns, adding more information to corroborate or alter the themes. Further theme development occurred after the in-home interview through follow-up phone calls to one of the parents. During the family interview, I identified a main informant, the parent who was most involved with the everyday media behavior of the children, and I called him or her for more needed information and asked them to check with the other family members.

The family members, who had been cautioned that they might learn about themselves as I learned about them, became collaborators in the investigation. It was common for family members to discover patterns and even specific behaviors of which they had been unaware. "I never thought about it that way before but that makes sense," was a typical response. Each family indicated that the process had been interesting and fun and invited me to call or come back if I needed more information, which allowed the follow-up telephone calls back to the main informant.

Method and Procedures

Evidence was collected in two phases. The first phase consisted of a survey that was used to identify individual patterns of selection and preliminary systemic patterns. In the survey, each family member was asked to identify their favorite media and their favorite pieces within each of listed media. Further, they were asked to identify the patterns of behavior surrounding each of their favorite pieces: With which family member(s) do they most often attend the media piece? Who most often initiates the interaction with the media piece?

The answers of the individuals were used to compose the stem questions for the second phase of data collection, an in-home interview of the family. The method of questioning used was a version of "circular questioning," a therapeutic method developed by Selvini Palazzoli and colleagues (Selvini Palazzoli, Boscolo, Cecchin & Prata, 1978, 1980) to discover family system patterns underscoring dysfunctional behavior. I first used circular questioning in 1985 (Parks, 1985), in what may have been its first nonclinical usage, and replaced the initial screening folder with the survey. Because circular questioning encourages family members to comment on the behaviors of other family members, it allows the interviewer to move quickly and deeply into the family system without appearing unduly intrusive. Family members discover patterns and even practices for the first time and should be made aware of this before the interview. Its power is also its major disadvantage; if used without proper training and practice with a practitioner, it has the potential to severely damage a family. Often circular questioning is used by research teams that include a clinical therapist; when used by one researcher, it is important to have an therapist on standby, as I did. I have used circular questioning in more long-term interview relationships with families and have allowed the audio or videotaped interviews to be reviewed by a therapist (Parks, 1985; 1987). Families emerged from the interviews more conscious of their patterns of behavior, and it was important that they not be damaged by their new knowledge.

This approach is consistent with the ethnographic method in which, rather than studying people, the researcher learns from them (Spradley, 1979). I took the ethnographic approach one step further—I learned with the participants. The ethnographic approach also limits the number of participants in the study because the purpose of the study is not to generalize to large populations but to move deeply into specific systems and cultures. The number of families interviewed in this study was actually large for an ethnography, but was necessary to compare the different racial and structural characteristics of the families. After the interviews, I used notes and audiotapes to draw specific evidence.

The Families

Family Number 1: White, Two-Parent. The two-parent, White family was of Irish origin and consisted of two public school teachers and two boys, one 9 and one 13 years of age. The wife married 15 years ago into a stem family arrangement (Verdon, 1983) and lived with her husband and his parents for several years. In a stem family, a new spouse joins the stable, multigenerational family structure of his or her spouse's family of origin rather than forming a separate nuclear family. In this family, the stem family arrangement meant that the grandparents were actively involved in the everyday life of the family I interviewed. Soon after the birth of their first child, the parents' grandparents built a new home in the adjoining lot and moved there and sold the family home to their son and daughter-in-law. Another house on a third adjoining lot had been sold out of the family but a younger brother and his new wife recently purchased a home up the street. Other siblings lived farther away but returned frequently for important rituals such as birthdays. These families maintained daily contact and sometimes vacationed together. The grandparents often commented upon and influenced the raising of the children. This was sometimes with some resistance from the wife. The wife, in turn, kept regular contact with her family of origin. The result was a large, stable extended family structure. I chose not to interview the grandparents because they no longer resided in the house of the interviewed family, but I did question the parents and children about the roles of the grandparents. Until 2 years ago, the mother operated a licensed in-home day-care business. She also had finished her undergraduate degree. When the youngest child was considered old enough, the mother obtained a public teaching job in an inner-city school with predominately poor and Black students, where she said she was "needed most." The father commuted to work in another county.

Both parents were highly active in the daily lives of their children. The two boys were enrolled in selective public schools, and both children were very active, participating in one or more sports per season. The father coached soccer and softball teams in the same area league and the mother regularly attended games and practices. According to the parents and children, most of the children's activities included one or both parents. Other activities included regular trips to the library and to purchase additions to collections. The older son read approximately one book a day, and punishment for the most serious offenses warranted reduction or elimination of before-bed reading time. The younger son read less but was more involved in video games and computers, both of which the family owned and kept updated. The "library"-size CD player was in the kitchen-dining area and appeared to be of secondary importance to the family group.

The family reported that they liked to be together. The mother said, "We follow each other around. One person will be in a room and someone else will come in ... You look around and everyone is in there." Their media behavior followed closely the overall family pattern of togetherness. The "hearth room," or family gathering room, was the living room, which was furnished with chairs and a sofa that were purchased for their comfort and ability to withstand use (Tichi, 1991). The sofa and one chair were recliners, the other two were wing chairs with lamps nearby. The family watched the most television in the hearth room and the largest television and video games were located there. The smaller televisions were located in the kitchen, the parents' bedroom, and the younger son's bedroom. The upstairs televisions were used primarily in the morning as the family dressed. Most programs were watched by the children and at least one parent. The favorite shows were watched by the entire family. The reclining chair, opposite the television, was the father's chair. When he was out of the room, the use of this chair went to the youngest son, who moved from the wing chair with the second best vantage point for viewing.

The oldest son (the avid reader) often positioned himself at one end of the recliner sofa or one of the wing chairs, arranged perpendicularly to the television but near the lamps, so he could read and be with his family at the same time. The mother often sat at the other end of the sofa so that the older son was sitting nearest his mother, often placing his head on her lap. "He is the cuddler of the family," the mother said. "You are more comfortable," replied the son. Some sporting events were watched by the father and sons, with the youngest son being the most avid sports fan of the two boys. The father was a self-described "sports nut" and was highly involved in television sports. (A recent vacation was planned so that hotel check-in times would coincide with starting times of televised international soccer championship games.) This was the one activity that the mother avoided by going into the kitchen and working on housework or schoolwork and using the smaller television. She said she would watch sporting events if they were very important to her husband or family, such as national titles, primarily as a way of communicating her support. The only show the parents watched alone as a couple was ER.

The family's power dynamic was traditional: The mother was involved in childrearing and decisions about the family's domestic life, and the father had veto power and weighed in for larger decisions and disciplinary matters. Monitoring and enforcement of television viewing followed this line of behavior. Keeping with their desire to be closely involved with their children, one or both of the parents were often in the room or within earshot when the boys were watching television. For nonsporting events, the mother took the responsibility for monitoring the viewing and censoring. (The family recently purchased a second remote so the mother could quickly change the channel when offensive content appeared.) If the boys wanted to watch a questionable show, both parents prewatched the program and decided if the boys would be permitted to watch. If the show was judged to be marginally appropriate, the parents would continue to watch with the boys and to discuss the show and its meaning. The most recent example of this was the series *South Park*, an animated show aired on Comedy Central with frequent ridicule, racial slurring, and mention of bodily functions. The show was popular among the boys' schoolmates, and the boys wanted to be allowed to watch. After watching the show and their sons' reactions to it, the parents decided they could watch but with a parent in the room to talk about what they were seeing. The mother reported remaining uncomfortable with much of the content but thought that the boys could be trusted not to imitate the most offensive program elements. The boys had subsequently taped episodes of the series so that the programs could be watched more often. With its cautious flexibility, the family fit Baumrind's (1971) description of "authoritative" families, who are characterized by reasoning and situationally tailored responses rather than by the strict enforcement of more overarching rules found in "authoritarian" families.

The most elaborate and far-reaching relationship with the media centered around the family collections of memorabilia related to videotaped films. The mother had enjoyed the *Star Wars Trilogy* (originally released 1977–1983) as a high school student and introduced the films to her sons. Because one of her hobbies was attending yard sales, she began to pick up related memorabilia in the 1980s just as other people began to get rid of them. The sons began attending the yard sales to augment their collection, selling off lesser items and duplicates to other collectors. They also purchased new *Star Wars* merchandise releases when they became available. The mother estimated that the family *Star Wars* collection was the fourth most valuable collection in the state. The sons could report the monetary worth of the individual items in their vast collection, stored in a special room of the house and in the attic playroom, but did not see the collection as an investment. "It is just to know that what you have collected is worth something," said the mother. This is an example of consumption as communication. Kline (1993), for example, argued consideration must be given to the impact of things given to a child. I would add that when the thing has a media tie-in, the communication becomes fuller, carrying the mythological information through the interpreted media content. The gift is a way of saying "who we are."

The oldest son knew the most *Star Wars* trivia because he had not only seen the films but also read the original books which contained more background and detail. The family had recently obtained a cast bronze statue of Darth Vader, which sat on a table in the living room. Although the entire family worked on their *Star Wars* collection, there were also other collections holding meaning for individual family members. The father collected memorabilia connected with the film *It's a Wonderful Life,* and other family members supported him by finding items to add to his collection. Recently, they had found Christmas decorations of the buildings shown in the film and had purchased them for him. Media, primarily television and videotaped films, were fully integrated into the rich patterns of leisure-time activities. The family used media and media-related behavior to act as a family.

Family Number 2: African American, Two-Parent.   The Black, two-parent family included a father, who was college educated and had opened his own home improvement business, and a mother who, similar to the White, married mother who worked and went to college, was working as an assistant office manager and was completing her own college education. Married 15 years, their family also included two children: one girl, 14 years old and one boy, 10 years old. Both children were enrolled in public schools. A year before, the family had moved from a neighborhood near the city to a more upscale development in a county that, until recently, had been rural but was being developed as the suburbs moved outward. The old neighborhood was all Black; the new was nearly all White. They were the only Black family in their immediate development.

The home had three televisions, one in the family room, facing a sofa; one in the parents' bedroom; and a smaller set, which "floated" between the children's rooms. Most of the family viewing activity occurred in the family room. Because the family was still purchasing furniture for their new home, the hearth room was not fully furnished. A "daddy chair" was "definitely" on the list of planned purchases but, as in the old house, other family members would also use the chair, particularly if the father were out of the room. The family style appeared to be one in which there was a high degree of parity between the parents, more egalitarian than was evident with their White counterparts, in which the father exercised more veto power. This father was also more involved in the daily domestic duties, perhaps because of an African-American tradition of fathers being highly nurturant (McAdoo, 1979) and/or because this mother worked out of the home and went to school at night, leaving him to interact with the children in the evenings.

In this family, the television was more important to the males than the females. The mother, even more than the other mothers, rarely sat down to watch television. Like the other mothers, she was often in the room or within earshot of the main television but she was often working, either on schoolwork or housework. She rarely made program choices but moved around her family as they watched. Although the mother was often physically in the room, her attention was often on something else. The parents watched little television as a couple, seeing it as "not that important." The daughter cared for television less and watched somewhat less than her brother but did watch somewhat more than did her mother. Music was important to all of the members of this family but tended to be a private activity with much more individual variability.

The parenting style was kind yet firm, fitting into Baumrind's (1971) description of authoritative parents but exercising more direct control than did the White, married parents. Parental control was clear and seemingly unquestioned. The parents could identify no major difference in the ways in which they were raising their children and the ways in which their parents raised them. When asked who usually held the remote control, the family identified an unspoken rule that nobody held it. However, a difference in power became obvious in the way in which a program change was facilitated. The father was able to enter the room and change the channel at any time. The children could not themselves change the channel if the father were watching. (It was unclear if the mother could because she rarely cared what program was on.) The father would say "Let me hold the remote," a friendly but direct command, and then he would start changing the channel. The children would say, "Can I see what else is on?" a question that required an answer and that created the possibility that a program change could then be requested if a more desirable alternative was discovered. The general rule was that whenever father was watching a sporting event, then that was what stayed on. The parents were so confident in their authority that they were not concerned with their children imitating what they saw. Unlike their White counterparts, they felt that their children "know not to try it." Although Baumrind's (1971) typology of permissive, authoritative, and authoritarian has been found to work across race, the two married families demonstrate the continuum within the category of authoritarianism. Although authoritative, the Black family demonstrated some authoritarian leanings in their valuing of obedience and a code of conduct but they did not fit the authoritarian category because they also reasoned with their children and did not favor punitive or forceful means. Children were allowed their individual opinions within certain boundaries; delineation of the boundaries was more absolute and closely maintained than in the White two-parent family, who considered the circumstances presented by each new situation. Sudarkasa (1997), who has researched the African influences still present in the African-American family, described a characteristic termed *restraint*, the necessity to curb the individual will for the good of the whole. When combined with another characteristic identified as *respect* for elders, the origins of a firm style of parenting becomes clearer.

Family Number 3: African American, Single Parent. The mother of the Black, single parent family is a personnel management analyst, an upper-middle-level government employee who also operated a small in-home cosmetic business. Her son was 9 years of age and enrolled in private school. She never married, deciding to have a child and raise him on her own. The father, whom she defined as a "coparent," was a longtime friend, himself a single government professional, who was very active in the daily life of the child. They were not dating at the time of the interview, and their relationship was defined by a level of cooperation in carrying out the routine duties of parenting, such as picking the child up from school and activities and purchasing clothing. The father lived approximately 10 minutes' drive from the mother and son, and the child moved between the two houses, having a bedroom in each but living primarily with the mother. The child moved between the two parents several times a week, according to the demands of his and their schedules.

The mother and son had a history of leisure time activities together, such as roller skating, going to the library, or to church, and visiting other families with children. They went to the beach in the summer. "Dinner time is an important time, too," the mother said. The family history also included watching television together. Until recently, a weekly ritual had included watching *Touched by an Angel* together. The program was still the mother's favorite show but the son had come to prefer Black situation comedies, such as *Family Matters* and programs carried on the Warner Brothers network, after being introduced to them by a friend. At that point, their favorite shows were on at the same time on different stations, and they often watched on separate televisions. She appeared to see his viewing of them as a form of play and watched "his little shows" with him primarily "to keep an eye on what he is watching." There were five televisions in the house, one each in the recreational room, the den, and the kitchen, and one in each person's bedroom. There was no clear hearth room: "We float all over the house," she said. The room in which they were most likely to watch television together was her bedroom. After school, homework, and dinner, the son watched his favorite shows while the mother worked around the house or spoke with clients. She watched the late night news by and for herself after the son had gone to bed. Music, particularly gospel music, was "very important" to her, but she was seldom able to sit down and listen to it except on weekends. Similarly, although she liked to read, she had little time for newspapers or books. She said, "By the time I come home, get through homework, dinner, with everything I have to do, I'm exhausted. I watch the news nearly all the time and go to bed."

As in the other families, the boy's interest in sports had drawn him closer to the father and away from the mother. "Now he is focused on bowling," she said. The father played tournament-level bowling, and the son had recently begun to play in junior tournaments, doing well and enjoying himself so much that many Friday evenings and Saturdays were taken over with bowling. His father took him to the tournaments, and they talked often about the game. His mother attended some tournaments but did not go often. Like the children in the other families, he too had become an avid viewer of the sport he played, another activity which his mother did not share. One Saturday morning, he awoke his father at 6:30 a.m. with a phone call to find out who had won a televised tournament the night before, because his mother had made him go to bed before the tournament ended. The call was reportedly met with delight by the father.

Like the married parent families, the mother expected her son to carry through with her television rules on his own. Specifically, as was the married Black family, she was confident in her authority and seemed to worry little that her son would transgress her rules. "He knows what he can't watch." Also as with the Black married family, her style was authoritative but with some authoritarian leanings. When the son wanted to see a show of which she disapproved, "we generally talk about it ... about what's wrong with it. I try to reason with him." When reasoning did not succeed, "I put my foot down. No because I said so." Otherwise, the son controlled much of the programming of the television. Her firm style was in marked contrast to the White single mother discussed next.

Family Number 4: White, Single Parent. The single, White mother was an associate professor at a small, Catholic college. She was of southern, Scotch-Irish heritage. Her son was 12 years old and enrolled in a private school. The mother and father had separated within the past year and had joint custody of their son, who spent one half the week with each parent. Most weekends were with his father. Having separated only 4 months earlier, they were still working on new patterns and rituals. As with the Black single mother who had been living alone with her child all of his life, this mother also reported that they had no single room that served as a hearth room, but she did not know if this would become a permanent pattern. "We are still new at this," she said. The house, the same one lived in before the separation, held two televisions, one downstairs in the living room and another, which was moved between the two bedrooms upstairs. The original upstairs television was with the father, and the mother and son had purchased a new one. The choices surrounding the new television took on important symbolism. The original set had been located in the parents' bedroom. The new set was set up to be mobile, to move between the son's and mother's bedroom. The son also chose to use his own money to pay for one half the cost, using funds from odd jobs and allowance. Of all of the children, he emerged as the one with the most power in the family system, with control over his own viewing as well as other aspects of his life.

Although the mother reported that her son primarily controlled the television, he said that it was not that he controlled the television but that he viewed television when his parents were busy and they both worked at home. The father had cable television at his house; the mother did not and reported that she was uneasy about the lack of control that she had over his viewing there. The son reported that cable gave him "more of the same thing" and that the only programming he added at this father's was soccer games. Similar to the other families, the father, rather than the mother, shared the child's interest in sports. (Like most of the other mothers she did not often attend his matches.) The son also kept his Playstation video game at his father's, because that was where he often was on weekends.

The mother originally reported that she and her son only "occasionally" watched television together because they preferred different shows, but what emerged suggested a more complex pattern. The book-lined living room in which the television sat was furnished with a sofa and a love seat, with the sofa facing the television. However, the furniture arrangement did not reflect this family's most common way of watching television. The living room was flanked by a dining room on one side and an enclosed sun room on the other. As with the other mothers in the study, this mother often worked while the television was on. The researcher observed a situation in which the mother was in the dining room and the son, newly interested in body image, worked out with weights in the sun room. The television in the living room was on, tuned to the shows that the son enjoyed, but the mother and son easily conversed from the adjoining rooms. When the researcher asked if this was a common arrangement, the mother reported that it was. Although she did not define herself as "watching," she did say that she was aurally monitoring the television content and conversing with her son. The two also watched *The X Files* together in this way.

The mother had a very different media pattern when the son was away. The television was on much less. When it was on, she watched *Masterpiece Theatre, Mystery,* and *Homicide.* She read and listened to music much more when alone. An important difference between music and television became apparent. Although she had given her son control of the television, she had not done the same thing with music, about which she cared very much. She listened to female artists such as The Indigo Girls and reggae, whereas he preferred mainstream rap, of which she held a low opinion. They had a "compromise radio station," which played a "mix" format. Both single mothers reported that they did not know or directly control what their children saw at their father's house, but the White mother did not report trying to extend her influence into the fathers' homes whereas the Black mother assumed that her influence held regardless of context.

INTERPRETING THE INTERVIEWS

Racial Differences

Mass media played a different role in each family system and was informed by a number of other system patterns. Family structure clearly played a major role in the family systems; however, some of the differences between the families appeared to be related to race. All of the Black parents reported no great departure from ancestral values or the way in which their parents had raised them, except that they talked to their children more. They retained expectations of obedience and responsibility to the collective that traditionally have been found in African and African-America families (Sudarkasa, 1997). The White parents felt that they had made significant changes in the way they were raising their children; they negotiated more than their own parents had. In keeping with their overall styles, the Black parents exercised more direct control over their children's viewing whereas the White children exercised more control over their own viewing. The cultural and familial grounding of the Black parents may have helped the level of confidence they reported in their decisions and rules about media behavior.

The cultural differences can be seen most easily in comparing the two single mothers for it is with them that the greatest differences arose. The Black mother was authoritative but firm, whereas the White mother was permissive in her parenting style. The Black mother reported feeling more confident in her ability to control her son's viewing than did the White mother. Race appeared to play a role in the confidence of the one and the lack of confidence of the other. Race informed many aspects of their lives, even in the way they became single, which, in turn, informed media-related patterns. The White mother took on her role as a single parent in a common manner for White women, separation in anticipation of divorce. The Black mother was single in a way common for Black women. The percentage of single African-American mothers is three times that of White mothers. In 1992, they represented 31% of African-American families as opposed to 10% of White families (U.S. Bureau of the Census, 1993). Although social class is often confounded in racial analysis, it does seem to have a role in marriage. Professional Black women are less likely to be married than working-class women (Staples & Johnson, 1993). In the context of this social reality, the Black woman had chosen to be a single mother and had been one for all of her child's life. Her life situation was stable. Single parenthood had been a very recent byproduct of a dissolved marriage for the White mother, and her life situation was destabilized.

The Black mother spent more time with her son and expected to exercise a high level of control, which may also be related to race. Willie (1984) concluded that Black mothers provided relatively high emotional, academic and financial support across class and marital situation. Staples and Johnson (1993) suggested that Black parents and children may have closer relationships than White families, a finding which reflects the value of the collective. It should be noted that differences in support and closeness were not noted in the married-parent families but differences may become more acute with the differences in resources and support mechanisms that often come with single parenthood. For instance, the Black coparents worked more closely to parent their son than did the White coparents. They were a family unit, a collective, despite living in two houses. The single mother reported feeling distant, saying that she did not know "what they do over there." For all of these reasons, the Black mother was surer and more authoritative in her expectations for her son's media behavior.

Although the two married-parent families were similar in a number of ways, there appeared to be a higher level of parity in the Black family. Staples and Johnson (1993) found that Black families displayed more egalitarian relationships and economic parity between men and women. The parity of the Black family meant that the father was highly involved in daily decisions about viewing and related behavior and that he was intimately involved in the life of the collective.

Racial identity marked a drastic difference in the ways that the families treated the topic of race in the media. Racial socialization is a central function of the Black family. (For a historical overview of this research, see Jackson, McCullough, & Gurin, 1997; Daniel & Daniel, chap. 2, this volume; Diggs, chap. 6, this volume.) More than two-thirds of Black parents provide racial socialization messages (Taylor, Chatters, Tucker, & Lewis, 1990), and media selections have been found to play a major role in the racial socialization of children (Parks, 1983). If Black parents are aware of media's racial potential, then it might be expected that media program selection would reflect the desire for racial socialization. The single Black mother spoke about the role of race in her selection of her favorite show, *Touched by an Angel*. She originally identified the program through an advertisement featuring Black star Della Reese and Black guest star Natalie Cole. "I thought it was a movie with these two Black women." She said that when she first saw it, "I felt good. I like the theme and that they deal with everyday situations … I don't want to say that I limit what I watch to only Black shows but I find that a lot of those other shows are not relevant to me. I can't relate. They are simple, there is no meat, no depth." When her son began to watch "his own" shows, they too starred African Americans.

The Black, married-parent family primarily watched televised sports together. In discussing the role of race in his family's viewing, the father noted that his family watched sports such as basketball, baseball, football, and track and field, in which African Americans were prominently featured. "The NBA is almost all Black," he said. He and the children appeared to be very conscious of the race of the players, and the father reported feeling that his children had racial role models because they saw African-American sports figures, such as Michael Jordan, who were also good people. Racial socialization went beyond self-identity to scripts for interaction with others; the father of the Black married-parent family also felt his children learned this from sports. The lessons they learned were that skill and persistence might overcome racial attitudes, "everyone is equal," "when you are out there on the field it does not matter who you are," team mentality might override racial prejudice, and "regardless of how you feel off the field, you have to work as a team." The family agreed that the children's socialization by sports and their continued involvement with sports had eased their transition into a new, predominately White neighborhood.

In contrast, race seemed to matter little in the viewing selection of the White families, who often made choices for reasons other than race. The White married-parent family made its viewing selections from the whole universe of cable television, easily crossing racial lines of programming. The family watched *Family Matters* for years, only recently stopping as the primary character, Steve

Urkel, grew into college age and the mother began to feel that the plotlines became "too mature" for the sons. The race of the star and most of the costars was not a factor in choosing to view and, eventually, choosing not to view the program. Race was a topic of discussion in the other White family but did not affect viewing. One area of dispute between the single White mother and her son was his viewing of *South Park*. He said that he knew it was "racist, sexist and badly drawn but it is funny anyway." It was the difference between viewing in part because of race and that of viewing "anyway" factor that distinguished the role of race in the families. It should be noted that although all of the White children listed *South Park* as a favorite, the very popular program did not come up at all in the discussions with the Black families. When I asked the Black, single mother and the Black, married father about the program, both said than no members of their families wanted to watch the show, in keeping with Black audiences preferring shows which depict positive images of African Americans. The Black, married father expressed surprise that the question would even be raised. The White families recognized the mediated bigotry but could look past it; the Black families could not.

Trust and Control

Because all of the parents worked, trust was an important element for all of them. The White, married family, with two relatively healthy grandparents next door, had the largest support network and the least uncertainty. When both parents were away, the boys were likely to be with their grandparents, who were reported to uphold the parents' media rules. For instance, the younger boy left for school 45 minutes later than the rest. Rather than spending the time alone, he went to his grandparents and watched weekday morning cartoons in their living room until his grandmother walked him to the school bus stop and waited with him.

At the other end of the spectrum, the single mothers with nonresidential coparents had to hope that their children would follow their wishes. The White mother said that she did not know what her son watched at his father's house. During the interview the son told her that it was primarily soccer games that he could not see without cable. The Black mother reported being more confident that her son watched in accordance with her wishes but did not offer evidence. Discipline, including media-related discipline, was the area in which the two single mothers differed greatly. The Black, single mother appeared to always remain in an authoritative position and reported very little uncertainty. The White mother negotiated more with her son, was more permissive, and reported a higher level of uncertainty (Baumrind, 1971).

The most elaborate portrait of the role of trust and control emerged with the Black, married family. The daughter was highly successful in school and did not view much television, so the parents did not control her viewing much. The son, although talented, had been less successful in school. He was seen as someone who would "watch television all day if we let him," and they had identified a relationship between periods of heavy viewing and lower grades. Therefore, they created rules for him. He was to view no television until his homework was done, sometimes hours after school was out. The father, who was often not home yet, trusted that his son carried out his parents' wishes but made a point of checking for evidence of television viewing, both immediate (homework and household chores not finished, snack food in front of the television) and long term (poor grades) to support his trust. He knew that his son could not accomplish his tasks while also watching television because television commanded his entire attention.

The Black children had less negotiation power than their White counterparts. Although the parents were kind and allowed their children to voice their opinions, the parents' decisions were more final, reflecting some authoritarianism leanings within otherwise authoritative families. An interesting comparison arose between the married Black family and the single White mother family. The parents were asked what happened when their children wanted to watch a program of which the parents disapproved. The initial answers were very similar but further questioning revealed very different meanings. For example, the words in the answers of the White single mother and the Black married father seemed to convey similar meaning. The Black father said, "I talk to them to let them know why I think they should not watch the show." The White mother said, "I tell him why I do not like the show." However it became clear that the first indicated an intent to control behavior. The second was a voicing of opinion. Their elaborations reinforced the difference in meanings and outcomes. The Black father said that statement meant that his children did not watch the show. It was a gentle way of saying "no." The White mother's meaning was more literal, she had never disallowed her son's viewing of a program. She simply wanted him to understand why she disapproved of his behavior. The single, Black mother indicated a position similar to that of the Black father.

Like the other parents, the single, White mother was concerned about the content that her child favored. His favorite shows, although including some age-appropriate shows such as *Saved by the Bell* and *The Wonder Years,* also included several shows of which his mother strongly disapproved, including *South Park, The Simpsons,* and *Seinfeld.* Her concern about the shows went to the heart of the family mythology and the values which she was consciously passing on to her son. She was most concerned that he be concerned with issues of "social justice, respect for other people ... issues of poverty and racism and feeling that you ought to do something about it." Yet, consistent with her negotiational, more permissive style of parenting, she had never stopped him from viewing particular shows and, instead, "gives him a hard time about it," pointing out what she considered to be sexist and racist content. Like the other parents, she made her feelings known and hoped to influence his interpretation of the content. Unlike the other parents, she did not censor his viewing.

Racial Similarities

Some similarities existed across race. All families reported being more involved with their children's daily lives than their parents were, and of doing activities with and talking to them more. One similarity appeared to be related to family structure. The married-parent families had well-established hearth rooms and routinely used them together. Although there were other televisions in the house, they gathered at predictable times to watch together. Watching together was participation in a rich family ritual, which was informed by family mythology—the importance of sports, of collecting, of elaborate lessons to be learned. Sometimes, family members joined in to be able to be with the rest of the family. The single parent families had a much less elaborate hearth behavior, which was spatially looser, less predictable, and less stable over time.

Another across-race similarity emerged with the interest of all of the children in sports. In early childhood, viewing had been influenced by the mothers in most of the families. As the children became interested in sports, participation in sports and viewing of sports became more tightly linked with the father. In each instance, the mother verbally expressed a sense of loss but continued to avoid the sports-related viewing and activities. Even the mother who attended practices and games left the room for most televised sports. The meaning system and the value that went with it shifted as the children became older and interested in outside activities that favored the fathers' personal interests.

CONCLUSION

Families are complex systems in which meaning is often unstated but understood by members (Kim & Ruben, 1988). Rather than seeing television as erasing childhood, which critics of the medium have charged, parents in this study used television as a starting point for a common aesthetic culture between parents and children that was driven by children and was therefore childlike. The families enveloped media with related activities to create a child-centered culture in their homes. Media consumption and related behavior are richly meaningful interactions within the family systems, often because they are leisure-time activities and because they can convey meaning in indirect, comfortable ways. It allows families to manage space, either togetherness or separation, in ways that are not disruptive to the system as a whole. The families examined here demonstrated a rich array of media-related behaviors as they accepted, rejected, and reinterpreted media influence. Race informed many points of interaction, overtly in the lives of the Black families and less overtly in the lives of the White families. The traditions, attitudes, and patterns that often accompanied racial identity were woven into the context for media interaction and the ways in which the families managed media and related behavior (see also Diggs, chap. 6, this volume). Race appeared to play a major role in the selection and interpretation of favorite television programs for Black families.

They also identified those programs as playing a role in the racial socialization of their children. Although racial identity did not appear overtly to factor into the selection of programs for the White families, the tendency to choose programs from across the racial spectrum may be an indication of racial privilege. It seemed that the racial stakes were not as high for the White families. When race did emerge as an issue for the White families, it led to a period of negotiation but did not lead to a change in selection behavior.

Race also appeared to interact with family structure, which, in turn, informed patterns of behavior. The parity of the Black two-parent family seemed to allow the father to intervene more often in daily television attendance as well as interpretation, whereas the White father intervened only in larger decisions of selection and interpretation. The Black single mother and father, in a family in which nothing had been broken or dissolved, appeared to the mother to work rather seamlessly to govern their son's media behavior, whereas the separated White mother worried but did not act to control her son's media behavior at his father's house. Race played an important and complex role in the active family system and racially informed media behavior. Family television viewing emerged as an important indicator of family system behavior and meaning patterns.

REFERENCES

Alexander, A. (1994). The effect of media on family interaction. In D. Zillman, J. Bryant, & A. C. Huston (Eds.), *Media, children and the family: Social scientific psychodynamic, and clinical perspectives* (pp. 51–59). Hillsdale, NJ: Lawrence Erlbaum Associates.

Andreasen, M. S. (1994). Patterns of family life and television consumption from 1945 to the 1990s. In D. Zillman, J. Bryant, & A. C. Huston (Eds.), *Media, children and the family: Social scientific psychodynamic, and clinical perspectives* (pp. 19–36). Hillsdale, NJ: Lawrence Erlbaum Associates.

Baumrind, D. (1971). Current patterns of parental authority. *Developmental Psychology Monographs, 4*(1, Pt. 2).

Bower, R. T. (1973). *Television and the public.* New York: Holt, Rinehart & Winston.

Braxton, G. (1998, May 12). For many Black viewers, Seinfield's end is non-event television: Much of the African American community appears indifferent to the show. *Los Angeles Times*, p. F2.

Business report: Black and White in color. (1992, November). *American Demographics, 14*(11), 9–10.

Cronen, V. E., Pearce, W. B., & Tomm, K. (1985). A dialectical view of personal change. In K. Gergen & K. Davis (Eds.), *Social construction of the person* (pp. 203–224). New York: Springer-Verlag.

Economics and Statistics Administration. (1995). *Statistical abstract of the United States.* Washington, DC: U.S. Bureau of the Census, Department of Commerce.

Economics and Statistics Administration. (1997). *Statistical abstract of the United States.* Washington, DC: U.S. Bureau of the Census, Department of Commerce.

Farhi, P. (1994a, December 1). In Black homes, some TV hits are not so big ratings: Once small differences in viewing tastes have widened in prime-time viewing hours. *Los Angeles Times*, p. F10.

Farhi, P. (1994b, November 29). A television trend: Audiences in Black and White: Viewers split on racial lines: Networks find diversity sells—but critics see cultural risks. *The Washington Post*, p. A1.

Garbarino, J., & Abramowitz, R. H. (1992). The family as a social system. In J. Garbarino (Ed.), *Children and families in the social environment* (2nd ed., pp. 71–98). New York: Aldine De Gruyter.

Jackson, J. S., McCullough, W. R., & Gurin, G. (1997). Family, socialization environment, and identity development in Black Americans. In H. P. McAdoo (Ed.), *Black families* (3rd ed., pp.251–266). Thousand Oaks, CA: Sage.

Kantor, D., & Lehr, W. (1975). *Inside the family.* San Francisco: Jossey-Bass.

Kim, Y. Y., & Rubin, B. D. (1988). Intercultural transformation: A systems theory. In Y. Y. Kim & W. B. Gudykunst (Eds.), *Theories in intercultural communication* (pp. 299–321). Newbury Park: Sage.

Kline, S. (1993). *Out of the garden: Toys, TV, and children's culture in the age of marketing.* New York: Verso.

McAdoo, J. L. (1979). The study of father–child interaction patterns and self esteem in Black pre-school children. *Young Children 34*(1), 46–53.

McAdoo, J. L. (1997). The role of African American fathers. In H.P. McAdoo (Ed.), *Black families* (3rd ed., pp. 183–197). Thousand Oaks, CA: Sage.

Nielsen Media Research. (1991). *Media research news.* New York: Author.

Nielsen Media Research . (1994). *Media research news.* New York: Author.

Nielsen Media Research. (1997). *Media research news.* New York: Author.

Nobles, W. N. (1997). African American family life: An instrument of culture. In H. P. McAdoo (Ed.), *Black families* (3rd ed., pp. 83–93). Thousand Oaks, CA: Sage.

Parks, S. L. (1983). *Television and the racial and sexual socialization of the child.* Unpublished master's thesis, University of Massachusetts, Amherst.

Parks, S. L. (1985). *Family structure, myth, meaning and media behavior.* Unpublished doctoral dissertation, University of Massachusetts, Amherst.

Parks, S. L. (1987, November). *Always there is music: Mass media and the systemic life of a family.* A paper presented at the meeting of the Speech Communication Association, Boston.

Selvini Palazzoli, M., Boscolo, L., Cecchin, G. & Prata, G. (1978). *Paradox and counter paradox: A new model in the therapy of family in schizophrenic transaction.* New York: Jason Aronson.

Selvini Palazzoli, M., Boscolo, L., Cecchin, G. & Prata, G. (1980). Hypothesizing—circularity—neutrality: Three guidelines for the conductor of the session. *Family Process, 19*, 3–12.

Socha, T. J. (in press). Communication in family units: Studying our first group. In L. Frey (Ed.), *Handbook of group communication.* Thousand Oaks, CA: Sage.

Spradley, J. P. (1979). *The ethnographic interview.* New York: Harcourt Brace Jovanovich.

Staples, R., & Johnson, L. B. (1993). *Black families at the crossroads: Challenges and prospects.* San Francisco: Jossey-Bass.

Sudarkasa, N. (1997). African American families and family values. In H.P. McAdoo (Ed.), *Black families* (3rd ed., pp. 9–40). Thousand Oaks, CA: Sage.

Taylor, R. J., Chatters, L .M., Tucker, N. B., and Lewis, E. (1990). Developments in research on Black families: A decade review. *Journal of Marriage and the Family, 52*, 993–1014.

Tichi, C. (1991). *Electronic hearth: Creating an American television culture.* New York: Oxford University Press.

U.S. Bureau of the Census. (1993). *Household and family characteristics: March 1992* (Current Population Rep., Series P-20, No. 467). Washington, DC: U.S. Government Printing Office.

Verdon, M. (1983). The stem family: Toward a general theory. In M. Gordon (Ed.), *The American family in social-historical perspective* (3rd ed., pp. 24–37). New York: St. Martin's Press.

Willie, C. V. (1984). The role of mothers in the lives of outstanding scholars. *Journal of Family Issues, 5*, 291–306.

5

White Children's Talk About Race and Culture: Family Communication and Intercultural Socialization

Roberta A. Davilla
University of Northern Iowa, Cedar Falls

The cornfields and gently rolling hills of Iowa seem too tranquil a setting for issues of race and culture to exist, let alone generate debate. From appearances and perceived stereotypes, diversity does not exist in this agricultural state. The Scandinavian, German, and Irish immigrants of the region created a European-American environment where a seeming absence of race and a secure, unquestioning culture were certain to thrive. Yet, from its very beginnings, Iowa has grappled with racial and cultural diversity. The indigenous Native American presence, the bringing in of African Americans to the manufacturing centers, and the Hispanic appearance along the railroad and seasonal migrant farming communities have long existed here. The uneasy marriage of race and culture as community issues, although sometimes quietly ignored, overlooked, or entirely dismissed, has been a part of the fabric of this otherwise "removed" Midwestern state.

Children in Iowa, as other children, seldom have occasion to express their understanding of the world in the company of grown-ups. When they do make the attempt to voice their opinions, children may be chastised for speaking out of turn. Yet, children live increasingly complex lives, and from their lived experiences, they develop a way of knowing. The purpose of this study was to provide an opportunity for children to express their ideas, in general, and to reveal their way of knowing and expressing their understanding of race and culture, in particular. It is important to listen to children's sense of social reality and their expression of the slippery terms of *race* and *culture*. Adults may erroneously presume attitudes and understandings of children that, in reality, simply do not exist. Adults often misattribute adult qualities to children as well.

In the controlled environments of family, child-care centers, school, and church, children undergo transformations. They are transformed cognitively, emotionally, physically, and morally (e.g., Bandura, 1973, 1977; Erikson, 1985; Gilligan, 1982; Piaget, 1954, 1969; Skinner, 1989, 1990) into the generally socially approved ways of functioning in Western society.

Children (defined here from age 5 to age 12) are, of course, members of families. Families contribute to the acquisition of worldviews and understandings of the complex world within which children live. As a part of this, families produce a discourse that is used by their members to understand both the immediate events of everyday living and the larger social occurrences and structures. Families are shaped and transformed, in part, by this discourse. Through their talk, attitudes, beliefs, and values are produced, perpetuated, and practiced. One of the discursive practices that emerges from this interaction includes talk about the topics of race and culture. Families are key sites for children to learn and understand these concepts. Wartella and Reeves (1987) asserted that, through their interactions with parents, siblings, friends, teachers, and other community members, children are socialized to the dominant cultural values and beliefs. Families' biases and prejudices affect the family members' perceptual filters and habits of understanding about race and culture. Ultimately, family experiences and interactions are key to shaping the ideas and beliefs about race and culture.

Children are active participants in families. They play a part in the shaping of everyday living practices, and thus, the shaping of family values. Learning and understanding the complexities of race and culture are two important developments for children. Families present the sites where the dark sides of prejudice, fear, and misunderstanding as well as the positive sides of empathy, enrichment, and understanding often occur about race and culture. Because children can be thought of as examples of "society-becoming" (Davilla & Pearson, 1994), the influence of families on children's attitudes, values, and beliefs about race and culture cannot be overlooked. Of particular interest for this study was how children learn and understand their families' discursive practices of race and culture. Holmes (1995) stated that it is "children to whom we should be listening" (p.7) if the development of educational strategies, multicultural curriculum, and multicultural interactions is to be achieved.

In addition to being producers of discourse, children are also consumers of social practices. Their uses of imitation and fantasy are part of the consumption of the discursive practice. To view children as consumers is to shift attention from interpreting the discourse messages and texts as already constituted to seeing how the discursive practices organize those messages and texts.

PURPOSE OF THE STUDY AND QUESTIONS

This research study attempted to illuminate how elementary school children in Grades 2, 4, and 6 talk about "race" and "culture." These grade levels were selected because of the varying cognitive and multicultural developmental levels thought to be represented in the different grades. Prior to second grade, children's communicative competence is limited. Kindergarten and first graders are just beginning to understand the world beyond their own homes, preschools, and child-care centers and are adjusting to full-time schooling away from these more limited and controlled environments. Second graders have adapted to the new experiences of school and the many people with whom they must interact every day. The sixth grade was the upper cutoff because, in the school district of interest, students entered junior high during the seventh grade year. The junior high experience is yet another level of academic, cognitive, physical, and emotional development.

For the purpose of this study, the focus was on the elementary school years and the understandings these children have about "race" and "culture." The issue of racial homogeneity is of concern as well, because of the overwhelmingly White dominance in the community. The midsize Iowa metropolitan area in which the study was conducted is among the most culturally diverse populations within the State. Yet, the predominance of White people and culture limits the immediate and consistent exposure to other races and cultures for the people who live there. Through the discourse, the children's talk can reveal the complexities of these abstract concepts and the children's understanding of them. The illumination of their understandings of the difficult dialogues of "race" and "culture" may help parents, teachers, counselors, law enforcement personnel, clergy, and other adults who work with children in dispelling prejudices and incorrect assumptions. The organizing research question asked was: "How do 2nd-, 4th-, and 6th-grade children talk about "race" and "culture" and where and how do they learn these constructs?"

METHOD

The investigation of the concepts of race and culture was fulfilled through the methodology of phenomenology. The tripartite method of description, reduction, and interpretation was described by Lanigan (1988) as synergistic in nature. The aim of phenomenology is to illuminate the basic structures of lived experience (see Merleau-Ponty, 1962, 1964a, 1964b, 1964c, 1968; Patton, 1990; Polkinghorne, 1983) and to derive insights from prereflective experiences (see Van Maanen, 1990). Because much of children's experiences are formed primarily through unique and previously unconstructed consciousness, phenomenology fits well as an analytical methodology.

A goal of the study was to present an illustrative, but not necessarily defini-tive, understanding of a unique group of predominately White children's lived experiences about race and culture. Grown-ups frequently assume that chil-dren reflect the adult version of knowledge (Mackay, 1991). Yet, children may differ significantly in their discursive structures and discernment. Programs for education, advice, and information offered to children may be erroneous in fun-damental assumptions about race and may be based on faulty assumptions. In-deed, learning children's discourse in illustrating the lived experience of race and culture can enrich adult ways of knowing.

The physical body is of an intersubjective nature. The body does not derive its intersubjectivity from a principle that is distinct from itself (Kwant, 1963). What this meant for this study was that children experience the world through their bodies and senses. Their development moves from body to world (or not body). Children move through the concrete world from the perspective of body/not body. They move from what is known within their bodies to what is known outside their bodies. Children experience what they know by what they embody in the world. The interview protocol developed for this study reflected this assumption. Through the tripartite method of phenomenological descrip-tion, reduction, and interpretation, the goals of revealing the essence of chil-dren's understanding of race and culture can be achieved.

PARTICIPANTS AND PROCEDURES

Two elementary schools in a midsize Iowa university town were selected for in-vestigation. These schools were chosen, in part, because the researcher had been a parent-volunteer in one of the schools and had stepchildren who at-tended the other school. As a qualitative researcher who studies children, the necessity to cultivate and maintain relationships with schools, in general, and with children, in particular, cannot be adequately emphasized. Children are protected by school administrators, teachers, and parents and are taught to be distrustful of strangers. In order to create a comfortable environment in which the children can express their experiences and ideas, the researcher must be known to the children and to the school personnel. Another reason that these schools were selected is that the researcher wanted to stay away from the uni-versity-sponsored school in which children are often research study partici-pants. A fresh perspective was sought by including students who had never before participated in a research study.

The researcher received permission from the University's Human Subjects Review Board to conduct the research. She then completed the necessary pa-perwork to obtain permission to conduct research in the school district. She met with the District Director of Elementary Education and one of the school principals to review the interview questions and then received permission to proceed with the study. After the school year began in September 1997, the researcher sent letters of intent and informed consent forms to the parents/guardians of all students in the selected classes. Students became researcher participants with the return of the signed informed consent permission slip from parents/guardians.

Twenty-one 2nd-grade children, twenty-one 4th-grade children, and eleven 6th-grade children were interviewed from the two elementary schools. Demographically, one school educates middle- to upper-middle-class students from many professional families. At this school, student scores on the Iowa BASIC school achievement test are the highest in the school district. Of the school population, 94.5% is White; 5% is Asian; and .5% is Hispanic. No African-American students attend this school. The second school is not much different, with 95% of the children coming from White; 4% from African-American; and .5% from Hispanic-American, and .5% from Asian backgrounds, respectively. These children also come from middle-class homes. See Table 5.1.

In addition to the interviews, 129 students participated in class units/lessons that dealt with some aspect of race and culture. Forty-eight 2nd-grade students, forty-two 4th-grade students, and thirty-nine 6th-grade students participated in the all-class activities. The researcher planned the class lessons in consultation with each class teacher, but the teacher was ultimately responsible for designing and implementing each lesson. The purpose of the activities was to introduce the ideas of race and culture in as nonintrusive a way as possible to

TABLE 5.1
Study Participants by Grade, Sex, and Race

Participants	Grade 2	Grade 4	Grade 6
By Sex:			
Females	9	10	7
Males	12	11	4
Total	21	21	11
By Race:			
White	20	20	8
African-American	0	0	1
Hispanic	0	0	1
Native American	1	0	0
East Indian	0	0	1
African-American/White	0	1	0
Total	21	21	11

the children while, at the same time, to incorporate these concepts into the existing curriculum.

The researcher was introduced to each class and observed the students as the teacher or student-teacher led each class lesson about race and/or culture. Every teacher conducted an all-class discussion about the topic. After the lesson was completed, the researcher approached the student participants and asked them if they would be willing to go with her to the interview site. Interviews were conducted in groups of 3 to 5 participants and ranged in length from 15 to 30 minutes. The interview questions were asked of all participants (see Appendix). All interviews were recorded on audiotape. The interviews were transcribed by a transcriptionist. The thematizations and interpretations of the transcripts were based in the phenomenological methodology tradition described next, along with the themes and interpretations by individual grade levels.

THEMATIZATION OF THE DATA BY GRADE

All 53 interviews were analyzed by using the tripartite method of phenomenology developed by Merleau-Ponty (1962) and practiced and expanded by Lanigan (1988), Nelson (1989), Jenkins (1988), and Peterson (1987). The phenomenological description is the first order of signification. Through their talk, the children express their experiences (signified) in speech (signifier). The group conversations, as recorded on audiotape, were transcribed for content to detail the experiences into signifying form. Each participant was assigned a letter (i.e., "A," "B," or "C"), and the interviewer was identified as "Q" on the transcripts. The intersubjective nature of the lived experiences was isolated and then clustered into groups of similar statements, called *phenomenological thematization*, or revelatory phrases.

The phenomenological reduction is the second order of signification. Here, the focus is on the correlations and interrelations among the signs (the signifier plus the signified equal the sign; Eco, 1979; Fiske & Hartley, 1978). In the reduction, the statements of each cluster are reduced to brief descriptions that characterize the theme.

After several readings of the transcripts, researchers begin to identify emerging themes. In the reduction, these emergent themes from the participants' speech are analyzed. The themes are created by listening, reading, re-listening, and re-reading the transcribed text and the audiotapes. Redundant patterns emerge from the repetition. The clusters merge into themes that share similarities of conscious experience. The children expressed their understanding of race and culture by definitions of the words, the family circumstances under which these meanings were learned, and the desired social goals to achieve harmony among people of different races and cultures. The family's place in these socialization processes was of central interest.

Grade 2 Themes

"In the Olympics I see some people race and that means they have culture." The second graders had very limited understanding of and vocabulary with which to express the concepts of race and culture. Race was primarily described as a car, motorcycle, or go-cart race. The quote, "Race is like you have to go faster and then you can win and get a trophy," aptly describes the majority of children's responses to the question, "What does the word, *race*, mean?"

The term *culture* was even more vaguely described by the second graders. One respondent replied, "What or how you were born," to the question, "What does the word, *culture*, mean to you?" and then quickly stated, "No, that's race. [Culture is] what you eat." Language was the key concept used by the majority of the children to describe the essence of culture. Language constraints limited understanding other cultures. Culture was described in concrete terms such as "food" and "ways of doing things." To the children, if people from different cultures were to achieve better understanding, learning English was the preferred way to achieve this end. Learning the other person's language was viewed as too difficult. A frustrated/polite ethnocentrism was communicated by the respondents. One respondent stated that people from different cultures should speak "nicely" to each other. "Don't say anything bad about them, like if you don't like their hairdo, don't say anything about it, just keep it to yourself or something."

The effort to be "nice to them" illustrates a personal opinion that sets up an "us" versus "them" dichotomy. As a family member and student, propriety and politeness are social skills that a person exhibits to "other" people in the public domain. Families do not always have to demonstrate such social skills at home, but if a guest or outsider enters into the private domain of the home, members are called upon to be "nice to them." Likewise, if families are out in public, such social graces are expected when interacting with friends, acquaintances, and other people who are encountered in a public setting. Thus, to be nice to them implies a guest behavior and separation from an inner social circle that can occur within a family or more intimate setting. A clear distinction is made between "us" and "them" that separates and excludes intimate knowing and understanding of other people, whether they are from another race, culture, or family. If one does not cross over to include "them," then the status quo is maintained and security and certainty are conserved. This notion can illustrate the distinctions made between families and can be extended to other groups that are different and apart from what is known and accepted. In the present circumstance, to be "nice to them" suggests that anyone of another race or culture is worthy of respect while still being kept at a safe interaction distance. At the demonstrated level of understanding description, children recognize that differences exist among races and cultures. Dissimilarities reveal curiosity, uncertainty, and risk in the exposure and learning about them. To know and to understand another race and culture are risky and dubious undertakings. Protection and absolutes are lost or challenged, and the return to certainty is not assured. Hence, to be nice to them implies respect and regard while at the same time maintaining a safe space from which to view the curiosities of an unknown and not understood person/event. (For additional information about racism see Katz, 1978 and Kivel, 1996.)

Grade 4 Themes

"Culture is what you do and how you do it." Fourth graders have a considerably more elaborate understanding of the concepts of race and culture than the second graders. The site described for hearing information about race and culture was frequently the media. This makes sense because the exposure and interaction with varying racial and cultural groups within the community are quite limited. Viewing differences among racial and cultural groups also suggests a voyeuristic vantage point. To be a voyeur, one is distant while viewing the enticement/provocative scene. Five fourth graders, in particular, described in great detail violent confrontations between races in movies. Five respondents stated that they heard the words *race* and *culture* in their Social Studies class. Two children discussed talking with their families about issues of race and culture. One narrator was particularly descriptive in relating a family story about her Hispanic relatives. She commented, "They treated her (aunt) like she was not even like she was Mexican, they treated her like she was their real sister and they were being kind to her and stuff.… " Another narrator stated, "Sometimes parents say, 'Don't talk to Black people cause they are different from us,' but they really aren't. It's just their skin color and their hair color." This narrator continued,

> They (White people) used to call them that (n———) back then because they thought Black people were stupid so they made up names for them. And Black people made up names for White people. They call us cracker. They did. That's insulting.… I think that Black and White people shouldn't scream and swear at each other and call bad names to each other. I think that we should speak to each other with respect and not with rudeness but with kindness.

The fourth graders indicated, however, that primarily they learned about race and culture by watching television shows, films shown on television, videos, and through classroom discussions with teachers. The narrators mentioned *Oprah*, *Rescue 911*, *Family Matters*, and *Candyman* as the television shows and films in which cultural and racial differences were discussed. The majority of the interview discussions involved relaying the storylines of these mediated sources and the unkind statements and actions that Blacks and Whites made toward one another.

Eighteen respondents described race as having "different skin color and hair color." Race still meant "to get in a line and start running" to 3 respondents. Culture, was frequently described as the "ways people do things in a special way." One respondent indicated that she/he experienced a "family culture." Language was still viewed as important to culture but the descriptions broadened to include customs, dress, and ways of doing things.

Grade 6 Themes

"Just different colors of the world." As anticipated, sixth graders have a more sophisticated vocabulary with which to describe race and culture. Their global understanding of countries was more apparent than the fourth and second graders. Sixth graders referred to African and Asian countries and different religions as examples of different cultures. European subcultures were mentioned also, such as the Nazis and the Aryan race. Sixth graders heard about the words *race* and *culture* at school, on television news and shows, and on the radio. Their more expansive awareness of the concepts may, in part, be influenced by their more regular exposure to various forms of mass media. The respondents talked about discussing race and culture with their family but did not develop their responses beyond "the rightness or wrongness" of the differing ways of doing things. They may not want to be seen as judgmental or wrong in front of their peers or may be at an early stage of keeping culture and race abstract and distant. Finally, learning the languages of other cultures was confirmed by the sixth graders. The difficulty of understanding an entire system of customs and words was expressed: "Well, when we talk they can't understand us and we can't understand them, so there is no use in having a conversation if you can't understand what they are saying." A suggestion to overcome this difficulty was "I think that everyone should learn to speak their own language. And like learn a new one or something. Learn one that is nobody's so it is kind of like a universal one."

Interpretation of the Themes

The framework for the interpretation of the themes of the respondents was the intercultural transformation systems theory model developed by Kim and Ruben (1988). These researchers suggested that intercultural communication studies of travelers and immigrants have been categorized into two approaches: the "intercultural communication-as-problem" and the "intercultural communication-as-learning/growth" (p. 301). In the first approach, disorientation and "cultural fatigue" (p. 302) are frequent experiences of individuals who are placed in a foreign environment. A person must go through several adjustment stages to become acclimated to the foreign culture. These stages include (a) a "honeymoon" stage characterized by fascination, elation, and optimism; (b) a stage of hostility and emotionally stereotyped attitudes toward the host society and increased association with fellow sojourners; (c) a recovery stage characterized by increased language knowledge and ability to get around in the new culture; and (d) a final stage in which adjustment is about as complete as possible, anxiety is largely gone, and new customs are accepted and enjoyed (p. 302).

Thinking about, experiencing, and adjusting to a new culture is viewed as a problem that must be worked through. A schism is created for people by the uncertainty and strangeness of customs and language in the new environment. Gradually, through exposure and a personal experience of sense making, people overcome the problem of the foreign nature of things (Kim & Ruben, 1988).

The second perspective, the intercultural communication as "learning/growth" approach developed originally by Adler (1975), views the progressive shifts coming from a change in personal identity and through experience learning. The five phases include: (a) a contact phase characterized by excitement and euphoria during which the individual views the new environment ethnocentrically; (b) a disintegration phase marked by confusion, alienation, and depression, during which cultural differences become increasingly noticeable; (c) a reintegration phase characterized by strong rejection of the second culture, defensive projection of personal difficulties, and an existential choice to either regress to earlier phases or to move closer to resolution and personal growth; (d) an autonomy stage marked by increasing understanding of the host culture along with a feeling of competence; and (e) a final independence stage marked by a cherishing of cultural differences and relativism, creative behavior, and increased self- and cultural awareness (p. 304). Adler's phasic model influences the move away from viewing intercultural communication as problematic and provides a foundation for Kim and Ruben's (1988) systems theory of intercultural transformation. Key terms for the transformative model are *culture* and *intercultural transformation*. *Culture* is defined as "collective life patterns shared by people in social groups such as national, racial, ethnic, socioeconomic, regional, and gender groups" (p. 305). A *communication event* is defined as intercultural if attributes of differing cultures and subcultures are present. Then, to experience *intercultural transformation*, a person must move beyond the original cognitive, affective, and behavioral patterns learned in the first culture. Transformation implies movement and differing levels of interculturalness (p. 306). Hence, the intercultural transformation as a systems theory recognizes the ebb and flow and interdependence of cultural knowledge and understanding. The person's ability to "self-organize," which is highly individual (see Jantsch, 1980), is central to the sophistication and acceptance of alternative cultures.

Awakening Multiculturalism.   The Adler (1975) and Kim and Ruben (1988) theories of interculturalness and intercultural transformation function in helpful but limited ways to account for the Iowa children's understanding and expression of race and culture. The responses of the second, fourth, and sixth graders reflect a primitive, but evolving, awareness and sophistication in expressing ideas and understanding about the slippery and politically charged concepts of race and culture. The Iowa children of European heritage must rely on media to inform their frameworks of thought about race and culture. This is highly problematic given the negative stereotypes and underrepresentation of

African Americans, especially on television. This places extraordinary burdens on education and other institutions (e.g., churches, temples, and child-care facilities) to fill the gap. The limits of exposure to other races and cultures in the predominately European-American culture of northern Iowa were reflected in the confined responses of the children. This finding was not surprising. The second graders, in particular, were quite limited in their expression and understanding of the key concepts of this study. Other than the concrete "race is something you run" idea that all the respondents have experienced on numerous occasions, the vague notions of race and culture remained remote.

The children, as the different grade level responses demonstrate, grow in sophistication of language expression. Yet, the notions of race and culture remain limited and distant even at the fourth and sixth grades. The children expressed that they do hear about and discuss the terms *race* and *culture* with their family. The more disquieting finding, however, is that the children were much more animated, expressive, and knowledgeable during the interviews when they described the media influence on their understandings of race and culture. The children were able to offer specific examples about the racial and cultural themes they had seen on television or had seen in films shown on television; specific comments about family conversations were infrequent and only discussed in general terms.

Clearly, media are predominate in knowledge acquisition and representation of race and culture. A sad protest with this finding may lead to admonishing these media for failure to accurately depict varying races and cultures on television and in films. Yet, it may be these media that are key to implementing the push for more multicultural perspectives. Coupled with family influence, television programming, including films seen on television, may be among the forces that will help achieve multicultural sensitivity and transformations of ethnically homogeneous populations.

The television might very well be a legitimate family member. The television is often switched on during family meals, if a common mealtime is enjoyed by a family; it serves as the focus of family rooms; and a family may spend "time together" by collectively watching TV (see Parks, chap. 4, this volume). Television is often used for background noise in homes, and power in the family is measured by who has the television remote control. Recognizing that television and other mediated sources have profound influence on children's lives, researchers may take this cue to serve as the starting point for encouraging and enhancing multicultural perspectives for children.

Educational efforts to create multicultural perspectives should capitalize on television's influence. Education empowers people; educating all cultures creates advantage for everyone. Media are driven by and responsive to the desires and needs of viewers as well as the advertised products that viewers purchase. Given this supply–demand relationship, multicultural perspectives and interests can be represented and advocated if the educated people demand and insist on multicultural transformation.

Multicultural perspectives should not be limited to the social levels of the media and formal education; such efforts must be advocated from multiple sites. To incorporate individual families into this process and to encourage conversations about race and culture, some activities, adapted from Kivel (1996) and Katz (1978), are offered (see also Socha & Beigle, chap. 10, this volume for a discussion of education issues). These activities are useful for all families, but especially families living in remote, culturally homogenous communities:

Activity 1: Assess your home for the books, art, calendars, music, computer games, sporting equipment, and religious materials present. Name the decorations and items that are either created by or represent race or culture. Consider the contributions that each of the races and cultures made to the creation of these objects. Discuss the common interests and experiences that may exist among the races and cultures, such as in the areas of music, art, sports, religion, and so forth.

Activity 2: Ask family members to write a description of a situation in which they interacted with another person from a different race or culture. This experience can be either positive or negative. Shuffle the descriptions. Have each family member select a description and role play the situation. Discuss observations made about the situation and offer alternatives for interaction. Talk about the common interests and similarities among the various races or cultures as well as the differences that created the unique situation.

CONCLUSION

The limited views of Iowa children about race and culture will not be transformed overnight. With awareness and a willingness to discuss and to use the institutions already in place to advocate multicultural perspectives, teachers and parents may give children the opportunities to learn alternative viewpoints. These children will, it is hoped, grow up to become multiculturally transformed so all races and cultures can feel that a comfortable place for them can be found and maintained.

ACKNOWLEDGMENT

The author thanks the students and teachers who participated in this research study and the administrators who gave their permission to make this study possible. Without their enthusiastic interest, the completion of this project would not have been possible. Thanks also to the following people who provided their comments and insights for this chapter: Tom Socha, Rhunette Diggs, Edward Ellis, and Brad Craig.

APPENDIX

As topics arose during the interview, these topics were followed up. Particular topics/questions asked during the interview included the following:

1. Describe your picture to me (if applicable).
2. What does the word *race* mean?
3. What does the word *culture* mean?
4. When have you heard these words (*race* and *culture*) used? Where have you heard these words (*race* and *culture*) used? Please explain.
5. Are there differences in the way that people from different cultures and races talk with each other? Are there differences in the way that people from different cultures and races talk with other people? Explain.
6. How would you like to see people from different cultures and races talk with each other? Explain.

REFERENCES

Adler, P. S. (1975). The transition experience: An alternative view of culture shock. *Journal of humanistic psychology, 15*, 13–23.

Bandura, A. (1973). *Aggression: A social learning analysis.* Englewood Cliffs, NJ: Prentice-Hall.

Bandura, A. (1977). *Social learning theory.* Englewood Cliffs, NJ: Prentice-Hall.

Davilla, R. A., & Pearson, J. C. (1994). Children's perspectives of the family: A phenomenological inquiry. *Human Studies, 17,* 325–341.

Eco, U. (1979). *A theory of semiotics.* Bloomington: Indiana University Press.

Erikson, E. H. (1985). *Childhood and society.* New York: Norton.

Fiske, J., & Hartley, J. (1978). *Reading television.* London: Methuen.

Gilligan, C. (1982). *In a different voice: Psychological theory and women's development.* Cambridge, MA: Harvard University Press.

Holmes, R. M. (1995). *How children perceive race.* Thousand Oaks, CA: Sage.

Jantsch, E. (1980). *The self-organizing universe: Scientific and human implications of the emerging paradigm of evolution.* New York: Pergamon.

Jenkins, H., III. (1988). "Going bonkers!": Children, play and Pee-wee. *Camera obscura: A journal of feminism and film theory, 17,* 169–192.

Katz, J. (1978). *White awareness: Handbook for anti-racism training.* Norman: University of Oklahoma Press.

Kim, Y. Y., & Ruben, B. D. (1988). Intercultural transformation: A systems theory. In Y. Y. Kim & W. B. Gudykunst (Eds.), *Theories in intercultural communication* (pp. 299–321). Newbury Park, CA: Sage.

Kivel, P. (1996). *Uprooting racism: How White people can work for racial justice.* Philadelphia: New Society.

Kwant, R. C. (1963). *The phenomenological philosophy of Merleau-Ponty.* Pittsburgh, PA: DuQuesne University Press.

Lanigan, R. L. (1988). *Phenomenology of communication: Merleau-Ponty's thematics in communicology and semiology.* Pittsburgh, PA: Duquesne University Press.

Mackay, R. W. (1991). Conceptions of children and models of socialization. In F. C. Waksler (Ed.), *Studying the social worlds of children: Sociological readings* (pp. 23–37). New York: The Falmer Press.

Merleau-Ponty, M. (1962). *Phenomenology of perception* (C. Smith, Trans.). London: Routledge and Kegan Paul.

Merleau-Ponty, M. (1964a). *The primacy of perception and other essays.* Evanston, IL: Northwestern University Press.

Merleau-Ponty, M. (1964b). *Sense and non-sense.* Evanston, IL: Northwestern University Press. (Original work published 1948).

Merleau-Ponty, M. (1964c.) *Signs.* (R. C. McCleary, Trans.). Evanston, IL: Northwestern University Press. (Original work published 1954).

Merleau-Ponty, M. (1968). *The visible and the invisible.* (A. Lingis, Trans.). Evanston, IL: Northwestern University Press. (Original work published 1964)

Nelson, J. L. (1989). Phenomenology as feminist methodology: Explicating interviews. In K. Carter & C. Spitzack (Eds.), *Doing research on women's communication: Perspectives on theory and method* (pp. 221–241). Norwood, NJ: Ablex.

Patton, M. Q. (1990). *Qualitative evaluation and research methods* (2nd ed.). Newbury Park, CA: Sage.

Peterson, E. E. (1987). Media consumption and girls who want to have fun. *Critical Studies in Mass Communication, 4,* 37–50.

Piaget, J. (1954). *The construction of reality in the child* (M. Cook, Trans.). New York: Basic Books.

Piaget, J. (1969). *The child's conception of the world* (J. Tomlinson & A. Tomlinson, Trans.). Totowa, NJ: Littlefield, Adams & Co.

Polkinghorne, D. (1983). *Methodology for the human sciences: Systems of inquiry.* Albany: State University of New York Press.

Skinner, B. F. (1989). *Recent issues in the analysis of behavior.* Columbus, OH: Merrill.

Skinner, B. F. (1990). *Walden two: With a new introduction by the author.* New York: Macmillan.

Van Maanen, M. (1990). *Researching lived experience: Human science for an action sensitive pedagogy.* London, Ontario, Canada: The State University of New York Press.

Wartella, E., & Reeves, B. (1987). Communication and children. In C. R. Berger & S. H. Chaffee (Eds.), *Handbook of communication science* (pp. 619–650). Beverly Hills, CA: Sage.

6

African-American and European-American Adolescents' Perceptions of Self-Esteem as Influenced by Parent and Peer Communication and Support Environments

Rhunette C. Diggs
University of Louisville

The lengthy research history of sociocultural and identity[1] differences between African Americans and European Americans serves as the background to examine the communication influences and issues related to the self-esteem of African-American (or Black) and European American (or White) adolescents. The rationale for the inclusion of this chapter in a book devoted to the family communication of Blacks and Whites rests in its emphasis on those whom are regarded as our future—especially young adults who will inherit adulthood in the near future. In this chapter, the terms *adolescent*, *youth*, and *students* are used interchangeably. Adolescence is viewed as a stage of development and as a circumstance in which certain personal needs are emphasized (Pearl, 1981). The most well-known way

---

[1]*Sociocultural* is defined as the resultant outcomes on a person because of the intersection between social context and a person's psychology (Hauser, 1971). A sociological and social psychological understanding of identity may be useful. "Identity refers to who or what one is, to various meanings attached to oneself by self and other" (Gecas and Burke cited in Adams, Montemayor, & Gullotta, 1996, p. 134). This definition references personal and social identities. Gecas and Burke add that the postmodern self is not characterized as having a core or essence.

that identity theorists have defined and characterized adolescence is from the Eriksonian perspective (see Erickson, 1968). The Eriksonian model emphasizes phases of development throughout the life cycle (from infancy to old age). In the adolescent phase, as in all other phases, "there is a phase-specific developmental task which must be solved by the growing-individual in order to continue in his [sic] psychological maturation" (Hauser, 1971, p. 2). The aspect of Erickson's conceptualization of interest here is the social aspect—"the society into which the individual is born makes him a member by influencing the *manner in which* he [sic] solves the tasks posed by each phase of his [sic] epigenetic development" (quote from Rapport, in Hauser, 1971, p. 2).

Pearl (1981) described the adolescent in U.S. society as those individuals 11 to 18 years of age who attend school and, perhaps, are not old enough to work independent of parental awareness. U.S. adolescents follow different paths culturally by participating in varied cultural group lives in the quest to understand who they are. Furthermore, the view of the adolescent-self incorporated within this chapter is consistent with a systems theory perspective (see Kim & Ruben, 1988; Adams, Montemayor & Gullotta, 1996) in that, in light of culture, self-concept issues are a significant consideration for adolescents. Who am I? Do they like me? Where do I fit in? Scholars from various disciplines (e.g., see Adams et al., 1996, for a social psychological developmental viewpoint; Gilligan, 1982, for a feminist viewpoint; Asante, 1988, for an Afrocentric viewpoint) who study identity and culture state that by experiencing and conceiving of the world differently, many and varied issues can be raised in terms of developmental tasks and resultant communication. Such distinctions would imply that the communication of Black and White adolescents could lead to similar and divergent explanations for how self-esteem is influenced and enacted within ethnic families. This volume emphasizes that the family is where the first exposure and first teachers of many of life experiences can be found. But who in the family, primarily, communicates with youth about self and what is being communicated and incorporated about self and others?

The world is changing demographically (Chadwick & Heaton, 1996); and how we think and feel about ourselves may have important implications for living together successfully in a multicultural or diverse world (e.g., Takaki, 1993). In general, self-esteem is important to almost every aspect of our lives (e.g., psychological well-being, Rosenberg, 1965; being achievement-oriented, pro-social, independent, and creative, Coopersmith, 1967/1981; making judgments, relationships, cooperating with others, Branden, cited in Gudykunst, Ting-Toomey, Sudweeks, & Stewart, 1995; Cardinal, 1998; Leary, Tambor, Terdal, & Downs, 1995). Communication and the varied aspects of self-esteem for Black and White youth ultimately point to self-esteem's (debatable) role in realizing the aims of a pluralistic, collective society (see Kohn, 1994) and point to problems surrounding cultural values and worldviews (see Cross, 1991, for an extensive analysis of Black personal and racial identity orientations).

The social science literature examining self-esteem emphasizes two aspects: the personal or unique, and the social or collective (e.g., Mead, 1934; Gudyskunst et al., 1995; Wood, 1997). The language about self-esteem in this literature is often either ambiguous or uses similar terms for slightly different concepts.[2] Rosenberg and Simmons (1971) stated that self-concept has widespread agreement on its importance but equally widespread disagreement on terminology. Synonyms for self-esteem found in this literature are self-image, self, self-concept, proprium, self-feelings, self-evaluation, self-worth, ego, ego identity, and identity. In this chapter, the term *self-esteem* is used interchangeably with the term *self-feelings* as this term reflects the meaning of self-esteem utilized by Rosenberg: "the individual's conscious beliefs, opinions, attitudes, values, and feelings about himself [sic]" (Rosenberg & Simmons, 1971, p. 9). Rosenberg (1965), often credited with the early large-scale sociological survey research on self-esteem, viewed self-esteem as *global,* defined as a disposition or a general tendency to respond a particular way, and *area-specific,* which is an assessment in a particular area, such as school, physical areas, or sports.

The research on self-esteem has a lengthy history in sociology, social-psychology, and psychology in locating group traits and psychological correlates to self-esteem. However, in the interpersonal and family communication areas, there are few studies that specifically highlight the communication influences on adolescent self-esteem (see McDermott, 1983; McDermott & Greenberg, 1984). There has also been limited utilization of Afrocentric theorizing and sociocultural models of difference versus deficit models[3] to explain behaviors related to self-esteem (e.g., Asante, 1981; Hare, 1977; Nobles, 1973, 1978) and limited utilization of multiple research methodologies or triangulation, which "involves a comparative assessment of more than one form of evidence about an object of inquiry … typically a method of verification … explanations become more credible" (Lindlof, 1995, p. 239). Exploring communication influences on self-esteem between White and Black adolescents within the framework of past literature may enhance our understanding of the kinds of communication that can affect communication in interpersonal, intergroup, and interethnic settings. The terms *interethnic* and *intercultural* are also used interchangeably in this chapter, but refer to "race" or color as an aspect of culture.

---

[2]Self-esteem is a part of the self-concept. Self-concept is a "complex, intricate and multifaceted structure" (Rosenberg, 1965, p. 232). The personal or unique aspect refers to Mead's *I;* the social or collective refers to Mead's *Me;* and Nobles' (1973) Afrocentric view of self-esteem emphasizes the holistic view of self or *We* (discussed within chapter).

[3]Sociocultural models of difference point to the distinct culture of a social group to explain behaviors versus a deficit model that explains behavior of a social group in comparison to the dominant social groups' patterns. For example, a deficit model might suggest that the Black family is a different family form in the negative sense, and its positive aspects would be attributed to dominant cultural standards (e.g., see Allen, 1978; Nobles, 1978).

The purpose of this chapter is to (a) discuss the theoretical bases of adolescent identity within the self-esteem research tradition; (b) report two studies of communication influences on adolescent self-esteem; and (c) make recommendations for parent–child communication based on research findings. The chapter is organized into three sections. The first presents a review of relevant literature; the second summarizes two studies (one quantitative and one qualitative) that investigated influences on African-American and European-American adolescents' self-esteem; and the third concludes with a discussion and recommendations for future scholarship and family esteem communication practices.

REVIEW OF LITERATURE

The review of literature examines selected intellectual voices who offer theories on conceptualizations of self and Black and White adolescent identity. Also, research that addresses historical adolescent self-esteem studies and incorporates communication variables is highlighted.

Black and White Identity

An underlying assumption of this chapter is that Whites and Blacks may differ in the degree of emphasis placed on the self as I *(unique, personal)*, the self as Me *(collective, social)*, or the self as We (e.g., Crocker, Luthanen, Blaine, & Broadnax, 1994; Nobles, 1972, 1973; Phinney & Chavira, 1992; Taylor & Dubé, 1986). Such differential emphases are assumed to be learned, primarily within the family, and are a recognition of possible core differences in thinking (or worldviews) that may manifest varied behaviors and perceptions. In symbolic interaction theory, Mead (1934) saw the self as a social process involving two distinguishable phases, the I (spontaneous, individual) and Me (reflective, evaluative, societal-based). Children are both active and reactive organisms. As an active and reactive organism, the child interacts with the environment and uses information from that interaction to assist with future interactions and understanding of the self. For example, a child learns by interacting in the community that she or he is valued/not valued and good/not good. These interactions also help the individual to learn about others in relation to the self. A child may choose to accept, resist, or generate new views of self (e.g., Baldwin, 1986; Mead, 1934). Their choice is affected by their developmental levels (e.g., infant, early childhood, adolescence, adulthood).

Maccoby and Martin (1983) noted that an additional aspect in the socialization of self is the contribution of the individual's self-component. That is, what influence does the individual's own behavior have on an outcome of interest? James (1890/1918) seemed to address this aspect of the self when he stated that "our self-feeling in this world depends entirely on what we back ourselves to be and do it" (p. 310). For James, self-esteem is determined by the ratio of successes to the pretensions, which implies an active view of self (e.g., self-agency) than more passive views such as locus of control and efficacious actions (e.g., see Coleman & Hendry, 1990; Nobles, 1972). In this view, the person possesses the power (or agency) to create a social being that is not solely the product of the processes of social influence. Such an internal perspective combined with the effects of the social environment help to provide a more holistic view of the importance of all the variables that reflect an individual's evaluation of self (Baldwin, 1986).

The critical theory Afrocentricity (sometimes labeled Africentricity), as are most critical theories, is concerned with issues of power and legitimacy. Asante (1988) noted that "an Afrocentric base of scholarship is rooted in the social, political, and economic values of our people ... recognizing that the care begins with African Americans" (p. 59). Afrocentric scholars seek African- or African-American-derived perspectives to approach the human condition or to address social problems. Afrocentricity complements symbolic interaction with its interest in understanding the lived experience of people. In addition, an Afrocentric focus on identity issues is interested in understanding messages and structures that may diminish individuals' or groups' well-being and the actions that may be undertaken to restore, maintain, or improve well-being. Asante (1988) and Myers (1993) noted that Afrocentricity is only superficially related to skin color. Nobles (1973), an Afrocentric psychologist, offered an analysis of Mead's *I* as the "perception of oneself as reflected by the shared meanings and values of others" and *Me* as "representing the incorporated other within the individual," and *We* as the extended self or "feelings or perceptions one has toward the group and being (or interacting) with the group" (pp.16–17).

Nobles raised controversy when he stated that "most students of Mead would suggest that the 'we' is handled in Mead's analytical thinking by the 'me'" (p. 16). For example, researchers view collective self-esteem as grounded in social identity theory where "social identity is a function of how one privately evaluates one's groups, how one believes others evaluate those groups, and how identified one is with those groups" (Crocker, Luthanen, Blaine, & Broadnax, 1994, p. 504). Yet, Nobles argued that a closer examination makes it clear that "Mead meant for the 'me' to stand for the incorporation of *others'* attitudes and feelings about oneself; the 'I' stood for one's perception or feelings about the organized 'me.'" (pp 16–17).[4] West (1993), in historicizing European male cultural critics, offered a similar perspective in which "we" as "universalizing

---

[4]The example Nobles' (1973) provides: The "other" for someone could be American psychologists. Then, that someone's "me" would be the internalizations of the attitudes and feelings the "other" has toward him. The someone's "I" would be the feelings and attitudes the person has about the organized "me." The "we" would be the feelings the person has about other American psychologists and his interaction with them (pp. 16–17)

gestures exclude (by guarding a silence around) … "(pp. 7–8) peoples of color and women.

Nobles' analysis of Mead's conceptions of self introduced a theoretical controversy. Nobles' perspective places emphasis on self that exists because of others. In everyday practice, it is common for people to identify themselves as both unique and connected with others. These distinctions are relevant to the present discussion of the *self* concept and opens the possibility that cultural awareness of these concepts and their explanations may yield some new insights concerning race and self-esteem bases (e.g., see Cross' critiques of historical Black identity studies, 1991; Harrison, 1985; Horowitz, 1997; Martin, Krizek, Nakayama, & Bradford, 1996; Nobles, 1973; Peters, 1985; Takaki, 1993; Will, 1997).

Black and White Self-Esteem Research

The most visible self-esteem research is found in quantitative studies in sociology and social psychology that examined self-esteem within the symbolic interaction perspective (see Coopersmith, 1967/1981; Rosenberg, 1965, 1985). Coopersmith and Rosenberg developed and validated indices of self-esteem, concluding that the perceived attitude and treatment of significant others are important to enhancing or diminishing self-esteem. Coopersmith's study utilized all White male youth and Rosenberg's utilized White and Black youth. The assumption of these studies was that in understanding ourselves we compare ourselves to others who are significant to us and to those who are part of the larger community, labeled *generalized* others (e.g., Baldwin, 1986; Mead, 1934). The social comparison perspective within a racist context and deficit framework (in which Blacks are seen as being in some way less prepared for societal life) led early sociology theorists and researchers to view African Americans as deficient in self-esteem because, in comparison to the majority, White societal groups, the assumption was that African Americans lacked role models, social status, and material goods. The prime error in this interpretation was making Whites—people far removed from Black's home and culture—significant sources for Blacks rather than other Blacks or their own families. Reflected appraisal suggests that people internalize the perspective others have of them or that assessments by the other are reflected back to the self. This perspective led to the notion of *self-hatred* within a deficit framework. Later, Rosenberg and associates and others rejected the deficit self-esteem findings for Blacks (e.g, see Cross, 1991; Hare, 1977; Hauser's summary of select quantitative comparative studies of Black and White adolescents, 1971; Rosenberg & Simmons' discussion, 1971).

Yet, the prevailing popular belief for too many U.S. readers and scholars is that Blacks within U.S. culture (because of their skin color, race, generally lower socioeconomic condition, and political minority status) still somehow need to gain the "approval" of those who are White (because of their skin color, race, generally higher socioeconomic condition, and political majority status). However, little attention or consideration is given to the notion that Whites should gain the "approval" of Blacks in order to assess themselves positively (see Orbe's discussion of interracial couples, chap. 8, this volume). This popular belief is continually being challenged in communities and academic settings and currently in President Clinton's "Conversations on Race" (e.g., see Horowitz, 1997; Will, 1997).

The scholarship of critical and feminist researchers often approaches the topic of identity and self-esteem from a qualitative perspective (e.g., Gilligan, 1982; Rotheram-Borus, Dopkins, Sabate, & Lightfoot, 1996; Ward, 1990; Waters, 1996). Qualitative studies of identity and adolescent self-esteem typically question preexisting theories and challenge the typical path and conceptions of identity formation and gender. Gilligan (1982) stated that "different judgments of the image of man as giant imply different ideas about human development, different ways of imagining the human condition, and different notions of what is of value in life" (p. 5). Qualitative studies examined social contexts' influence on youth identity, values and self-esteem (Rotheram-Borus, Dopkins, Sabate, & Lightfoot 1996), Black adolescent girls' and parents' socialization scripts (Ward, 1990), and adolescent racial identity (Waters, 1996) and argued for a different theoretical understanding of identity for women (Gilligan, 1982). By accessing the voices of the study participants, the findings show that adolescents' understanding of themselves reflects their interpretation of their world and the implications for their lives (see also Davila, chap. 5, this volume). The socialization environments appear quite deterministic in constructing youth ideas about the self.

The social-scientific research on Black and White adolescent identity and self-esteem in general concludes: Self-esteem is conceived to arise out of social interaction, which is culturally situated. Generally speaking, Black and White adolescents are adequate and comparable in their global self-esteem. White and Black adolescents have similar and different ideas or beliefs about factors that influence self-esteem. But racial esteem is assumed to be correlated to self-esteem, particularly for Blacks (e.g., Diggs, 1994; McDermott, 1983; Phinney & Chavira, 1992; Rosenberg & Simmons, 1971; Ward, 1996). The next section addresses the role of communication in the construction of self-esteem for the adolescent.

Family and Peer Communication Influences and Self-Esteem

Research on families and adolescents point to the child's general perception of the social environment as an important influence on self-esteem (e.g., Buri, Louiselle, Misukanis, & Mueller, 1988; Demo, Small, & Savin-Williams, 1987; Gecas & Schwalbe, 1986; Hoffman, Usphiz, & Levy-Shiff, 1988; Margolin, Blyth, & Carbone, 1988; Walker & Greene, 1986). And, according to Demo, Small, and Savin-Williams (1987) family and parent–child studies published in the 1980s concluded that positive environment and positive parent attitudes are related to self-esteem. These conclusions rest primarily on quantitative studies of White middle-class participants and excluded race-related concepts as independent variables.

Parental and Peer Communication

Studies of family and child development that utilized predominantly White participants indicate that perceived parental attitudes are highly significant for the child, and, as the child reaches adolescence, peer interactions also become important for self-esteem (e.g., Felson & Zielinski, 1989; Openshaw, Thomas, & Rollins, 1984). Parents and society are often concerned about the influence of peers due to the appeal of adolescent peer relationships and the negative trends that are often associated with adolescent behaviors (e.g., see Chadwick & Heaton, 1996). According to Clark (1988), "peers serve as a baseline for social comparison and thus are able to either strengthen or weaken the developing self-concept" (p. 175). In light of this, the relative importance of parent and peer communication on self-esteem becomes a logical concern.

Several recent studies on parental and peer influences on self-esteem suggest that, although peers are influential, parental influence continues to surpass that of peers and that boys' self-esteem is more strongly influenced by parent–adolescent interaction than that of girls (e.g., Demo et al., 1987; Gecas & Schwalbe, 1986; Smith, 1985; Walker & Greene, 1986). Among Black adolescents in particular, the family is perceived as a strong source of influence (Clark, 1988). Even so, few communication studies have actually examined the communication aspects of self-esteem and connections to culture; therefore, there is uncertainty about who influences adolescent self-esteem more, parents or peers.

Based on the conceptualization that a child's self-esteem may be based on unique personal traits or on race, McDermott (1983) proposed two major types of communication that influence self: direct (about self) and indirect (about race). Even though European Americans may not think of themselves in racial terms (e.g., Martin et al., 1996; Nakayama & Krizek, 1995), race affects the results of interpersonal and family communication studies (see McDermott, 1983). What occurs in the family communication environment of adolescents in particular that affects their everyday communication, which, in turn, influences self-esteem?

Social Support and Self-Esteem

In discussing the historical context of research on parental behavior (i.e., support and control) that influences self-esteem, Thomas, Gecas, Weigart, and Rooney (1974) found parent support to be consistently related to self-esteem. Support is often assumed to be found in natural, physical locations that have an ongoing interest and investment in the care of children: homes, schools, and churches. From a symbolic interaction framework, the concept of *support* refers to the "quality of the interaction which is perceived by the investee (self) as the significant others establishing a positive affective relationship with him [sic]" (Thomas et al., p. 10). The symbolic interaction perspective of support places importance on the child's perception of her or his socialization (see Davilla, chap. 5, this volume). A critical perspective seeks to understand how the person's construction of support and existing support structures benefit the optimal goals for the self. In their extensive quantitative studies on support, Thomas et al. (1974) utilized the Cornell Parent Behavior Description measure (see Siegelman, 1965). This measure is intended to measure children's perception of parental treatment. A variety of social support studies show that support contributes to general adjustment and well-being (e.g., Coates, 1985; Isberg et al., 1989; Maton et al., 1996; Peterson & Rollins, 1987). The context in which such support is given includes home, church, and school. However, what is the unique relationship of parental and peer support to self-esteem in the context of race? And, what is the description of a supportive context for Black and White adolescent self-esteem?

RESEARCH STUDIES

Two studies were conducted to examine communication and Black and White adolescent self-esteem. Study 1 used a quantitative methodology and examined the relative importance of parent and peer communication, racial esteem, and support variables on self-esteem of African-American and European American adolescents. Study 2 used a qualitative methodology and addressed some of the questions raised in Study 1 (Diggs, 1994). Questions included (a) what are adolescents' beliefs about their self-esteem, (b) what are the sources of those beliefs and their meanings as well as descriptions of everyday communication that helps construct self-esteem, and (c) how does race relate to self-esteem. Together, these studies provide insight into how family communication helps to construct the perceptions that both Black and White youth have of themselves. From these studies we may draw implications of how Black and White adolescents' perceptions and their communication support environments might help to advance dialogue between people and communities.

Study 1: Effects of Parent and Peer Communication, Racial Esteem, and Support on Adolescents' Self-Esteem

Questions

Study 1 desired to reexamine previous findings about the inferred relationship between self-esteem and racial esteem and to describe the similarities and differences between communication influences on Black and White adolescents' self-esteem. Specifically, these research questions were posed:

RQ 1: What is the relationship between self-esteem and racial esteem for African-American and European-American adolescents?

RQ 2: What is the relative importance of African-American adolescents' perceived parent communication, perceived peer communication, racial esteem, and perceived support on their own self-esteem?

RQ 3: What is the relative importance of European American adolescents' perceived parent communication, perceived peer communication, racial esteem, and perceived support on their own self-esteem?

Participants

There were 192 6th- and 7th-grade African American (100 females, 92 males) and sixty-two 6th- and 7th-grade European-American (32 females, 30 males) participants from two different racially mixed urban middle schools. Participants ranged in age from 10 years to 15 years with a mean age of 12.2 years (*SD* = .48). Data were collected during spring 1993. Permission to conduct this study was granted by the Behavioral and Social Sciences Human Subjects Committee at The Ohio State University, the Columbus Board of Education Research Division, and each school principal.

Procedures and Measures

Questionnaires were administered at the schools to all Grade 6 and 7 students from whom permissions to participate were received. Questionnaires contained five demographic items and 11 Likert scales, which measured the independent variables, and concluded with four demographic items. The communication measure from McDermott and Greenberg (1984) was used to measure parental and peer communication by asking the amount and content of communication the adolescents engage in with parents and peers about self and race and peer communication about self and race. A sample item is: "How often does your (mother, father, friend) tell you that you are good, important, friendly, kind, as good as or as equal to anyone?" The same statements were used to obtain data about racial communication. For example, "How often does your (mother, father, friend) tell you that (own race) kids are good, important, friendly, kind, as good as or as equal to anyone?" This measure of racial esteem used a validated index taken from McDermott (1983), which stated: "I think (own race) kids in real life are good, important, friendly, kind, as good as or as equal to anyone"

The measure of support used was a subscale of the short form of the Cornell Parent Behavior Description (Siegelman, 1965; Thomas et al., 1974). The support for mother, father, and peers was measured by the following items: "If I have any kind of a problem, I can count on … to help me out. She … says nice things about me. She … teach(es) me things I want to learn. She … make(s) me feel she ... is there if I need her." The response categories were *very often, fairly often, sometimes, hardly ever,* and *never.*

The five-item index of self-esteem was taken from McDermott's (1993) study that utilized concepts from the validated indices of Rosenberg (1965) and Coopersmith (1967/1981) and is a shortened version of a measure designed and validated by Schwartz and Tangri (1965). The measure states "I think I am ... " followed by response categories from *very (concept), pretty (concept),* to *not (concept).* The concepts were *good, important, friendly, kind,* and *as good or as equal to anyone else.* Results show reasonable means for the self-esteem measure (M = 16.79, SD = 3.27) and good reliability measures (.76–.90).

The primary analyses consisted of Pearson correlations and regression analyses. A decision was made early in the process to separate the adolescents' responses about mother and father. In accordance with symbolic interaction perspective, the child's experience with each parent can be uniquely different (e.g., Hinde & Stevenson-Hinde, 1988).

In consideration of the two schools, *t*-tests were performed to address possible group differences on dependent and independent variables. *T*-test results revealed that the null hypothesis of no difference was partially rejected, suggesting that the two groups were somewhat similar in responses.

Results and Discussion

Pearson product moment correlation coefficients for interval variables were calculated for each of the independent variables and the dependent variable for research question 1 (RQ1) and were preliminary steps to answering research questions 2 and 3 (RQ2 and RQ3). For the Black and White sample, all of the independent variables, with the exception of father's support (for Blacks) and father's communication about race (for Whites), were low to moderately significantly related to the dependent variable. Significant correlations ranged from $r = .156$ to $r = .439$, $p < .05$ for Blacks, and $r = .276$ to $r = .475$, $p < .05$ for Whites (see Tables 6.1 and 6.2). The mean self-esteem levels for the two groups were positive: the Blacks, 16.85 (SD 3.14) and Whites, 16.48 (SD 3.30). They were consistent with past research that found comparable global self-esteem levels between Black and White adolescents (see Rosenberg & Simmons, 1971). The significant correlational finding between racial esteem and self-esteem ($r = .44$ for Black adolescents; $r = .32$ for White adolescents) seems to reflect the interrelatedness between the personal self and the racial aspect of self (Rosenberg, 1965; Taylor & Dubé, 1986), which is assumed for Blacks but seldom considered for Whites (see Cross, 1991; Martin et al., 1996; Nakayama & Krizek, 1995). Crocker et al. (1994) found that White, Black, and Asian college students' personal self-esteem scores were correlated to general and race-specific collective self-esteem with unique variations among the racial groups. They stated that "self-esteem was predicted by *evaluations* of one's groups and one's role in them, rather than the importance of those groups to one's identity" (p. 511).

TABLE 6.1

Pearson Correlation Coefficients for Independent Variables for African-American Adolescents

	Selfscal	Racescal	Mselfscal	Fselfscal	Pselfscal	Mracescal	Fracescal	Pracescal	Msupscal	Fsupscal	Psupscal
Selfscal											
Racescal	.439**										
Mselfscal	.368**	.223**									
Fselfscal	.156*	.105	.472**								
Pselfscal	.385**	.283**	.408**	.203**							
Mracescal	.348**	.457**	.539**	.301**	.389**						
Fracescal	.239**	.373**	.397**	.835**	.338**	.683**					
Pracescal	.217**	.480**	.381**	.270**	.479**	.635**	.589**				
Msupscal	.407**	.230**	.548**	.268**	.306**	.403**	.317**	.321**			
Fsupscal	.114	-.020	.225**	.627**	.150**	.170*	.551**	.189**	.329**		
Psupscal	.343**	.334**	.215**	.107	.585**	.341**	.330**	.411**	.332**	.189**	

* p < .05; ** p < .001; Selfscal = self-esteem; Racescal = racial esteem; Mselfscal = Mother's communication about adolescent; Fselfscal = Father's communication about adolescent; Pselfscal = peer's communication about adolescent; M-F Pracescal = Mother's, Father's, and Peer's communication about the adolescent's race, respectively; M-F-P- Supscal = Mother's, Father's, And Peer's support toward adolescent, respectively.

TABLE 6.2

Pearson Correlation Coefficients for Independent Variables for European-American Adolescents

	Selfscal	Racescal	Mselfscal	Fselfscal	Pselfscal	Mracescal	Fracescal	Pracescal	Msupscal	Fsupscal	Psupscal
Selfscal											
Racescal	.323*										
Mselfscal	.475**	.315*									
Fselfscal	.348**	.345**	.530**								
Pselfscal	.398**	.176	.165	.223							
Mracescal	.278*	.410**	.518**	.303*	.396**						
Fracescal	.236	.621**	.457**	.625**	.315*	.558*					
Pracescal	.276*	.553**	.261*	.324**	.488**	.573**	.566**				
Msupscal	.444**	.293	.597**	.232	.167	.193	.292*	.185			
Fsupscal	.299*	.251	.167	.682**	.105	.008	.422**	.241	.421**		
Psupscal	.342**	.338**	-.020	.296*	.448**	-.000	.243	.284*	-.068	.296*	

* $p < .05$; ** $p < .001$; Selfscal = self-esteem; Racescal = racial esteem; Mselfscal = Mother's communication about adolescent; Fselfscal = Father's communication about adolescent; Pselfscal = peer's communication about adolescent; M-F Pracescal = Mother's, Father's, and Peer's communication about the adolescent's race, respectively; M-F-P-supscal = Mother's, Father's, and Peer's support toward adolescent, respectively.

Research questions 2 and 3 ask what is the relative importance of all the independent variables on self-esteem for each group. Using the stepwise regression method, multiple regression coefficients were first calculated together and then separately for each group on all independent variables. Table 6.3 shows the results of the Black and White participants combined and finds an adjusted Rsquare of 37%. The variables racial esteem, mother's support, and peer's communication about self account for the most significant variation in self-esteem for Blacks and Whites. This finding suggests that the Black and White adolescents in this study see their race, in general, as a significant frame of reference, and this consciously impacts their self-feelings or vice versa. Socialization studies indicate that mothers are highly influential for the developing self. The regression results for peers (Table 6.3) suggest that the role of White and Black peers' may focus on specific self-oriented content and support for self-esteem in that peer communication about self was more influential on self-esteem than peer communication about race for Blacks and peer support rather than peer communication about self or race for Whites (see Table 6.4). This finding suggests that peer-to-peer interactions may be more focused on personal and relationship issues both within and across racial groups. Maton et al. (1996) found evidence for the cultural meanings of events framework to explain the relationship for support to adjustment in their study of older Black and White adolescents. The cultural meanings of events framework indicates that "when support from a given source has greater value, appropriateness, meaning, or efficacy in one culture than another" (p. 579) that source will reflect a stronger relationship to well-being in that culture than the other. In this study, it seems that Black and White adolescents do share a cultural value of emphasis on uniqueness and support in their friendships.

Table 6.4 shows separate stepwise regressions for each ethnic group. The Beta's represent a standard slope that is interpreted to mean that for every standard deviation change in the independent variable, there is a particular Beta change or increase. The stepwise regression for the African-American group

TABLE 6.3

Results of Stepwise Multiple Regression of Self-Esteem on Selected Independent Variables for African-American and European-American Adolescents

Variable	Beta	Adjusted R2	F	Significance Level
Racescal	.285	.187	64.62	.0001
Msupscal	.116	.277	54.00	.0001
Pselfscal	.159	.339	46.64	.0001
Pracescal	-.116	.346	37.34	.0001
Mselfscal	.116	.355	31.58	.0001
Psupscal	.076	.366	27.45	.0001

TABLE 6.4

Stepwise Multiple Regression of Self-Esteem on the Selected Independent Variables for African-American and European-American Adolescents

Variable	Beta	Adjusted R2	F	Significance Level
African-American				
Racescal	.285	.187	64.62	.0001
Msupscal	.116	.277	54.00	.0001
Pselfscal	.159	.339	46.64	.0001
Pracescal	-.116	.346	37.34	.0001
Mselfscal	.116	.355	31.58	.0001
Psupscal	.076	.366	27.45	.0001
European-American				
Mselfscal	.260	.201	14.81	.0003
Psupscal	.226	.319	13.85	.0000
Msupscal	.177	.362	11.39	.0000

yielded five significant variables presented in the order of the highest to least variable that accounts for the change in the dependent variable: race esteem, mother support, peer communication about self, peer communication about race, and mother communication about self (e.g., as racial esteem increases one standard deviation unit, self-esteem increases .29 when other variables are held constant or not included; 36% of the variation in self-esteem is explained by the set of independent variables combined). The stepwise regression for the European-American group yielded three significant variables, which are also presented in the order of highest to least in accounting for variation on self-esteem: mother's communication about self, peer's support, and mother's support (e.g., as mother's communication increases one standard deviation unit, self-esteem increases .26 when other variables are held constant or not included; 36% of the variation in self-esteem is explained by the set of independent variables combined). These results suggest that Black adolescents have a broader base for self-esteem in comparison to White adolescents. The findings in Tables 6.3 and 6.4 also suggest that Black and White adolescents differ on the salience of the racial group in defining self. This finding, in some ways, brings attention to Noble's conceptualization of the Afrocentric *We* concept. Nobles' (1973) emphasis is on belonging and affect toward the group. Crocker et al.'s (1994) finding showed that collective self-esteem is correlated or predictive of psychological well-being for Blacks when personal self-esteem is controlled, but for Whites, general collective self-esteem is not related to psychological well-being when personal self-esteem is controlled. They speculated that "ascribed social group memberships are not particularly central or salient for Whites in predominantly White environments" (p. 505). Recall that collective self-esteem is defined as the evaluation of our social groups.

Not shown are additional regression analyses that were designed to further clarify communication influences, given the results of the earlier regression analyses and correlational matrices. For example, when racial esteem was selected as the dependent variable, for Blacks, mother's communication about race, self-esteem, peer's communication about race, followed by father support were significant predictors. For Whites, however, only father's and peer's communication about race were significant predictors. The particular parent that the adolescent perceives as talking about race is interesting from a sociocultural perspective. Black and White parents appear to have different roles in the esteem construction process. Specific communication from Black mothers about race, and communication from White fathers about race, were strong predictors of racial esteem, which indirectly influenced self-esteem. Historically, European-American families' experiences in Western society have not warranted the comparatively lengthy history of "warning against" the world that is found among Blacks but rather, showed a preparation for a world that values the White race. Thus, it seems that with this sample, the White fathers may be instrumental in communicating messages about "racial socialization." Historically, in considering Black and White interactions, Blacks have typically perceived White males because of positions of power in United States and the execution of that power (in comparison to White females) as more negative and antagonistic. The context of White male racial socialization messages (in the past) have overtly and covertly conveyed less than favorable perspectives of the Black race (e.g., Takaki, 1993, provides a historical glimpse inside White slave owners' homes through Thomas Jefferson's notes: "It [slavery] also had a pernicious and 'unhappy' influence on the masters and their children"; p. 70). Even though researchers have explored White and Black experiences with race (e.g., Hecht, Larkey, & Johnson, 1992; Orbe, 1994), these studies have not focused on familial contexts.

Study 2: Everyday Interactions and Adolescent Self-Esteem

Questions

In studying communication influences on global self-esteem, Diggs (1994) suggested that a better understanding of adolescents' perceptions could be obtained by focusing on their beliefs about their self-esteem, sources and meanings of self-esteem, and natural communication contexts that influence self-esteem over time (longitudinal data). This study was grounded in the premise that self-esteem or self-feelings arise out of interaction and that people use their perceived understanding to frame their actions (see Cardinal, 1998; Gudykunst et al., 1995; Jones, 1973, in Leary et al., 1995). Meanings of objects evolve from the interactions between people. *Meanings* are "creations that are formed in and through the defining activities of people as they interact" (Blumer, 1969, p. 5). Symbolic interaction and Afrocentricity both place persons in their environments at the center of interactions (Asante, 1988; Blumer, 1969). Here, the qualitative research approach was utilized. Several preliminary research questions were posed, which were expected to yield future questions and explanations (Lindlof, 1995):

RQ 1: What beliefs, sources, and meanings do Black and White adolescents and supportive adults report for self-esteem?

RQ 2: What do Black and White adolescents' interactions suggest about the construction of self-esteem?

RQ 3: What is the influence of race for adolescents' self-esteem?

Participants

Twenty-four 8th-grade students and the female teacher (White) in a Language Arts (Whole Language Writing Lab) classroom of a racially mixed urban middle school consented to participate in the study. The students were 7 Black females, 5 White females, 1 Asian female, 1 Bi-racial male (Black and White parents), 3 Black males, and 7 White males. Two parents of adolescents who are unrelated or not associated to this 8th-grade class were interviewed: 1 African-American female parent, married, and the mother of an adolescent girl, 13 years old; and 1 African-American female parent, married, and mother of seven children including two adolescent boys between ages 13 and 16 years. The teacher and parents are viewed as part of the adolescents' support contexts. Data were collected in spring 1996. In qualitative studies, the researcher is also seen as a participant. Descriptions of the researcher and research assistant are provided later.

Procedures and Measures

Blumer (1970) stated that exploration and inspection are "the two modes of inquiry that clearly distinguish direct naturalistic examination of the empirical social world" (p. 32). Exploration is a flexible procedure that moves from a broad purpose to a narrowing or sharpening as the inquiry progresses. Its focus is "to learn what are the appropriate data, to develop ideas of what are significant lines of relationships" (Blumer, 1969, p. 40). Inspection is the ongoing analytical phase of the research process. The following procedures and others were used as the study progressed. After obtaining permission to conduct research from the Jefferson County Public Schools Research Division and the school principal, I interviewed the female teacher (a member of a supportive school context) using an unstructured interview format. After meeting with the classroom teacher, I met with the adolescent students in their classroom and gave them: (a) a description of the research project and the questionnaire to obtain demographic information, (b) A questionnaire was prepared by the author to obtain identifying information, self-expressions of feelings about oneself (Day 1), the source of those feelings, persons who influence their thoughts about self, thoughts about culture/race, 10 days of interaction (or journal), parent interview format, and self-expressions of feelings about oneself (Day 10). The journal prepared by the researcher obtained recent remembered interaction or recalled messages and pre- and post-information about self-esteem on Day 1 and Day 10.

The journal consisted of individual 8½ × 11" sheets of paper with space for daily interaction entries: "Who said or did anything to you today or recently that you remember? What was said or done? Did you have any reaction to what was said or done? And If 'Yes,' describe how you reacted." The content of the journal was based on self-esteem research and the researcher's judgment as to the pertinent data that provided a picture of the adolescents' communicative contexts and interactions over time. For example, an incomplete phrase to assess how the students feel about themselves ("I believe that for the most part I feel good/do not feel good about myself because … ") and how well they get along in life ("I think I get along/do not get along well in life because … "), and one adolescent-conducted interview with a mother and/or father (Day 9).

The journal activity was part of regularly scheduled assignments (i.e., the students received feedback by the teacher in the form of a check mark for participation and zero (0) if not participating) and took 10 to 15 minutes of class time each day. Writing complete thoughts was emphasized for journal writing. The journals were kept at school. I visited the classroom on two different occasions during the journal-writing process to check with the teacher about any concerns.

The memory literature indicates that asking adolescents to recall contextualized information may say a great deal about what adolescents already know about themselves. "What we already know shapes what we select and encode; … Our memory systems are built so that we are likely to remember what is most important to us" (Schacter, 1996, pp. 45–46). However, to minimize varied interpretations of what to include, the students were asked to note what they remembered from the weekend, same day, or previous day.

A focus group was designed to pursue this study's preliminary findings and to obtain further reflections and thoughts about the sources of adolescents' self-feelings. The focus group provided an additional kind of interaction in which I could obtain more information about how the students represented themselves. Therefore, focus group questions were finalized after the journal entries. Two separate focus groups consisting of 12 students each were conducted by the researcher and the research assistant[5] within a 2-week period following the journal data collection. Each focus group met for one 50-minute class period. There was no audiotape recording. Preliminary questions consisted of "What activities do youths your age who feel good about themselves participate in? What is the best/worst thing about what is happening today that affects your lives? Do you think most of the youths you socialize with feel OK with how things are going for them? How can you tell when someone your age is feeling OK about herself or himself?" Only the responses to questions about self-esteem were analyzed.

The one Black mother and one White mother were interviewed separately on the telephone 2 weeks after adolescent focus group data were collected. The interview protocol was piloted on one Black mother of adolescents known to the researcher. The purpose of the interview was to add further insights into adolescents' responses and more insight into family support contexts that construct self-esteem. Each parent was known by the researcher in the roles of acquaintance (Black mother) and work (White mother). These parents were selected by the researcher because of the potentially sensitive nature of one of the interview questions regarding race. It was believed that our relational knowledge would limit the need to respond in a socially desirable manner (Fontana & Frey, 1994). The interviews were recorded on audiotape.

Analysis or Inspection

Inspection refers to "clear, discriminating analytical elements and the isolation of relations between analytical elements" (Blumer, 1970, p. 37). In this study, elements were the instances of participants' reports of beliefs about self-esteem, sources and meanings of self-esteem, everyday communication interactions, aspects of race, and support environments' perspective on self-esteem. "The meanings assigned to an event are closely tied to the language used to account for the event in communication among participants" (Shotter's social construction perspective as cited in Littlejohn, 1992, p. 197). The empirical instances of analytical elements were examined from different vantage points. Each instance of responses to analytical elements were written on individual index cards; the researcher and the research assistant then separately and together organized these data. Topical and ideational categories were created. That is, a categorizing scheme and reliability for categorizing recalled messages were obtained by the reading and re-reading between the researcher and student assistant until 90% agreement was reached. The isolation of relations between analytical elements only happens if "such a relation presumes the existence of a meaningful connection between the components *in the empirical world*"

---

[5]The student assistant was present to take notes of adolescent content and to describe the environment and other environmental cues during the focus group. The teacher and I agreed that the student assistant's race would not affect students' responsiveness. I agreed because (a) one-time class period interaction would not pose a great threat for the kind of data requested; (b) students were frequently exposed to Black and White races in the school context; and (c) separation by race did not appear necessary in that the students were given the freedom to say what they felt in response to esteem questions addressed previously on the questionnaire, without focusing specifically on race.

(Blumer, 1970, p. 37). My roles as an African-American parent of adolescents, a volunteer mentor with African-American adolescents, a resident in a Black community, a communication researcher, and a college professor often exposed to older predominantly White adolescents come to bear on my interpretations. The student assistant's roles as an African American, 21-year-old college student, sibling with several male and female adolescents, and a Communication major in a predominately White college atmosphere are important to the interpretation of data. Such relevant roles have the potential of bringing credibility and insight into interpretations of the data (Lindlof, 1995).

Italics are used to represent spoken and written words from the participants and students' written journal entries, and parents' interviews. An ellipsis (...) indicates that some of the written or spoken words of the participants have been omitted for clarity and/or information was a repetition or an additional example of information already provided. For example, "Trying to guide trying to be supportive helping to try to get to all the little places they need to go get to ... whatever would be wholesome." In this instance the ellipsis indicates information that is redundant or additional examples: "trying to help them find activities."

Findings and Discussion

Self-Esteem Beliefs.   The majority of students reported their self-esteem to be adequate. This finding supports the quantitative finding in Study 1. The first set of responses (Day 1) indicated that 20 of the 24 adolescents (83%) indicated that they feel good about themselves (Table 6.5). The last set of responses (Day 10) indicated that of the 18 students who responded to the question, all reported feeling good. The dynamics observed during the focus group appear to support the interpretation that most of these students were adequate in their self-assessments.

Sources and Meanings of Self-Esteem.   When the 24 students were asked where their good/bad beliefs about self came from, parents (generally mothers) were overwhelmingly identified as the source of positive feelings for Black and White adolescents. Parents were identified in 83% of the responses; friends, 29%; God, 25%; and myself or unique, 21% (see Table 6.5). When asked, why do you feel good about yourself ("I feel good/bad about myself because ... "), the adolescents identified 13 different reasons for their positive and negative feelings about themselves. Sources and reasons are used interchangeably because the adolescents sometimes listed the source as a reason and vice versa (the focus group revealed additional influences on adolescent self-esteem; see Table 6.6). There were some distinctions along racial lines, which are reviewed next.

Black girls drew their reasons for positive self-esteem from their uniqueness (see Table 6.5): *don't act like everyone; no one else like me; my own person; I am who I am; I don't act like everyone; no one else approaches their self like me.* These responses may appear to be antithetical toward a cooperative ethos. However,

TABLE 6.5

Results of the Survey of Beliefs and Sources of Self-Esteem
of Black and White Adolescents

	Black		White	
	Female	Male	Female	Male
Beliefs (Day 1)				
I feel good	6	1	5	7
I do not feel good	1	1	-	-
N/R	-	1	-	-
Sources and Reasons				
Parents	7	1	5	7
Positive role model	-	-	1	-
No problems	-	-	-	1
Live my life	1	1	-	1
Lots of friends	-	-	3	4
Many talents	-	-	-	3
Unique	4	-	-	1
Like myself	-	-	1	-
Do my best	-	-	2	1
Easy to get along with	1	-	3	1
Material	-	-	-	1
God/Jesus	4	2	-	-

Note. One Asian American did not feel good about herself; one Bi-racial male reported feeling good; negative reason for African-American male (susceptible to things). Other sources: media (1), teacher (1), preacher (1), and sister (1). Dash indicates zero frequency for category.

Black feminist researchers have sought to explain Black girls' behaviors from their socialization in the nonconsonant or contradictory environments in which they often cope. Collins (1994) stated that "a key part of Black girls' socialization involves incorporating the critical posture that allows Black women to cope with contradictions" (p. 171). For example, in the urban United States in the late 1990s, all must get an education but the people who teach are more likely than not to be of a different race, not Black. Ward (1996) also stated that Black girls exhibit a certain resistance that is interpreted as a remedy to negative attributions that adolescents believe are imposed from without. Ward stated that such resistance strategies are passed down from the Black parent to the ad-

TABLE 6.6

Focus Group Discussion Themes: What Makes You Feel Good or Bad?

Positive Treatment by Others

1. The way I'm treated. (BF)

2. I do good things and help people. (Bi-raM)

Abilities/Skills

1. I love to speak my mind. (WF)

2. Just let it out. (BF)

Achievement

1. I do good in school. (WM)

2. I can do anything if I try. (BM)

Unique

1. I am original. (BF)

2. I'm different from others by going to church, learning about God. (BM)

Media Images

1. <u>Roots</u> made me feel bad because he didn't want to change his name. (BM)

Expressiveness

1. Should just let it out—say what you want to say. (BF)

2. I love to speak my mind. (WM)

Own Will/ Self Agency/Opposition

1. Because I'm opinionated and if I have something to say I'm gonna say it, not let anybody tell me otherwise. (BF)

2. I know that I can move on in this world, make it without having friends because one day they may be your friends, one day they might not. (BF)

Note. White, Black, Asian-American females = WF, BF, and As-AF; White, Black, Bi- racial males = WM, BM, Bi-raM. Themes are not based on any hierarchical order.

olescent child. For these girls, these reasons for self-feelings appear to be affirming. Black female and male youth were distinctive in their reference to God as a source or reason for positive self-esteem. This God consciousness is supported in other theoretical and empirical research about Black culture and Black family relationships (e.g., Dainton, chap. 7, this volume; Diggs & Stafford, 1998; Manns, 1988; Myers, 1993). Television images were captured by a Black male during the focus group as another potential source of influence for self-feelings (also see Parks, chap. 4, this volume).

White females and males offered similar reasons for basing self-esteem in friendships. Only White males noted "talents" as another reason for positive self-esteem, whereas White females viewed getting along with others as a source of positive self-esteem. According to Rosenberg and Simmons (1971), White youth may find the societal bases consistent with creating positive self feelings, whereas the Black youth may not. In other words, the society may reflect values and beliefs that are more consistent to Whites than to Blacks. The inferred cooperative ethos seems predominant in the White adolescents responses (*I like having friends; I get along with others*). Identity and esteem studies indicate that Blacks and Whites may differ on bases for self-esteem (e.g., Erkut, Fields, Sing, & Marx, 1996; Rosenberg & Simmons, 1971; Rotherum-Borus, Dopkins, Sabate, & Lightfoot, 1996).

Researchers differ on the value of different orientations to self-feelings. Crocker et al. (1994) suggested that Blacks, in comparison with Whites, rely less on social comparison as the basis of self-esteem. Communication texts such as Beebe, Beebe, and Redmond (1996) discouraged judging one's value in comparison to that of others, whereas Gudykunst et al. (1995) advocated a balance of the basis of one's self-feelings between unique and social comparison. Research is needed to further explore adolescents' interpretations of their self-esteem. The observation that parents, friends, and God-consciousness sources are influential to adolescent self-esteem clearly reflects certain kinds of messages that adolescents value and enact: positive, unique, social comparison, oppositional, and God-consciousness. Thus, for these adolescents, self-esteem means one's feelings or regard for oneself secured from varied sources, with different emphases and functions within the Black and White cultural communities. The belief that parents, particularly mothers, are primary communicators who enhance positive self-esteem is evident in this data.

Support Contexts

Prior to the adolescent data collection, the teacher provided a perspective on self-esteem and rated the students' self-esteem as "lacking." The teacher gave the following account:

> Self-esteem is how you feel about yourself and others; and how you think others perceive you. I want the kids to see they have some type of value. I would know by their nonverbal expressions—a sparkle in their eyes ... Everyday, at least one child will say they're stupid. Academically, they are on the average of 2.5 (G.P.A.) About one-third would see themselves as high self-esteem.

In light of the different perceptions between teacher and students, I asked the teacher to keep a weekly checklist for 8 weeks, in which she noted observations with a brief comment as to why she agreed or disagreed with the students' general positive self-feelings. It was not obvious if the teacher made weekly comments, but she entered a concluding statement at the end of the 8 weeks. She stated that she believed that the students' classroom group affiliation resulted in their positive self-esteem. It appears that the teacher, after being informed about the students' higher self-assessments, sought to find reasons for the scores. It might be inferred that adolescents make an implicit distinction between self-feelings and their academic behavior whereas someone in the teacher role does not make that distinction, typically. However, the observation that the teacher adjusted her response after she was informed of the students' responses indicates that it is possible to take another perspective and broaden or incorporate additional bases for self-esteem. This broadening might be more consistent with the way adolescents view themselves. Simultaneously, it suggests the challenge of motivating U.S. adolescents and learning about what motivates them over the course of time. Public educational settings are locations in which the assessment of others potentially affects individuals' personal and social self-feelings (e.g., see Dukes & Martinez, 1994).

What are parents of adolescents teaching their children to believe about themselves? Seven students (29%) completed an interview with their own parent, which asked "what do you want your child to remember about himself/herself?" The six parents of three Black students and four White students offered 25 messages (see Table 6.7). These messages were interpreted and categorized in several ways (see Tables 6.8 & 6.9). First, concrete or topical categories were created by simply reading and re-reading the parents' messages. This process yielded the following categories from Black and White parents: self-affirmation (e.g., *I'm smart, I'm handsome*); spiritual (*God will be with you*); and 14 other messages of advice that were achievement focused (e.g., *study hard; stand tall*) and self-caring (e.g., *love yourself*). Not shown is an analysis utilizing McDermott's conceptualization of esteem communication, direct (about self) and indirect (about race). All of the messages except one seemed explicitly about self. The one message, *Make us proud*, did not explicitly fit into the indirect category in that the term race or discussion of ethnicity was not obvious. Yet, from a Black culture perspective this is a statement that both data analyzers responded to similarly and quite spontaneously as discussed later. Table 6.9 shows an analysis that utilizes *I*, *Me*, and Nobles' (1973) concept of *We*. Remember, Nobles indicated that *We* messages are not simply about an individual or a group but about how the two coalesce or come together, *I am because of you*. Nine messages were viewed as *I* messages because they seemed to focus on ways to affirm oneself and often used the word "I" (e.g., *I'm smart, I'm handsome, exercise more*). Fifteen messages seemed tied to the social aspect of self (or *Me*) because they can help relationship building (e.g., *be honest, be kind, enjoy life, do my work, no bad habits, go out more*). Finally, one message was categorized as a *We* message because its meaning within the context of a Black family seemed tied to the value of the primacy of family or parents and ancestors (*make us proud*). In the context of this

TABLE 6.7

Parent Interview Responses to the Question: "What do you want your child
to think about himself/herself?"

STUDENT	PARENT	PARENTAL MESSAGE
BF	Mom	You're a good child: Make us proud; God will be with you.
WM	Mom	Be honest; Be kind; Enjoy life.
WM	Dad	Do my work; No bad habits; Go out more often.
	Mom	Study hard; Exercise more; Do some family chores.
BM	Aunt	I'm smart; I'm a Christian; I'm handsome.
WF	Mom	Respect yourself; Love yourself; Trust yourself.
BF	Mom	You're beautiful inside/outside; Don't let others hold you down for what you believe; Stand tall, pursue your goals.
WM	Dad	Don't accept put-downs; Don't take anything; Do your best.

Note. 29% response rate; B = Black; W = White; M = Male; F = Female.

mother's several messages to her child, this interpretation seems reasonable
(see Table 6.7). Fordham and Ogbu (1986) discussed the fictive kin concept,
which not only conveys a kind of "brotherhood" and "sisterhood" of all Black
Americans but is a kind of mindset that references the "behavior, activities, and
manifest loyalty" of its members (pp. 181–182). It is also consistent with the
theme of collectivism (see Socha & Diggs, chap. 1, this volume).

It is interesting to note that the Black families' messages are viewed as balanced between the unique and social self whereas the majority of the White
families' messages are about the social self (see Table 6.9). Recall that Crocker
et al.'s (1994) findings of college adolescents' beliefs supported that Blacks in
comparison to Whites rely less on social comparison as the basis of self-esteem.
This data of parental messages is consistent with Crocker et al.'s findings for
perceptions of Whites but not for Blacks. It seems that Blacks receive messages
that are balanced or holistic in the creation of bases of self-feelings, but in their
beliefs (what is salient to how they think/cognition) the unique or I messages
predominate. These data suggest that Blacks do not predominantly rely on
uniqueness or social comparison when it comes to the reality of living in the
world that they face and must face differently than Whites. Several of the messages organized under Me might be construed as protective of the self or
oppositional (e.g., *don't let others put you down, stand tall, don't accept put-downs,
don't take anything, God will be with you*). When engaged in Black–White
intercultural communication, perhaps these messages are encoded and de-
coded differently between the two groups (recall the theoretical controversy

TABLE 6.8

Topical Categories of Parent Interview Responses

Self-Affirmation
You're a good child. (BF)
I'm smart. (BM)
I'm handsome. (BM)
I'm a Christian. (BM)
You're beautiful inside/outside. (BF)

Spiritual
God will be with you. (BF)

Achievement Focused
Do my work. (WM)
Study hard. (WM)
Do some family chores. (WM)
Pursue your goals. (BF)
Don't let others hold you down for what you believe. (BF)
Don't accept putdowns. (WM)
Don't take anything. (WM)
Do your best. (WM)

Self/Other Caring
Be honest. (WM)
Be kind. (WM)

Self-Caring
Enjoy life. (WM)
Respect yourself. (WF)
Love yourself. (WF)
Trust yourself. (WF)
No bad habits, exercise more. (WM)
Go out more often. (WM)
Exercise more. (WM)

Note. B = Black; W = White; M = Male; F = Female.

TABLE 6.9
Categorizing Parent's Messages to Their Children Using I, Me, and We Conceptualizations.

I (Individual, Personal)

I'm smart. (BM)

I'm handsome. (BM)

I'm a Christian. (BM)

You're a good child. (BM)

You're beautiful inside/outside. (BF)

Respect yourself. (WF)

Love yourself. (WF)

Trust yourself. (WF)

Exercise more. (WM)

Me (Social, Collective, Group)

Be honest. (WM)

Be kind. (WM)

Enjoy life. (WM)

Do my work. (WM)

No bad habits. (WM)

Go out more often. (WM)

Study hard. (WM)

Do some family chores. (WM)

Don't let others hold you down for what you believe. (BF)

Pursue your goals. (BF)

Stand tall. (BF)

Don't accept putdowns. (WM)

Don't take anything. (WM)

Do your best. (WM)

God will be with you. (BF)

We (race, ethnicity, cultural)

Make us proud. (BF)

stated earlier about the distinctions among *I*, *Me*, and *We*). Fordham and Ogbu (1986) discussed Black people's sense of collective identity, which is in opposition to White identity (but not to the person, relationally). The messages parents want their adolescents to remember are reflected in several of the sources that the adolescents identified (Table 6.5). During the focus group, students were asked to reflect on their parents' messages. Because peers are also supportive of other adolescents, it is important to know what they think and how they act toward other cohorts. It appears that these students are internalizing the messages from their parents—reflective of intergenerational transmission. Using topical categories, 14 students talked about achievement in some fashion: *doing work, give 100%, keep up good grades, do your best in school, study hard—exercise more, and do your best.* Self-caring was interpreted in such responses as *always respect yourself, remember who I am; no bad habits.* Independent or self-agency was suggested in such comments as *be strong, be what you want to be; don't follow anybody, be yourself; use good judgment.* Other responses from students regarding parental advice were *don't do anything they wouldn't do; care for sister, brother … ; just do what you do.*

Further probing on parental advice in one of the focus group situations yielded much energy and animation around the importance of *beauty inside and out.* Two students agreed with this statement as stated and two disagreed. Others offered some explanation or clarification:

> Personality is more important; just being nice is important; don't have to be pretty as long as your character is pretty; it is beauty that is inside that counts; people judge by looks is not right; must respect yourself; be yourself; don't have to have head swimming, if you like yourself, who cares what others think; important to think you're beautiful—can help you in life.

These students seem to believe that an external focus should be less important as a general measure of worth, but that it does matter if an individual is thinking about how this personally affects self-presentation. As cultural critics, this view reflects what U.S. adolescents have learned about the commodification of the body. They apparently have a negative view of physical beauty at the risk of feeling badly about oneself. Also, students overwhelmingly agreed that one should *not take anything from anybody.* These views by adolescents suggest that they could be supportive or understanding of another who is being evaluated from a destructive basis (physical beauty only) or in a restrictive manner. Apparently, they have a variety of perspectives on the basis of self-feelings.

Among the parents unrelated to study participants, the White mother and Black mother both view the parent's major task as listening to children (guiding and supporting). They felt that it is important for adolescents to have an understanding of self:

(White mother) Absolutely. She does from time to time make negative comments usually they are about her physical appearance—I hate my complexion, look at these zits, I can't get my hair to do anything—and I always try to counter those comments with 'all kids your age have zits'.

(Black mother) They need to understand ... a lot of the parents we need to under-stand ... what's going on the inside ... my son who just turned fifteen yesterday was concerned about the fact that he had acne.

These two mothers of an adolescent girl and boys, respectively, believe that their knowledge of their children's experiences helps to guide parental support and to create an adequate view of self.

(Black mother) The parent helping the child understand his thoughts would let the youngster understand that the [sic] they (the parent) were once in the same position ... just maybe there may be something that they (parent) can relate to.

The personal and collective aspects of self-esteem appear dominant in the beliefs of adult support environments. The teacher's response reflects a per-sonal (or *I*) and collective (or *Me*) perspective of self-esteem. However, she evaluates the youths' general well-being with an area-specific manner, which Rosenberg (1965) cautioned against. The parents seems to take the adoles-cents' personal or self-focus and extend it to the other (*all kids your age have zits; maybe something they can relate to*), which may serve to stimulate adolescent re-flection. To embrace an other seems naturally helpful for well-being. There is something comforting in reminding the adolescent that other youth are sharing in his or her experiences. This support seems helpful to the adolescents' needs of relationship building. It seems to reinforce a belief that self-evaluation is about the individual but also about other human beings with similar experiences.

Everyday Recalled Interactions

For a 10-day period, the 24 students generated 188 messages. The adolescents recalled interactions and were requested to explain their reaction to the mes-sage from others (e.g, feelings, thoughts). These students' accounts (or explana-tions) were analyzed to assess their meanings. The messages were categorized into the following hierarchical categories based on how often topics occurred: family (58), friend (57), peer (42), teacher (13), other (13), and activity (5). Friend and peer were distinguished by the adolescents use of the word *friend* ver-sus *someone in school*. The messages suggest that friends, family, peers, and teacher make up supportive environments. Further consideration of the holistic environment of messages between adolescents and others led to comparing and contrasting the recalled interactional entries. The tone of the messages seemed to be a distinguishing feature. The data analyzers used their knowledge of the English language and understanding of adolescent culture to interpret the tones of the messages when the adolescent did not assess the message himself or herself. Very conservative interpretations were made—deferring to neutral when there was no pattern of negativity or positivity, particularly for personality evaluations. The tones of positive equals happy or pleased; negative equals unhappy/angry, dislike; and neutral equals neither happy nor angry seemed to make sense in the mundaneness of what the students remembered as well their thoughts about the interactions (see exemplar in Table 6.10).

A higher number of neutral messages (105) with a small frequency difference between the positive (34) and negative (49) messages was observed. The one student who reported negative messages most consistently also reported low self-esteem. This finding suggests that the tone of everyday messages that ultimately influence self-esteem for adolescents may be a balance of positive, negative, and neutral messages that are normative for this sample and realistic for everyday life. A large body of parent–child research emphasizes the positive environment necessary for self-esteem to flourish but analyses of that communicative environment for children and adolescents have not been sufficiently addressed (McDermott, 1983; McDermott & Greenberg, 1984).

TABLE 6.10
Example of Recalled Messages

Exemplar of recalled messages of one Black female student over a 10-day period in response to the question: Who said or did anything to you today or recently that you remember?

Day 1: My brother scared me to death I was downstairs in the basement getting clothes out of the dryer. I was home by myself or at least I thought I was. Then all of a sudden the door at the top of the stairs slammed shut. Then, I heard footsteps upstairs. A couple of minutes afterwards I heard the door open. Someone was coming down the stairs. I started for some place to hide or a way to get out, but I felt trapped. There are bars on the basement windows, so I felt locked in. I started to scream. I was terrified. All of a sudden, my brother came around the stairway smiling (sic). It was my family (sic) returning home.

Day 2: My father congradualtions [sic] for my report card and promising me something nice

Day 3: My friend asked me to go to a concert I really wanted to go to

Day 4: My little brother told me that I was a conceited person.

Day 5: Nothing happened

Day 6: Absent

Day 7: I was honored for being a cheerleader

Day 8: My friend called me to tell me that we are going to Florida.

Day 9: I was elected by the class to be Valentine Queen

Day 10: (No answer given)

Race and Self-Esteem

How does the adolescent who possesses a certain assessment of self think about race? On the questionnaire, students were asked to consider the question "What do you think when people say something about someone's race that is good/bad?" Overall, these adolescents felt that those who speak negatively about race should be ignored. Based on frequency of responses, the Black adolescent females were most expressive on race:

> I just don't say anything; all people should have respect for other cultures and have sympathy for them; shouldn't be talkin about someone's culture if they don't want someone to talk about theirs; I don't worry about it; I don't believe what the person is saying because different people have different opinions; race don't matter.

The White adolescent males were the next most expressive on race:

> It keeps racism alive; I think there [sic] are disrespectful; make me mad because no one should be judged; get a bad impression; I think it is bad they don't have advantage in their culture; the people who said it are racist.

The White females were next in expressiveness on race:

> Felt that it's wrong to judge; people misjudge others race; all the same but different; it would get me angry—mean; can't trust them.

The Black males had no written responses to this question. The one Bi-racial male did not express an opinion and the one Asian American female was *pleased with good opinions about race and tried not to let bad things people say* affect her. It appeared that the students were aware of the negativity that may surround race issues. Although the question requested a good or bad perspective, most of the responses addressed the negative aspect of society's problem with race.

The adolescent responses to race issues may be further clarified by examining the interviews of the two parents who were not related to the students. The Black mother noted that she has a significant amount of contact with White people: *I would say a lot, a lot of interaction;* whereas the White mother says: *In the work place I had quite a bit, probably about 30%–40% of the people I have interacted with in a work place have been of another race ... socially, much less.*

The White and Black mothers' responses regarding contact with the other's culture reflect literature that indicates that Blacks believe they have more knowledge of the White culture than the Whites have of the Black culture (e.g., see Socha & Beigle, chap. 10, this volume). This knowledge is assumed to come from exposure and a willingness to discuss race issues (e.g., Ward, 1996).

In response to the question, "Do you teach your children to evaluate themselves in different ways than Whites?" the Black parent stated:

Yes. I think so. I really think so … there is a two-fold thing here. I try to teach them first, to react as a human being, to look at themselves as a human being first of all. But then I think given the situation that we have in this country, that you have to come back, and you do have to help them to be aware of themselves as an African-American child.

In probing further, the Black mother stated:

Well, to me I think that uh, you kind of have to point out to them some of the things that happen that are injustices. And they happened as a result of color. And I think I have to make my children aware of that.

The parent continued to tell of an incident in which her 18-year-old son encountered the police because of an altercation with several White male youths.

In response to the same question, "Do you teach your children to evaluate themselves in different ways than Blacks?" the White parent stated:

No, I never thought about that. I'm going to say that I don't teach her in different ways. I think I teach her different ways than other parents, but I wouldn't say another color.

When probed further about the cultural difference between Whites and Blacks, she stated:

Not from African Americans but perhaps from some others I can. Like from the middle-east where people have been raised and women are substantially second-class citizens and from those, absolutely.

It seems to be the case that in supportive home environments, the Black and White female parents may differ on the necessity of specific racial socialization. The Black parent's communication centered on the importance of one's humanity and making explicit the historical and cultural basis for African-American behaviors (or in Daniel & Daniel's terms, chap. 2, this volume, reacting to the hot stove). Racial communication from Black mothers was related to self-esteem in Study 1. Black adolescents often need this explicitly to deal with the ambiguities and discrepancies of a White majority society that values them differently than they value themselves (Daniel & Daniel, chap. 2, this volume; McAdoo, 1988; Ward, 1996; Will, 1997). Thus, it appears that Black parents are teaching some of the same lessons of the past to help their children to survive or to get along in the present (see Daniel & Daniel, chap. 2, this volume). The White parent's comments that she did not teach her child to evaluate herself differently than Blacks suggests that the notion of color or a race basis for parenting is not explicit or is viewed as a nonissue. Recent research has addressed the White perspective of the invisibility of Whiteness and the lack of family communication dealing with the issue of race in scholarship (e.g., Davilla, chap. 5, this volume; Martin et al., 1996; Nakayama & Krizek, 1995; Socha & Beigle, chap. 10, this volume; Ward, 1990).

DISCUSSION

Together, these two studies provide further evidence for the importance of family, particularly the presence and communication of a parent whom the adolescent perceives as caring and supportive in managing both self- and racial esteem. In the samples selected from these studies, that person typically was the mother. Evidence indicates, to a lesser degree, that adolescents (friends or peers) and fathers also convey information and influence on self- and racial esteem. Further research needs to examine fathers' and mothers' racial or ethnic communication and psychosocial outcomes more closely. Parental communication appears to be a crucial link for adolescents' self-esteem in both studies. Friendship or peer communication was secondary to parent communication in Study 1. However, the actual frequency of adolescents' interactions was greater with friends and peers than with parents, as evidenced in Study 2. Symbolic interaction theory often emphasizes perception or interpretation by the individual over actual events as a way to explain behavior (Blumer, 1969; Charon, 1985). The adolescents consistently expressed valuing and influence of parents over peers in both studies. Perhaps the impact of a supportive parental network runs deeper and lasts longer than an array of friends and acquaintances. Betty Bayé, an African-American journalist,[6] stated that her parents provided positive affirmation that she still "feasts on." The support environments of parents and peers are important to adolescent self-esteem. Support environments can create consistency or inconsistency about adolescents self-beliefs and self-esteem. In this research, parents, peers, and a teacher were designated as support persons. Racial esteem was correlated to adolescent self-esteem in Study 1 and was more influential on Black adolescent self-esteem than White adolescent self-esteem. This observation was explained somewhat by the qualitative findings of Study 2; specifically, Black and White parental support environments may differ in parental beliefs and actual behavior regarding racial socialization. The consistency and the distinctiveness of findings between the two studies, using different methodological assumptions, provide evidence for the relationship of adolescent self-esteem to parent and peer communication, support, and racial esteem.

The hypothesis generated from the findings in Study 1 and 2 and relevant communication, developmental, and self-esteem studies (e.g., Adams & Marshall, 1996; Isberg et al., 1989; Kim & Ruben, 1988; McDermott, 1983; McDermott & Greenberg, 1984; Newman & Newman, 1984; Nussbaum, 1989) is that communication's influence on self-esteem is cumulative. The messages are of varied quality and kind and are about the self that exists over the

---

[6]During a regular Sunday School session (June 14, 1998) at a local community church, Betty Bayé, a journalist for the *Courier Journal*, Louisville, Kentucky, newspaper, who writes often about African-American experiences, gave an unsolicited comment about the positive influence of her parents throughout her life.

life span of an individual's interactions in which a person forms some reasonable interpretations of who she/he is and how she/he values oneself. This perspective seems natural when what actually occurs over time in family and support environments is considered. Attempting to move children toward becoming self involves many messages. These messages, within a systems perspective, literally soothe, bend, stretch, and strain the psychic muscles of individuals. Such figurative language represents the interpreted quality or tones of messages (positive, neutral, negative). Kim and Ruben's (1988) discussion of "stress-adaptation-growth experiences" in the context of intercultural experiences appears relevant to the focus of communication influences on self-esteem because often stress accompanies growth and change. When confronted with goal-incongruent messages, emotions, or epiphanies that disrupt or question the self, people attempt to recover stability via a variety of sense-making strategies—ranging from obtaining information to creatively constructing new ways to think about events. The daily interactions of children and youth prompt growth and change, affecting self-cognition and self-feelings. Within the broader urban culture (which assumes contact with other races), Black and White youth experience similar and different communication interactions (within support contexts); therefore, a range of stress informs their views and evaluations of themselves.

The well-being of children suggests that there are tones (e.g., positive, neutral, negative) and acts (e.g., *I* /direct, *Me* /indirect, *We* messages) that affect the self in ways that may keep the self in balance (positive—*You are kind; You make me proud*) and others that may throw the self out of balance (negative—*I'm susceptible to things; I'm shy*). The balance of messages indicates that there is ongoing change within the environment—persons affect each other and persons take some perspective on these messages that soothe, bend, stretch, and strain cognition—leading to further change. The change in a person requires messages that enable him or her to continue to grow and to evolve into a person who has a sense of self and concomitantly evaluates the self. It is reasonable that these messages reflect what is internalized at various stages of development. A person's experience within a family (and an ethnic group in broader society) informs the self about those acts that promote or delimit well-being in that context or culture—or how to interpret messages. Interpretation of messages as positive, neutral, or negative may have a zero to high stress level. For example, Black females may believe they do not need friends compared to White females who may believe that having lots of friends is important to their well-being. For Black and White females the stress of the message appears minimal. Explaining such messages from the context of living in the United States and attending U.S. schools, Fordham and Ogbu (1986) might argue that the Black and White females exhibit appropriate (and seemingly oppositional) messages for well-being, learned from their community. In other words, these varied messages may provide cognitive stimulation to manage present and future messages—suggestive of different contexts and individual change and growth. Present and future messages imply a lifetime of interaction that may influence self. From a developmental communication perspective, then, positive or negative self-esteem may be acquired when a certain combination of perceived and culturally ascribed positive, negative, and neutral (quality) messages about self (*I*, *Me*, and *We*) occur over time, primarily within the family setting.

One may speculate that the combination of the quality and kind of self messages may be adjusted according to the developmental stage and unique needs of the child. For example, in constructing the well-being of young children, a parent would incorporate a higher frequency of positive direct messages because young children (infancy to childhood) are just beginning to learn about self. For adolescents who have positive self-esteem (as this sample), enjoy supportive environments, and have been exposed to many messages, there may be less need for an abundance of one quality type message and any one kind of message (direct, for example) because adolescents can better understand the basis of the messages they experience (cultural knowledge; previous messages). Rather than focusing on one quality and one kind of communication, there is a range of quality and kinds of communication that affects the adolescent self-esteem (see Tables 6.6–6.10). In keeping with a developmentalist perspective, the adolescent stage may be a critical time to insure that the influence of communication on self-esteem is understood. Complementary systems (e.g., Kim & Ruben's stress-adaptation-growth perspective), symbolic interaction, and critical models may be useful in further research to examine the natural environment of urban children and youth to better understand the proposed hypothesis for (parent, friendship, and peer) communication influences on self-esteem.

In general, natural contexts, and longitudinal studies might explore the variables of developmental level (i.e., identity stage), kind of communication about self, quality of communication, and culture to further explain self-esteem similarities and differences that promote optimal individuals and respect among societal members; specific future research and recommendations follow. Applied studies might incorporate known variables that influence self-esteem (positive communication and positive support models, for example) in contexts in which adolescents consistently evaluate themselves poorly and exhibit negative risk and self-destructive behaviors.

Future research is needed to understand the observation that these urban adolescents are adequate in their self-esteem and also perceive other races positively. The finding of positive attitude toward other races lets scholars, educators, and parents know that there is some desirability of adolescents and support environments (e.g., schools, homes, churches) to get along with others. Kim and Ruben (1988) discussed the motivation that is needed to acquire the understanding and skills to meet the challenge of the intercultural context. The adolescents' ideas about the issue of race may be quite different from those of their parents or ancestors (remember, Black mothers' communication about race and White fathers' communication about race indirectly influenced self-esteem through racial esteem). Although this may seem encouraging for a future world, there are counterarguments that suggest that Blacks and Whites need to be aware of racial realities (e.g., Bates, 1998; Hecht, Larkey, & Johnson, 1992; Hudson, 1998; Nakayama & Krizek, 1995; Orbe, 1994). Daniel and Daniel (chap. 2, this volume) emphasized that Black children still need to deal with the "hot stove" or the myth or illusion of always positive intercultural experiences (see Hudson, 1998; Rotherum-Borus et al., 1996; Ward, 1990;). In Study 2, it was evident from students' recalled interactions and teacher comments that Black and White students spent most of their in-class and free time with other same-race students. Rosenberg and Simmons' (1971) findings indicated that Blacks in integrated environments had lower esteem compared to Blacks in segregated environments. The implication was that Blacks who are in sustained interactions with those who evaluate them negatively in a nonconsonant racial context (not their race) will (perhaps in the recall of more negative messages) have lower self-esteem.

However, adolescents in urban schools, in close proximity to other ethnicities, may be able to offer insights to structured projects centered on developing culturally sensitized and skilled interactants (e.g., see Katz, 1978, on Whiteness and racism). There appear to be opportunities and obstacles to the positiveness that Black and White adolescents express about race. The pragmatic utility of the adolescent (and other support contexts) messages about self should be further explored over time to determine the benefits for such thinking. How does interethnic contact versus prolonged interethnic interactions affect adolescent self-esteem? Researchers might examine the cognitive distinctions and sense making between children who have positive versus negative perceptions of other cultural groups. Improving interethnic understanding may be addressed by creating opportunities for discussing values and providing cooperative and individual work/activities (e.g., Asante, 1981; Hudson, 1998; Kohn, 1994).

The similarities and differences between the Black and White samples are, perhaps, encouraging for scholars, families, and youth who are interested in locating common grounds for dialogue. It appears that the unique (*I*) and social (*Me*) aspects of communication are evident within both Black and White families but with different appearances and salience, perhaps from different parents (Table 6.7). The *We* concept when interpreted as strictly cultural (Noble's description) was less apparent—seen in two Black families (*you make us proud; the situation that we have in this country*). Such exploratory findings may be further examined in research and within family communication classroom activities and discussions. In my experience as a college instructor, it is not unusual for White college students in some geographic locations to deny an ethnic basis to their identity. Does this denial close down unity with an other? Does this acceptance create unity with an other? Does the presence of the We-ness language during intercultural encounters create more or less sensitivity to other? Martin et al. (1996) studied Whites' self-labels. They found that underlying Whites' resistance to self-labeling were issues of choice, related to power and domination. "Self-labeling for them may be an intrusion on choice and thus, engender negative associations" (p. 140). Family communication research could explore the meanings of the everyday usage of We, that is, who is really included/excluded; and classroom assignments that explore family ethnicity and communication may provide insight to methods that promote dialogue between and among diverse groups (e.g., Clark & Diggs, 1998; Diggs, 1995).

The topic of adolescent religiosity and self-esteem should be further explored. The internal orientation of Blacks (based on explicit talk in Study 2) suggests that messages incorporated from spiritual socialization may be the foundation for their beliefs and actions about self. Religious faith among African Americans reflects a strong cultural ideology (e.g., see Asante, 1988; Mindel, Habenstein, & Wright, 1988). For Blacks, the innate worth concept is garnered from Christianity and ancestral modeling, which says I am more than what others say that I am. Manns (1988) pointed out that the role of Black "individual's inner resources or self-directiveness" should not be ignored when considering important influencing factors (p. 282). Glover's (1996) study of religious White adolescents and young adults cited research that indicates that religious adults are more internally oriented and see their lives as more meaningful and integrated into society. Glover's own findings indicated religiosity scores would be lower for younger subjects. How does spiritual meaning of the self direct adolescent interactions with other races? What are the benefits and costs of a spiritual understanding of adolescent self (assuming visions of individual psychosocial health and a cooperative, pluralistic society)?

Methodologically, triangulation enabled further verification of the findings in each study. Utilization of methodological triangulation should be guided by philosophical assumptions and the hope of "obtaining a fuller understanding of complex, multi-faceted phenomena" (LeBlanc, 1995, p. 20). The focus groups and written journals helped obtain adolescent voices beyond the quantitative data gathered in Study 1. In addition, the focus group created some balance to the varied writing abilities of the adolescents. Future research should incorporate more participant observations and explicitly track and obtain participants' interethnic interactions. As noted earlier, the assumption of interethnic contact based solely on the study samples' urban school environment was challenged by the students' reported everyday communication interactions. Readers might view use of the terms Black, African American, White, or European-American as monolithic rather than diverse. The distinctions within the races are viewed based upon the data presented. Future studies are encouraged to remain sensitive to the diversity within racial groups.

The data in Study 2 suggest that family communication scholars, educators, adolescents, and parents might learn more about how adolescents with adequate self-esteem function within the school support context (and everyday context) and how Black families (who rear their children to be "biculturally competent," see Cross, 1991) might benefit from efforts to improve interethnic communication. For example, in these students' classroom, the teacher reported that Blacks tend to work—in teams and Whites preferred to work separately. Rotheram-Borus et al. (1996) reported that Latino and Black students were higher in group orientation and respect toward authority in comparison to Whites (consistent with the theme of collectivism, Socha & Diggs, chap. 1, this volume). My role of teaching a college small group process course affirms the possibility of how exposure to others and interactions in a "safe" structured learning environment can promote positive changes in attitude and actions—friendships often develop among those who were highly ambiguous of others, initially. Such observations might be explored by family communication researchers and instructors (using an interdisciplinary team) to create optimal learning and interethnic relationship-building environments for adolescents. For current, practical intervention, family communication researchers and instructors could be at the forefront of such current efforts as *dialogues for a purpose* (within school and family settings) then return by choice to separate environments. Hudson (1998), on discussing race relations in the late 20th century, stated that, "African-Americans must insist on the freedom to be as integrated or as self-segregated as they choose in those domains of life where such choices make sense" (p. 21). The implication is that this choice is status quo for European-Americans.

Diversity and multiculturalism are becoming a larger part of our real life (Takaki, 1993). Real life requires interactions inclusive of sensitivity to the communicators' needs and the current communication environment (e.g., Asante, 1981; Burleson, Delia, & Applegate 1995; Kim & Ruben, 1988). In our contemporary society, African-American and European-American children and adolescents are in close proximity, physically. Our old frames of references (about who we are and how we assess ourselves) or as Asanté stated, our "primordial errors of perception" (p. 408) will most certainly surface as we interact with others. Adolescents and their family support environments offer some traditional and additional considerations of communication influences on self-esteem that may help to revise our frames of references.

ACKNOWLEDGMENTS

The author thanks the principals, students, teachers, and parents of Columbus, Ohio, Public Schools and Louisville, Kentucky, Public Schools for their cooperation and participation in this study. Much appreciation goes to undergraduate student assistants, Ajeenah Sharif, for her tremendous help in the data collection and analysis of this research, and Shauna Taylor and Nicole Stevenson, for their assistance in word processing and locating bibliographic references.

REFERENCES

Adams, G. R., & Marshall, S. K. (1996). A developmental social psychology of identity: Understanding the person-in-context. *Journal of Adolescence, 19*, 429–442.
Adams, G. R., Montemayor, R., & Gullotta, T. P. (1996). Psychosocial development during adolescence. In G. R. Adams, R. Montemayor, & T. P. Gullotta (Eds.), *Psychosocial development during adolescence* (pp. 1–11). Thousand Oaks, CA: Sage.
Allen, W. R. (1978). The search for applicable theories of Black family life. *Journal of Marriage and the Family, 40*(1), 117–129.
Asante, M. K. (1981). Intercultural communication: An inquiry into research directions. In D. Nimmo (Ed.), *Communication Yearbook 4* (pp. 401–410). New Brunswick, NJ: Transaction Books.
Asante, M. K. (1988). *Afrocentricity* (Rev. ed.). Trenton, NJ: Africa World.
Baldwin, J. D. (1986). *George Herbert Mead: A unifying theory for sociology, masters of social theory: Vol 6.* Beverly Hills, CA: Sage.
Bates, K. G. (1998, May). Young, black and too white. *Salon Magazine* [Online]. Available address: (www.salonmag.com).
Beebee, S. J., Beebee S. A., & Redmond, M.V. (1996). *Interpersonal communication: Relating to others.* Needham Heights, MA: Allyn & Bacon.
Blumer, H. (1969) *Symbolic interactionism: Perspective and method.* Englewood Cliffs, NJ: Prentice-Hall.
Blumer, H. (1970). Methodological principles of empirical science. In N. K. Denzin (Ed.), *Sociological methods: A sourcebook* (pp. 20–39). Chicago: Aldine.
Buri, J., Louiselle, P., Misukanis, T., & Mueller, R. (1988). Effects of parental authoritarianism and authoritativeness on self-esteem. *Personality and Social Psychology Bulletin, 14*, 271–282.
Burleson, B. R., Delia, J. G., & Applegate, J. L. (1995). The socialization of person-centered communication. In M. A. Fitzpatrick & A. Vangelisti (Eds.), *Explaining Family Interactions* (pp. 34–75). Thousand Oaks, CA: Sage.
Cardinal, C. (1998). *The ten commandments of self-esteem.* Kansas City, KS: Andrews Mcmeel.
Chadwick, B. C., & Heaton, T. B. (1996). *Statistical handbook on adolescents in America.* Phoenix, AZ: Onyx.
Charon, J. M. (1985). *Symbolic interactionism: An introduction, an interpretation, an integration.* Englewood Cliffs, NJ: Prentice-Hall.
Clark, K. D., & Diggs, R. C. (1988). *Connected or separated?: Towards a dialectical view of interethnic relationships.* Manuscript submitted for publication.
Clark, M. L. (1988). Friendship and peer relations of black adolescents. In R. L. Jones (Ed.), *Black adolescent* (pp. 175–203). Berkeley, CA: Cobb & Henry.
Coates, D. L. (1985). Relationships between self-concept measures and social network characteristics for black adolescents. *Journal of Early Adolescence, 5*(3), 319–338.
Coleman, J. C., & Hendry, L. (1990). *The nature of adolescence.* New York: Routledge.
Collins, P. H. (1994). The meaning of motherhood in the black community. In R. Staples (Ed.), *The Black family: Essays and studies* (pp.165–173). Belmont, CA: Wadsworth.
Coopersmith, S. (1967/1981). *The antecedents of self-esteem.* Palo Alto, CA: Consulting Psychologists Press.
Crocker, J., Luhtanen, R., Blaine, B., & Broadnax, S. (1994). Collective self-esteem and psychological well-being among White, Black, and Asian College Students. *Personality and Social Psychology Bulletin 20*(5), 503–512.
Cross, W. E., Jr. (1991). *Shades of Black: Diversity in African-American identity.* Philadelphia: Temple University Press.
Demo, D. H., Small, S. A., & Savin-Williams, R. C. (1987). Family relations and the self-esteem of adolescents and their parents. *Journal of Marriage and the Family, 49*, 705–715.
DiCindio, L. A., Floyd, H. H., Wilcox, J., & McSeveney, D. R. (1983). Race effects in a model of parent–peer orientation. *Adolescence, 18*(70), 369–379.

Diggs, R. C. (1994). *Perceptions of parent and peer communication, racial esteem and support influences on self-esteem among African-American adolescents.* Unpublished doctoral dissertation, The Ohio State University, Columbus.

Diggs, R. C. (1995, June). *Black family communication: A course proposal.* Presented at the Speech Communication Association Black Caucus Summer Conference, Frankfort, KY.

Diggs, R. C., & Stafford, L. (1998). Maintaining marital relationships: A comparison between African American and European American married individuals. In V. J. Duncan (Ed.), *Towards achieving MAAT: Communication patterns in African American, European American, and interracial relationships* (pp. 191–202). Dubuque, IA: Kendall/Hunt.

Dukes, R. L., & Martinez, R. (1994). The impact of gender on self-esteem among adolescents. *Adolescence, 29*(113), 105–111.

Erickson, E. (1968). *Identity: Youth and crisis.* New York: Norton.

Erkut, S., Fields, J. P. F., Sing, R., & Marx, F. (1996). Diversity in girls' experiences: Feeling good about who you are. In B. J. R. Leadbeater & N. Way (Eds.), *Urban girls: Resisting stereotypes, creating identities* (pp. 53–64). New York: New York University Press.

Felson, R. B., & Zielinski, M. A. (1989). Children's self-esteem and parental support. *Journal of Marriage and the Family, 52,* 287–297.

Fontana, A., & Frey, J. H. (1994). Interviewing: The art of science. In N. K. Denzin & Y. S. Lincoln (Eds.), *Handbook of qualitative research* (pp. 361–376). Thousand Oaks, CA: Sage.

Fordham, S., & Ogbu, J. U. (1986). Black student's school success: Coping with the burden of acting White. *The Urban Review 18*(3), 176–204.

Gecas, V., & Schwalbe, M. L. (1986). Parental behavior and adolescent self-esteem. *Journal of Marriage and the Family, 48,* 37–46.

Gilligan, C. (1982). *In a different voice: Psychological theory and women's development.* Cambridge, MA: Harvard University Press.

Gilligan, C. (1990). Prologue. In C. Gilligan, N. P. Lyons, & T. J. Hanmer (Eds.), *Making connections: The relational worlds of adolescent girls at Emma Willard school* (pp. 174–193) Cambridge, MA: Harvard University Press.

Glover, R. J. (1996). Religiosity in adolescence and young adulthood: Implications for identity formation. *Psychological Reports, 78*(2), 427–432.

Gudykunst, W. B., Ting-Toomey, S., Sudweeks, S., & Stewart, L. P. (1995). *Building bridges: Interpersonal skills for a changing world.* Boston: Houghton Mifflin.

Hare, B. R. (1977). Black and White self-esteem in social science: An overview. *Journal of Negro Education, 46*(2), 141–156.

Harrison, A. O. (1985). The Black family's socialization environment: Self-esteem and ethnic attitude among Black children. In H. P. McAdoo & J. L. McAdoo (Eds.), *Black children: Social, educational, an parental environments* (pp. 174–193). Beverly Hills: Sage.

Hauser, S. T. (1971). *Black and white identity formations: Studies of the psychosocial development of lower socioeconomic adolescent boys.* New York: Wiley.

Hecht, M. L., Larkey, L. K., & Johnson, J. N. (1992). African American and European American perceptions of problematic issues in interethnic communication effectiveness. *Human Communication Research, 19,* 209–231.

Hinde, R., & Stevenson-Hinde, J. (1988). *Relationships within families: Mutual influences.* Oxford: Clarendon Press.

Hoffman, M. A., Usphiz, V., & Levy-Shiff, R. (1988). Social support and self-esteem in adolescence. *Journal of Youth and Adolescence, 17*(4), 307–316.

Horowitz, D. (1997, December). Perspectives on race. *Los Angeles Times,* [Online]. Available: http://www.elibrary.com/s/edumark/getdoc.cgi

Hudson, J. B. (1998, Summer). Race relations in the late twentieth century: Toward pluralism. *University of Louisville Magazine, Vol. 16*(4), 20–21.

Isberg, R. S., Hauser, S. T., Jacobson, A. M., Powers, S. I., Noam, G., Weiss-Perry, B., & Follansbee, D. (1989). Parental contexts of adolescent self-esteem: A developmental perspective. *Journal of Youth and Adolescence, 18*(1), 1–23.

James, W. (1918). *Principles of psychology,* New York: Holt. (Original work published 1890).

Katz, J. H. (1978). *White awareness: Handbook for anti-racism training.* Norman: University of Oklahoma Press.

Kim, Y. Y., & Ruben, B. D. (1988). Intercultural transformation: A systems theory. In Y. Y. Kim & W. B. Gudykunst (Eds.), *Theories in intercultural communication* (pp. 299–321). Newbury Park, CA: Sage.

Kohn, A. (1994, December). The truth about self-esteem. *Phi Delta Kappan, 272–283.*

Leary, M. R., Tambor, E. S., Terdal, S. K., & Downs, D. L. (1995). Self-esteem as an interpersonal monitor: The sociometer hypothesis. *Journal of Personality and Social Psychology 68(3),* 518–530.

LeBlanc, H. P. (1995). *Syncretism of qualitative and quantitative research paradigms: the case for methodological triangulation.* Unpublished manuscript, Southern Illinois University at Carbondale.

Lindlof, T. R. (1995). *Qualitative communication research methods.* Thousand Oaks, CA: Sage.

Littlejohn, S. W. (1992). *Theories of human communication.* Belmont, CA: Wadsworth.

Maccoby, E. E., & Martin, J. A. (1983). Socialization in the context of the family: Parent–child interaction. In E. M. Heatherington (Ed.), *Handbook of child psychology* (pp. 1–101). New York: Wiley.

Manns, W. (1988). Supportive roles of significant others in black families. In H. P. Mcadoo (Ed.), *Black families* (pp. 238– 251). Newbury Park, CA: Sage.

Margolin, L., Blyth, D. A., & Carbone, D. (1988). The family as a looking glass: Interpreting family influences on adolescent self-esteem from a symbolic interaction perspective. *Journal of Early Adolescence, 8(3),* 211–224.

Martin, J. N., Krizek, R. L., Nakayama, T. R., & Bradford, L. (1996). Exploring whiteness: A study of self-labels for White Americans. *Communication Quarterly, 44,* 125–144.

Maton, K. I., Teti, D. M., Corns, K. M., Viera-Baker, C. C., Lavine, J. R., Gouze, K. R., & Keating, D. P. (1996). Cultural specificity of support sources, correlates and contexts: Three studies of African-American and Caucasian youth. *American Journal of Community Psychology 24(4),* 551–637.

McAdoo, J. L. (1988). The roles of Black fathers in the socialization of Black children. In H. P. McAdoo (Ed.), *Black families* (pp. 257–269). Newbury Park, CA: Sage.

McDermott, S. T. (1983). A reconstitution of racial esteem with regard to communication. *Communication, 11(2),* 69–75.

McDermott, S. T., & Greenberg, B. S. (1984). Black children's esteem: Parents, peers, and television. *Communication Yearbook, 8,* 164–177.

Mead, G. H. (1934). *Mind, self, & society: From the standpoint of a behaviorist.* Chicago: University of Chicago Press.

Mindel, C. H., Habenstein, R. W., & Wright, R., Jr. (1988). Family lifestyles of America's ethnic minorities: An introduction. In C. H. Mindel, R. W. Habenstein, & R. Wright, Jr. (Eds.), *Ethnic families in America* (3rd ed., pp. 1–14). New York: Elsevier.

Myers, L. (1993). *Understanding an Afrocentric world view: Introduction to an optimal psychology* (2nd ed.). Dubuque, IA: Kendall/Hunt.

Nakayama, T. K., & Krizek, R. L. (1995). Whiteness: A strategic rhetoric. *Quarterly Journal of Speech, 81,* 291–309

Newman, B. M., & Newman, P. R. (1984). *Development through life: A psychosocial approach.* Homewood, IL: Dorsey.

Nobles, W. W. (1972). African philosophy: Foundations of Black psychology. In R. L. Jones (Ed.), *Black psychology* (pp. 19–32). New York: Harper & Row.

Nobles, W. W. (1973). Psychological research and the Black self-concept: A critical review. *Journal of Social Issues, 29,* 11–31.

Nobles, W. W. (1978). Toward an empirical and theoretical framework for defining black families. *Journal of Marriage and the Family, 40(4),* 479–688.

Nussbaum, J. F. (Ed.). (1989). *Life-span communication: Normative processes.* Hillsdale, NJ: Lawrence Erlbaum Associates.

Openshaw, D. K., Thomas, D. L., & Rollins, B. C. (1984). Parental influences on adolescent Self-esteem. *Journal of Early Adolescence, 4,* 259–274.

Orbe, M. P. (1994). Remember, it's always Whites' ball: Descriptions of African American male communication. *Communication Quarterly, 42(3),* 287–300.

Pearl, A. (1981). A phenomenological cost-benefit analysis approach to adolescence. In R. W. Henderson (Ed.), *Parent–child interaction: Theory, research, and prospects* (pp. 293–323). New York: Academic Press.

Peters, M. F. (1985). Racial socialization of young Black children. In H. P. McAdoo & J. L. McAdoo (Eds.), *Black children: Social, educational, and parental environments* (pp. 159–173). Beverly Hills: Sage.

Peterson, G. W., & Rollins, B. C. (1987). Parent–child socialization. In M. B. Sussman & S. K. Steinmetz (Eds.), *Handbook of marriage and the family* (pp.471–486). New York: Plenum.

Phinney, J. S., & Chavira, V. (1992). Ethnic identity and self-esteem: An explanatory longitudinal study. *Journal of Adolescence, 15,* 271–281.

Rosenberg, M. (1965). *Society and the adolescent self-image.* Princeton, NJ: Princeton University Press.

Rosenberg, M. (1985). Self-concept from middle childhood through adolescence. In J. Suls & A. G. Greenwald (Eds.), *Psychological perspectives on the self* (Vol. 3; pp. 107–136). Hillsdale, NJ: Lawrence Erlbaum Associates.

Rosenberg, M., & Simmons, R. G. (1971). *Black and White self-esteem: The urban school child.* Washington, DC: Arnold M. and Caroline Rose Monograph Series, American Sociological Association.

Rotheram-Borus, M. J., Dopkins, S., Sabate, N., & Lightfoot, M. (1996). Personal and ethnic identity, values, and self-esteem among Black and Latino adolescent girls. In B. J. R. Leadbeater & N. Way (Eds.), *Urban girls: Resisting stereotypes, creating identities* (pp. 35–52). New York: New York University Press.

Schacter, D. L. (1996). *Searching for memory: The brain, the mind, and the past.* New York: HarperCollins.

Schwartz, M., & Tangri, S. S. (1965). A note on self-concept as an insulator against delinquency. *American Sociological Review, 30,* 922–926.

Siegelman, M. (1965). Evaluation of Bronfenbrenner's questionnaire for children concerning parental behavior. *Child Development, 36,* 163–174.

Smith, D. M. (1985). Perceived peer and parental influences on youths' social world. *Youth and Society, 17,* 131–156.

Takaki, R. (1993). *A different mirror: A history of multicultural America.* Boston: Little, Brown.

Taylor, D. M. & Dubé, L. (1986). Two faces of identity: The "I" and the "We". *Journal of Social Issues, 42*(2), 81–98.

Thomas, D. L., Gecas, V., Weigart, A., & Rooney, E. (1974). *Family socialization and the adolescent: Determinants of self-concept, conformity, religiosity and counter cultural values.* Lexington, MA: Lexington Books.

Walker, L. S., & Greene, J. W. (1986). The social context of adolescent self-esteem. *Journal of Youth and Adolescence, 15,* 315–322.

Ward, J. V. (1990). Racial identity formation and transformation. In C. Gilligan, N. P. Lyons, & T. J. Hanner (Eds.), *Making connections: The relational worlds of adolescent girls at Emma Willard school* (pp. 215–232). London, England: Harvard University Press.

Ward, J. V. (1996). Raising resisters: The role of truth telling in the psychological development of African American girls. In B. J. R. Leadbeater & N. Way (Eds.), *Urban girls: Resisting stereotypes, creating identities* (pp. 85–99). New York: New York University Press.

Waters, M. C. (1996). The intersection of gender, race, and ethnicity in identity development of Caribbean American teens. In B. J. R. Leadbeater & N. Way (Eds.), *Urban girls: Resisting stereotypes, creating identities* (pp. 65–81). New York: New York University Press.

Weigart, A., & Rooney, E. (1974). *Family socialization and the adolescent: Determinants of self-concept, conformity, religiosity, and counter cultural values.* Lexington, MA: Lexington Books.

West, C. (1993). *Keeping the faith: Philosophy and race in America.* New York: Routledge.

Will, G. (1997, June 4). Clinton defends racial categories. *St. Louis Post-Dispatch,* [Online]. Available: http://www.elibrary.com/s/edumark/getdoc.cgi

Wood, J. T. (1997). *Communication theories in action: An introduction.* New York: Wadsworth Publishing.

7

African-American, European-American, and Biracial Couples' Meanings for and Experiences in Marriage

Marianne Dainton
La Salle University

One need look no further than the differing statistics in the marital status of African Americans and European Americans to determine that ethnicity matters in the marital experience. According to U.S. census figures (1993), 29% of Black men and women under the age of 35 are divorced or separated, whereas 15% of White men and women under the age of 35 are so designated. Moreover, 63% of African-American men and women under 35 have never married, whereas 41% of European-American men and women in the same age group have never married. Clearly, there are quantitative sociological differences in the marital experience between the two ethnic groups. But are there qualitative differences in the meanings for and experiences of marriage for these couples? This chapter addresses that question through an exploration of communication as a process of symbolic exchange between marital partners.

First, a central assumption is made that it is appropriate to frame this endeavor in symbolic interactionism (Blumer, 1969). An interactional perspective presumes that meaning is created socially through interaction with significant others. In this case, significant others are represented both by "ethnic culture" as well as "marital partner." That is, I assume that individuals' meanings and experiences are shaped by cultural norms regarding how to enact a relationship as well as by everyday interaction with one's spouse. Such a belief comports with previous investigations of ethnic communication. Hecht, Larkey, and Johnson (1992), for example, suggested that ethnicity incorporates both a meaning structure as well as expressed behavior. Gaines (1995), based on the work of Mindel, Habenstein, and Wright (1988), defined ethnicity as the "values, attitudes, lifestyles, customs, rituals, and personality types of individuals who identify with particular ethnic groups" (p. 63). Most scholars in communication agree that ethnicity is created and recreated through social interaction.

There are several theoretical reasons to expect differences in the experience of and meanings for marriage among African-American and European-American couples. Using an Africanist perspective, Sudarkasa (1981) argued that the African heritage emphasizes consanguinity (blood ties) to define the family experience, whereas European tradition emphasizes conjugality (marital kinship). A preference for consanguinity suggests that there might be few rigid boundaries as to what constitutes a family: extended family is indeed family (see also Socha & Diggs, chap. 1, this volume). Moreover, a focus on consanguinity might allow for maintaining broken relationships, as marital stability might not be understood or emphasized as an important factor in defining family stability. Further diminishing the relative importance of marital stability among African Americans was the impact of slavery, which did not allow for marital stability (Herskovits, 1958). Combined, these two historical forces imply that African-American couples might rely more heavily on extended family, and therefore marital stability might be perceived as relatively less important to family functioning than the processes in other relationships. On the other hand, European-Americans' focus on conjugality privileges the nuclear family over the extended family, and thus marital stability would become more emphasized in judgments about family functioning.

Similar to Sudarkasa's perspective, Gaines (1995) built on the work of Asante (1981) regarding the collectivistic heritage of African Americans. Collectivism focuses on the well-being of the entire ethnic group as opposed to individual well-being (Hofstede, 1980). Asante and Gaines argued that collectivism promotes more egalitarian decision making, mutuality in nurturance, more frequent and open displays of love, and visible displays of esteem among African-American couples.

These theoretical perspectives are complemented by empirical work that suggests that African-American couples and European-American couples do, in fact, experience marriage differently in ways other than reflected in marriage and divorce rates. One of the most consistent results of social scientific inquiries is that African Americans experience lower marital quality than European Americans (e.g., Adelmann, Chadwick, & Baerger, 1996; Glenn, 1989). Similarly, Black husbands and wives perceive that their happiness outside of marriage (i.e., if they were to divorce) would be higher than that perceived by White husbands and wives (Rank & Davis, 1996). These differences cannot be explained by demographic or socioeconomic differences (Rank & Davis, 1996; Timmer, Veroff, & Hatchett, 1996), financial satisfaction or spousal emotional support (Broman, 1993), presence of children (Glenn, 1989), or kin relations or status inequality (Adelmann et al., 1996). However, as Gaines (1995) implied, the measure of marital quality used in these studies may be ethnically biased in favor of European-American values of what constitutes a quality relationship (i.e., individualism). For example, one question of Spanier's (1976) Dyadic Adjustment Scale (one of the most frequently used measures of marital satisfaction) asks respondents to indicate which of several statements best describes how they feel about their relationship. The item that scored highest on marital quality reads "I want desperately for my relationship to succeed, and would go to almost any length to see that it does." Such a statement reflects an individualistic tendency to view personal desires and self-efficacy as the ultimate in importance (see Hofstede, 1980). Scoring lower on marital quality is the item that reads "I want very much for my relationship to succeed, and will do my fair share to see that it does." This item is more collectivistic in nature, as it recognizes shared responsibility. Moreover, items that reflect truly collectivistic values, such as obligation, loyalty, and dependency, do not appear in the measure at all. Accordingly, there are reasons to believe that differences in marital quality between the two groups might indeed reflect cultural biases in measurement.

Beyond differences in marital satisfaction, there are some clear similarities and differences in predicting a quality marriage for the two ethnic groups. For example, Veroff, Sutherland, Chadiha, and Ortega (1993b) found that, for both Black and White couples, focusing on the marriage as a unit as opposed to individual desires was predictive of marital quality. However, Timmer et al. (1996) found that close family ties predict Black couples' marital happiness, but the same is not true for White couples. In addition, Veroff et al. (1993b) found that the themes of finances and children were negatively associated with Black husbands' marital happiness, whereas the theme of religion was positively related to Black wives' marital happiness. Further, lack of time was negatively associated with White wives' marital happiness, but not Black wives' marital happiness.

Religiosity plays a central role in African-American marriages. Diggs and Stafford (1991), for example, found that African-American couples assert that they use spirituality to maintain their marriage more often than do European Americans. Indeed, relying on religion seems to facilitate marital functioning for African-American couples. Brody, Stoneman, Flor, and McCrary (1994) determined that, for rural, Southern Black families, higher levels of reported religiosity were associated with higher levels of observed marital interaction quality and cocaregiver support and lower levels of marital conflict.

Differences between African-American couples and European-American couples also exist beyond marital quality issues. Regarding interactional variables such as conflict and communication, Staples (1981) argued that Black marriages may be characterized by more egalitarian roles. Oggins, Veroff, and

Leber (1993) found that African-American couples report more disclosure, more positive sexual interactions, fewer topics of disagreement, and more conflict avoidance.

When considering the link between ethnicity and marriage, what has largely been left unexplored is the marital experience of biracial couples (although see Orbe, chap. 8, this volume). African-American–European-American marriages are still relatively uncommon (also see Orbe, chap. 8, this volume). According to Rosenblatt, Karis, and Powell (1995), the 1992 U.S. census reported just 246,000 such unions. However, there is increasing tolerance of interracial marriage in the United States (Schuman, Steeh, & Bobo, 1985). Increased tolerance does not mean universal acceptance however, as Rosenblatt et al. (1995) indicated: "There are still powerful forces in society that make Black-white interracial marriage difficult, unappealing to people who might be looking for a partner, or otherwise unlikely" (p. 5). Because of the societal pressures that biracial couples experience as well as the presumed differences in the meanings for marriage among African Americans and European Americans, it is assumed that biracial couples might be instrumental in providing insight into how ethnicity can be managed within marriage. Accordingly, this research also addresses the meanings for and experience of marriage among biracial couples (see also Orbe, chap. 8, this volume, for a discussion of this literature).

Much of the research on biracial couples has focused on sociological qualities, such as educational and social class similarity (see e.g., Gadberry & Dodder, 1993; Kouri & Lasswell, 1993). The evidence to date suggests that younger Black and White males, particularly those who are well educated, and African Americans in general are more likely to be involved with an interethnic relationship (Tucker & Mitchell-Kernan, 1995). Still, education and social class similarity do not entirely explain why couples become involved in interracial relationships. For example, Kouri and Lasswell (1993) found that most biracial couples say that they became attracted to each other because of compatibility. Considering the current climate of racial hostility that exists toward Blacks, it continues to be instructive to understand how and why interracial personal relationships develop.

Rosenblatt et al. (1995) found that most of the interracial couples in his interview sample did not see themselves differently than single-race couples. For them, being an interracial couple did not present internal tensions, but external problems. For example, Welborn (1994, cited in Rosenblatt et al., 1995) found that 64% of interracial couples experienced negative public reactions as compared with 4% of African-American couples and 7% of European-American couples. It is interesting that research indicates that the families of interracial couples are typically supportive, although White women reported experiencing more family criticism than Black women or Black or White men (Kouri & Lasswell, 1993; Tucker & Mitchell-Kernan, 1995).

QUESTIONS

In sum, there are both theoretical and empirical reasons to suspect that there are in fact differences in the meanings and experiences of marriage among African-American and European-American couples. Moreover, the experience of those couples who come from different ethnic backgrounds becomes paramount in understanding if ethnicity matters, in what circumstances, and how it matters in the marital experience. Accordingly, this research seeks to address the following descriptive research questions:

> RQ1: Are there differences in the meanings for marriage among African-American, European-American, and biracial couples?

> RQ2: Are there differences in the experience of marriage among African-American, European-American, and biracial couples?

METHOD

Orbe (1995; chap. 8, this volume) suggested that many methods used to study the communication patterns of African Americans are biased toward European-American values (and see also Socha & Diggs, chap. 1, this volume). Accordingly, he called for methods that allow African-American voices to be heard. Dilworth-Anderson, Burton, and Turner (1993) proposed that grounded theorizing will allow researchers to make conclusions based on the meaning systems of the respondents. Similarly, Veroff, Sutherland, Chadiha, & Ortega, (1993a) suggested that a narrative method might be particularly useful in the study of African-American couples, as there is a cultural comfort with storytelling. Narrative methods would serve to extend the ethnographic work that already exists (e.g., Kochman, 1981). Accordingly, this research incorporates inductive, narrative methods in addressing the research questions.

Participants

Because this was an exploratory study seeking to raise questions rather than come up with definitive answers, a convenience sample was deemed acceptable. Thus, a network sample of two African-American, two European-American, and two biracial couples was obtained through students at an urban university on the East Coast. Table 7.1 describes the demographics of each couple. The students made the first contact with the potential participants, describing the nature of the study and ascertaining the couples' willingness to participate. After the couple expressed interest in the study, the student then gave the names and phone numbers of the couples to the researcher. The researcher then called the couple, clarified the purpose and procedures of the study, and answered any questions that the couple asked. At this point, interest in participating was again ascer-

TABLE 7.1
The Couples

Couple 1	Couple 2	Couple 3
Jason & Rhonda	Jonathan & Tanya	Greg & Kathleen
Married 1 year	Married 5 years	Married 2 years
0 children	0 children	2 children
$30–$39,999/year	$20–$29,999/year	Over $50,000/year
Live in suburbs	Live in city	Live in suburbs
Jason: 27	Jonathan: 29	Greg: 28
African American	European American	African American
some college	college degree	college degree
Islamic	Christian	Baptist
Rhonda: 24	Tanya: 30	Kathleen: 26
high school degree	college degree	some graduate school
Presbyterian	No religion	Roman Catholic

Couple 4	Couple 5	Couple 6
Gene & Wilma	Joseph & Carol	Alexander & Kate
Married 1 year	Married 2 years	Married 3 years
0 children	1 child	0 children
Over $50,000/year	Over $50,000/year	Over $50,000/year
Live in city	Live in suburbs	Live in city
Gene: 31	Joseph: 38	Alexander: 47
African American*	Italian American	Ukrainian American
some college	college degree	high school degree
Baptist	Catholic	No religion
Wilma: 32	Carol: 32	Kate: 34
African American	European American	African American
college degree	high school degree	some college
Baptist	No religion	New Age Christian

* Gene identified both Black and White cultures as having an influence on him.

tained, and if both members of the couple felt comfortable with participating, an appointment was made. The researcher (a European-American woman) went to each of the couples' homes for data collection.

Procedures

There were three parts to the research process. First, demographic information was collected using a standard questionnaire. Then, following the methods of Veroff et al. (1993a), the researcher asked the couple to jointly tell the story of their relationship from their initial meeting to their current experience. Specifically, the researcher read the following instructions to the couple:

> I would like you to tell me in your own words the story of your relationship. I have no set questions for you, I just want you to tell me about your lives together as if it were a story with a beginning, middle, and an end that includes how things might look in the future. There is no right or wrong way to tell your story, just tell me in any way you feel comfortable. You can agree about the story, you can disagree about the story, any way that seems comfortable to you. While I would like to hear from both of you, if one person wants to take the lead that's okay too. To help you with your story, look at the page that says "the story of your relationship." Most marriages involve these elements. That might help you with the story you tell.

To assist couples, a sheet was provided that incorporated the elements identified by Veroff et al. (1993a) as central to the marriage experience. These elements included: How you met; how you got interested in each other; how you became a couple; planning to get married; the wedding itself; what life was like after the wedding; what married life is like now; what you think married life will be like in the future. The narratives were recorded on audiotape and later transcribed by the researcher. Lengths of the narratives were as follows: couple 1 (Jason & Rhonda, both African American) spoke for 39 minutes; couple 2 (Jonathon & Tanya, both European American) spoke for 22 minutes; couple 3 (Greg, an African American, and Kathleen, a European American) spoke for 43 minutes; couple 4 (Gene & Wilma, both African American) spoke for 30 minutes; couple 5 (Joseph & Carol, both European American) spoke for 76 minutes; and couple 6 (Alexander, a European American, and Kate, an African American) spoke for 41 minutes. Both members of all of the couples were active in the storytelling process.

For the final portion of the study, spouses were asked individually to respond to a question regarding his or her meanings for marriage. This procedure follows that of Abernathy (1981), who modified Kuhn-McPartland's 20-statements test. Specifically, each respondent was asked to list 10 answers to the following question: Marriage is … ? If the respondent was unable to come up with 10 responses, he or she was instructed to simply identify as many as he or she possibly could.

It should be noted that all of the couples appeared to be very comfortable with the research methods and in particular with the narrative portion of the study. Nearly all of the couples volunteered that the research process was "fun." Although none of the couples expressed discomfort because of the researcher's race, it is possible that some of the couples might have changed their responses because of it. However, because the participants were recruited by their own friends and family members who "vouched" for the researcher, it is hoped that the research process was one that was comfortable for the participants and that they therefore felt free to be honest.

RESULTS AND DISCUSSION

Research Question 1 asked about variations in the meanings for marriage among the three groups. Answers provided to the question "Marriage is … ?" were used to uncover potential differences. Abernathy's (1981) categories provided a foundation for a content analysis of this data, yet it quickly became clear that his category scheme did not adequately capture the answers provided by this sample. Accordingly, Abernathy's scheme was modified. First, two of his categories, *marriage as an institution* and *marriage as an economic arrangement*, did not appear in the responses given by the participants of this study and were dropped. Furthermore, although Abernathy did not include the category of *marriage as spirituality*, this category emerged from the data and was included in the coding scheme.

To provide an estimate of intercoder reliability and to make sure that there were no ethnic biases in the placing of the answers into categories, a male, African-American student was trained in the coding scheme and coded the data separately from the European-American, female researcher. Scott's Pi = .80 was deemed an acceptable indicator of reliability. A superficial review of the differences in the ways that the data were coded indicates that the African-American man was more likely to code the answers in the *marriage as companionship* category and less likely to code answers in the *marriage as positive* category than the European-American woman. Table 7.2 provides an overview of the meanings for marriage provided by the couples and the frequencies with which these meanings were nominated.

The three groups of couples held a positive view of marriage. However, the two African-American couples simultaneously held negative meanings of marriage. For example, two different African-American individuals used the word *hate* to describe marriage, with additional negative meanings such as "anger," "death," and "hell" identified. These results might indicate the reason for some of the quantitative differences described earlier. For example, it may be that fewer African Americans get married simply because marriage is not perceived by them as a wholly positive experience. Conversely, it may be that lower marital quality among African Americans (Adelman et al., 1996; Glenn, 1989) may lead to more negative mental associations with marriage. Because marital satisfaction was not assessed in this study, it might simply be that the African-American couples in this study were less happily married than the other couples.

TABLE 7.2

Reported Meanings for Marriage by Race

Thematic Category	African American	European American	Biracial
Companionship Focusing on togetherness, sharing	1	5	5
Family/Children Linking marriage to family functions	1	2	2
Love Focusing on romance, love	2	1	4
Negative (e.g, hell, hate, bad)	5	1	0
Positive (e.g, stability, trust, wonderful)	11	13	16
Sex Focusing on the passionate, sexual aspects	1	0	2
Spirituality Invoking God, religion, or spirituality	5	1	1
Work Focusing on responsibilities	8	5	10

The African-American couples did not have meanings for marriage that included companionship. It seems that the African-American couples interviewed for this study did not immediately associate marriage as providing inclusiveness and a clear sense of connectedness. This result might confirm Sudarkasa's (1981) assertion that African Americans have a cultural heritage of consanguinality, which focuses on the importance of extended blood family rather than on the importance of the marital dyad. Further, this finding resonates with the work of Rank and Davis (1996), who found that Black couples believe their happiness outside of marriage is higher than do White couples. Perhaps African-American couples' happiness outside of marriage is higher because they are less reliant upon the spouse for companionship than are European-Americans. Still, it should be noted that the African-American man who provided intercoder reliability was more likely to code responses as reflecting companionship than reflecting positive views. It may be that the meanings for companionship vary across ethnic groups, such that what is viewed as companionship by African Americans is different than what is viewed as companionship by European-Americans.

On the other hand, the African-American couples in this sample were more likely than the European-American or biracial couples to associate marriage with spirituality. This comports with previous research that indicates that African-American couples more frequently use spirituality to maintain their relationship (Diggs & Stafford, 1991) and that religiosity is positively associated with marital happiness for African-American couples (Veroff et al., 1993b).

All groups mentioned meanings of marriage associated with work or responsibility, but biracial couples seemed to identify marriage as "work" more frequently than the other groups. The biracial couples were also more likely to identify "love" as a meaning of marriage. Perhaps these couples are more likely to focus on their enduring emotional connection because of societal disapproval of biracial relationships (Rosenblatt et al., 1995). That is, the couple's love for each other must be strong enough to overcome societal pressures against biracial relationships. These external pressures might also be the reason the biracial couples in this sample focus on the "work" aspect of marriage; it might simply be harder work to maintain a relationship in the face of such strong external pressures (see Orbe, chap. 8, this volume).

The second research question focused on the experience of marriage among the three groups of couples. The narratives of the couples' story of their relationship served as data for this question. Although the analysis of the data was informed by the categories detailed by Veroff et al. (1993a), the method of analytic induction was used. Specifically, the transcripts of the narratives were reviewed to uncover potential themes relevant to answering the research question. Both the content and structure of the narratives were utilized in this process. After the creation of working themes, the narratives were reviewed again in order to modify or augment the themes that emerged during the first review. This process was continued until the researcher felt satisfied that the essence of the narratives was captured fully in the analysis. To ascertain whether there were cultural biases in the resulting analysis, the transcripts and final report were reviewed by a female African-American student, who supported the researcher's interpretations of the narratives.

The results of the analysis indicate that the tensions expressed by the African-American and European-American couples were quite similar. The problems these couples faced as well as the way these problems were framed by the couple centered on issues related to the internal dynamics of the couple, particularly their differences in communication styles. For example, the major tension expressed by Gene and Wilma (African Americans) was their problem of adjusting to each other and marriage.

> Gene: I had peaks and valleys, I think. I was here a lot longer, so I had a lot of time to think. So I was like "oh my goodness."
> Wilma: "What have I done?"

> Gene: "What's going on here, fella? What did you do now?"
>
> Wilma: It hit all of a sudden. I'm happy go lucky.
>
> Gene: And I'm laid back. She's like a little kid. I'm like super super super super … I can't explain how laid back I am. So you can imagine. She likes to talk.

Similarly, Kate (African American) and Alexander (European American) have problems associated with their different interaction styles.

> Kate: He likes to fight a lot. I don't do that. I'm not going to sit here and shout about it. After a while, I can see that he kind of misses it.
>
> Alexander: Yeah, it gets your juices going. There's always some kind of debate. It's kind of this Slavic torment where you have to analyze everything.
>
> Kate: Well, I wasn't going for the Slavic torment.
>
> Alexander: Yeah.
>
> Kate: I just say "That's okay, if that's the way you want it, that's fine."

Although Joseph and Carol's (European Americans) major tension was not their differences in interaction styles, problems with money affected the internal dynamics of their relationship.

> Carol: If all goes well with this job, and he starts making money, I think it [the future] will be very good. The past months, the past year, has been so much of a strain on our relationship.
>
> Joseph: 'Cause of the finances.
>
> Carol: Our relationship is very good, but, you know, we're at each other's throats a lot, with the financial situation. It shows to everyone. We're bitter. And I want to talk about it. It makes me feel better. If I could scream and get it out. He won't talk.

As described by Carol and Joseph, financial problems (an external problem) served as a catalyst for the internal problem of differing conflict styles.

Both a European-American couple and an African-American couple talked about the tensions associated with one partner maintaining his or her individual interests outside of the marriage and the problems that caused with the internal dynamics of their relationships. Jonathan and Tanya (European Americans) recounted the following story:

> Jonathan: I was young. Still had some wild oats to sow. We had problems. I mean, I would work every night, sometimes to 1 o'clock, and then I'd go out and close out an after hours bar until 3:30 in the morning. I'd come back whipped …
>
> Tanya: Broke!
>
> Jonathan: Oh yeah, I'd think nothing of making $100 and spending $80 of it. It was incredible. I wasn't considerate of anybody but myself still.

Similarly, Jason and Rhonda (African Americans) are still dealing with individual needs and frustrations.

> Rhonda: Because even though we're married I still go out with my girlfriends, we go out dancing and stuff.
>
> Jason: There are times I don't want you to go out. If I want you to stay home with me, it's very easy. You should think about it.
>
> Rhonda: I hate that. Even though we're married and I love Jason to death, sometimes I just need my space, you know what I mean?

What is interesting about the similarity of internal tensions among both African-American and European-American couples and particularly the presence of the internal tension of individual needs is that it seems to contradict the notion that African Americans are more collectivistic (Gaines, 1995). Nearly all of the couples interviewed in this study focused on the needs of the individuals and the couple as opposed to the good of the ethnic group or even the extended family. This result was not entirely unexpected, however. In partial support of this assertion, Diggs and Stafford (1991) found that there was no significant difference between African-American couples and European-American couples in their reliance upon family and social networks to maintain the marital relationship. Future research should examine more directly with a larger, random sample whether African Americans are indeed more collectivistic in the ways they enact their marriage, as theory suggests.

As further evidence of the lack of differences between African-American and European-American couples, there was little difference in the description of family involvement among the two groups. The African-American couples talked frequently about family and friends, particularly the families of the wives. In fact, one of the couples lives with the wife's brother. In short, the larger family network was important to them. However, the European-American couples also talked about family a great deal, and again, the wife's family was mentioned most frequently. One husband indicated that he had brought potential engagement rings to his wife's mother and sisters for approval before giving it to her. This same couple relies extensively on family for child care. In short, in this sample both ethnic groups were connected to extended family.

It is noteworthy that both of the biracial couples experienced tensions related to the intrusiveness of friends and family, which they described as external to the relationship.

> Kathleen: It was hard living down in Delaware because we were right in the heart of his family. He's from Chester. That's the siblings ... there's four in his family.
>
> Greg: I'm the third.
>
> Kathleen: Most of them all live right in Delaware. And that was hard. It was hard when we lived with my family, but then to get married and live in the heart of his family.

Greg: Yeah.

It is tempting to suggest that the problems with family experienced by Greg (African American) and Kathleen (European American) might be due to cultural differences related to collectivism, but there are insufficient data to support this claim. Moreover, in the second biracial couple interviewed, Kate (African American) is the one who had problems with the intrusiveness of Alexander's network.

> Kate: Well, I don't know, something about us, but the minute I came around all of a sudden he had all these friends.
>
> Alexander: It was strange. I had no friends for like nine months. I was here alone. It just stayed that way for so long. And then when Kate … what did I ask you for? That brunch thing again, weren't we? But before that all of a sudden all these other friends came around.
>
> Kate: Well I started thinking they were kind of, like, interrupting the relationship.

Aside from the differences in the types of tensions experienced by the couples, there were also differences in the way the stories were told. Both the European-American couples and the biracial couples spent roughly equal amounts of time talking about the three time periods of their relationships: meeting and dating, planning the wedding and the wedding itself, and after the wedding. Both African-American couples spent the longest amount of time describing life after the wedding (roughly two to three times longer than the other two periods combined). Neither couple spent much time with the wedding planning or ceremony; couple 1 talked about this period for only 1 minute out of their 39-minute narrative, and couple 4 talked about this period for 5 minutes out of their 30-minute narrative. In fact, couple 1, Jason and Rhonda, forgot to talk about getting married, focusing instead on her brief period of time in the service.

> Rhonda: I cried and everything like that. It was hard.
>
> Jason: I told her what it was going to be like. I said … before she left … she'd get mad at me.
>
> Rhonda: Oh, we left out the part when we got married! (Both laugh.) We got married before I left for the service. Totally forgot. We got married.

This lack of focus on the wedding among the African-American couples supports Veroff et al.'s (1993a) speculation that, for European Americans, weddings have more to do with public performance and social obligation whereas, for African Americans, the wedding primarily reflects a commitment between the two people.

Contrary to previous research, however, the African-American couples and the biracial couples were more interactive while telling their stories than were the European Americans (Veroff, Chadiha, Leber, & Sutherland, 1991, unpublished manuscript reported in Veroff et al., 1993a). Although the women in

both groups tended to do the majority of the talking, the men consistently inter-
jected their memories or thoughts into the story. It was interesting that the interruptions used by the biracial couples tended to be continuations of their
partner's comments. For example, in describing their trip to the Grand Canyon,
Kate (African American) and Alexander (European American) engaged in the
following exchange:

> Kate: We were looking for it, looking for it, and then
>
> Alexander: You don't see it.
>
> Kate: And then you drive up to it and it was like, you just stand there in awe.
>
> Alexander: And everyone there is the same.

On the other hand, the African-American couples' interruptions tended to
reflect conflict. In talking about planning the wedding, Gene and Wilma had
the following exchange:

> Gene: [It was] a pain in the butt.
>
> Wilma. I don't see how it was a pain in the butt for him.
>
> Gene: She asked a lot of questions. Unbelievable. "Whatever you like."
>
> Wilma: Like you were even …
>
> Gene: In the end I just stayed out of it.

Much of the conflict was related to jokes or exaggerations, for example:

> Rhonda: Actually, my mom made the first step. She went over and she asked him …
>
> Jason: She started hounding me!
>
> Rhonda: … his name and …
>
> Jason: She was hounding me!
>
> Rhonda: Well she asked you if you have a job and …
>
> Jason: (in falsetto) "Where are you from? Do you have a job? Do you have a car?"
>
> Rhonda: Well she was looking out for me!
>
> Jason: (still in falsetto) "My daughter's looking for a man!"

This is consistent with previous research, which indicates that when asked to
tell the story of their relationship, African-American couples conflicted with
each other more than European Americans and confirmed each other less
(Veroff et al., 1993a). However, the consistency with which the African-American couples had conflict during their narrative runs counter to research that indicates that there are fewer areas of disagreement among
African-American couples and more conflict avoidance (Oggins et al., 1993).

Perhaps the conflicts evident during the storytelling process would not be viewed as conflicts by the couples themselves, but instead reflect a communication style difference between African Americans and European Americans. Hecht, Collier, and Ribeau (1993), for example, suggested that assertiveness (which is frequently mistaken for disagreement) is a communication style typically used by African Americans. Further, these authors suggest that many forms of humor are ritualized in African-American speech. Given the exaggerated nature of the comments and the lightheartedness with which the couples enacted the interactions, it is likely that this does in fact represent a communication style difference between African Americans and European Americans (see Kochman, 1981).

Returning to a discussion of the style of the narratives, the European-American couples also interrupted each other, but they also tended to have more clearly defined and longer turns, making their narratives a bit less interactive.

> Jonathan: I came home from work and she had a list.
>
> Tanya: It was "Things I love about Jonathan," "Things I don't like about Jonathan," and "What I want out of the relationship." And then I wrote another sheet for him. "Things I love about Tanya, things I don't like about Tanya, and what I want out of the relationship." And then the last sheet was things we need to work on. Then we sat down and talked about it. We switched each other's sheets and we talked about it.
>
> Jonathan: I thought it was really corny at first, but after a while I thought "you know, we really do need to talk." 'Cause I realized, you know, I'm being a jerk again. I worked on it.

This subtle difference in the interaction style used by African-American and European-American couples during the narrative portion of this research might translate to different interaction styles used in everyday married life. Future research should strive to ascertain if this is indeed the case.

Finally, a discussion of ethnicity is important. None of the African-American couples explicitly mentioned ethnicity in their narratives or their answers to the question "Marriage is … ?" However, both members of one couple did respond "African American" to a query on the demographic questionnaire that asked "What ethnic or cultural background has had an influence on you (if any)?" None of the European-American couples listed an ethnic or cultural background on the questionnaire. This difference between the African-American participants and the European-American participants is consistent with the results of Martin, Krizek, Nakayama, and Bradford's (1996) study, which found that Whites are less likely to label themselves than are other groups, as Whiteness is viewed as "the norm" (see also Ellison, 1952). These authors conclude that for Whites "labels and interpretation of labels do not emerge in naturally occurring conversations, and do not function in the same way as they do for marginalized groups" (Martin et al., 1996, p. 129).

On the other hand, all of the individuals in biracial relationships noted a cultural influence on their questionnaires. Yet, their narratives did not address this issue other than in an almost tangential way. The only time race was mentioned by these couples was well into their narratives. For example, as Alexander and Kate recalled some of their trips, the following exchange took place:

> Alexander: I'm surprised, because for all these places we've been, like the middle of the "children of the corn" in Pennsylvania, or the middle of Arizona ...
>
> Kate: Oh yeah, that's where our races probably come into play.
>
> Alexander: Yeah, but we never have any trouble.
>
> Kate: No, we haven't, but that's when you kind of, like, think "Uh oh."
>
> Alexander: We think about it in the back of our heads, like "What are we doing here?"

It is interesting that this sparked a reminiscence about a particular trip that was notable not because of a racial incident, but because of bad food in a restaurant. Similarly, the only time Greg and Kathleen (the other biracial couple) mentioned race was a comment embedded in a discussion of her premarital pregnancy. In describing her parent's anger about her situation, Kathleen asserted: "The interracial thing was never ... it was a separate thing [from the pregnancy]. Being Catholic and being pregnant before marriage was the big issue."

Clearly, then, for the couples interviewed in this study, ethnicity may have an influence on their meanings and experiences of marriage, but it may not be a conscious issue to them related to the daily experience of their relationships. Ethnicity might matter, but not in terms of everyday marital life for the relational partners.

CONCLUSION

In conclusion, the results of this study indicate that, although there were some differences in the experiences and meanings of marriage for the African-American and European-American couples, there were also many similarities. Both groups viewed marriage as positive, although African Americans also recognized negative meanings of marriage. The African-American couples tended to view marriage in more spiritual ways than did European Americans, and they were less likely to focus on the companionate aspects of marriage.

Still, African-American and European-American couples' experiences of marriage were similar, with both groups primarily experiencing internal tensions related to issues such as communication style differences, individual needs, and the extended family system. Although the African-American couples in this study tended to talk about their marriage in different ways than did the European-American couples, these differences seem to reflect overarching communication style differences rather than differences in the experience of marriage itself. However, the data reported here are insufficient to support or refute this. This study did not find any strong evidence that marriage among African Americans is experienced more collectively than is marriage for European Americans. In fact, both groups seem to reflect the larger, individualistic U.S. culture. This is consistent with the insights of Bell, Bouie, and Baldwin (1990), who noted that many African Americans have adopted European-American worldviews. There was, however, tentative evidence in this study that perhaps African Americans hold consanguinal views of marriage. This possibility deserves further empirical study.

It is interesting that rather than reflecting one or the other ethnic group, the biracial couples in this study seemed to reflect a unique culture. These couples focused more on their emotional attachments to the partner than did African Americans and European Americans and also focused more on the work associated with marriage. The biracial couples did not seem to experience internal tensions to the same extent as the other couples, however, with the majority of their problems framed as problems external to the relationship. These couples were very interactive and in tune with each others' thoughts, as they frequently continued their partners' narratives. It may be that the biracial couples represent an emerging "subculture" of marriage, one in which the spouses have undergone a cultural transformation (see Kim & Ruben, 1988). In becoming intercultural persons, the biracial couples may have increased their capacity to affirm others and become more behaviorally flexible, as Kim and Ruben (1988) predicted.

Finally, it should be noted that as an in-depth, qualitative endeavor, the results of this study cannot be generalized. Although there certainly were some trends associated with ethnicity among the couples interviewed, the sample size is too small to draw any significant conclusions regarding ethnicity and marriage. Moreover, the demographics of the couples (other than ethnicity) have not been examined. These couples were all fairly young, and only two of the couples had children. Previous research has established that marital interaction is different for parents and nonparents and that interactional patterns change over the life span (see Sillars & Wilmot, 1989). As Oggins et al. (1993) noted, demographic variables need to be considered when assessing the marital experience. Still, the trends found in the study reported in this chapter are consistent with previous research; where the results are not consistent provides room for future research.

ACKNOWLEDGMENTS

I express my gratitude to the eight couples who opened their homes and their personal lives to me during the course of this study. I also thank the students who recruited these couples for me: Melissa Robinson, Vonda Page, Monique Holland, Carol Matthews, Meredith Martino, Annie Blackson, Lilli McNally, and Terry Aisenstein. Finally, I thank Boyd Wareham and Annie Blackson for reviewing my data and providing their insights.

REFERENCES

Abernathy, T. J. (1981). Adolescent cohabitation: A form of courtship or marriage? *Adolescence, 16,* 792–797.

Adelmann, P. K., Chadwick, K., & Baerger, D. R. (1996). Marital quality of Black and white adults over the life course. *Journal of Social and Personal Relationships, 13,* 361–384.

Asante, M. K. (1981). Black male and female relationship: An Afrocentric context. In L. Gary (Ed.), *Black men* (pp. 75–82). Beverly Hills, CA: Sage.

Bell, Y. R., Bouie, C. L., & Baldwin, J. A. (1990). Afrocentric cultural consciousness and African-American male–female relationships. *Journal of Black Studies, 21,* 162–189.

Blumer, H. (1969). *Symbolic interactionism: Perspective and method.* Berkeley: The University of California Press.

Brody, G. H., Stoneman, Z., Flor, D., & McCrary, C. (1994). Religion's role in organizing family relationships: Family process in rural, two-parent African American families. *Journal of Marriage and the Family, 56,* 878–888.

Broman, C. L. (1993). Race differences in marital well-being. *Journal of Marriage and the Family, 55,* 724–732.

Diggs, R. C., & Stafford, L. (1998). Maintaining marital relationships: A comparison between African-American and European-American married couples. In V. J. Duncan (Ed.), *Towards achieving MAAT: Communication patterns in African-American, European-American, and interracial relationships* (pp. 192–202). Dubuque, IA: Kendall Hunt.

Dilworth-Anderson, P., Burton, L. M., & Turner, W. L. (1993). The importance of values in the study of culturally diverse families. *Family Relations, 42,* 238–242.

Ellison, R. (1952). *Invisible man.* New York: Random House.

Gadberry, J. H., & Dodder, R. A. (1993). Educational homogamy in interracial marriages: An update. *Journal of Social Behavior and Personality, 8,* 155–163.

Gaines, S. O., Jr. (1995). Relationships between members of cultural minorities. In J. T. Wood & S. Duck (Eds.), *Understudied relationships: Off the beaten track* (pp. 51–88). Thousand Oaks, CA: Sage.

Glenn, N. D. (1989). Duration of marriage, family composition, and marital happiness. *National Journal of Sociology, 3,* 3–24.

Hecht, M. L., Collier, M. J., & Ribeau, S. A. (1993). *African American communication.* Newbury Park, CA: Sage.

Hecht, M. L., Larkey, L. K., & Johnson, J. N. (1992). African American and European American perceptions of problematic issues in interethnic communication effectiveness. *Human Communication Research, 19,* 209–236.

Herskovits, M. J. (1958). *The myth of the Negro past.* Boston: Beacon.

Hofstede, G. (1980). *Culture's consequences.* Beverly Hills, CA: Sage.

Kim, Y. Y., & Ruben, B. D. (1988). Intercultural transformation: A systems theory. In Y. Y. Kim & W. B. Gudykunst (Eds.), *Theories in intercultural communication* (pp. 299–321). Newbury Park, CA: Sage.

Kochman, T. (1981). *Black and white styles in conflict.* Chicago: The University of Chicago Press.

Kouri, K. M., & Lasswell, M. (1993). Black–white marriages: Social change and intergenerational mobility. *Marriage and Family Review, 19,* 241–255.

Martin, J. N., Krizek, R. L., Nakayama, T. R., & Bradford, L. (1996). Exploring Whiteness: A study of self-labels for White Americans. *Communication Quarterly, 44,* 125–144.

Mindel, C. H., Habenstein, R. W., & Wright, R., Jr. (1988). Family lifestyles of America's ethnic minorities: An introduction. In C. H. Mindel, R. W. Habenstein, & R. Wright, Jr. (Eds.), *Ethnic families in America* (3rd ed., pp. 1–14). New York: Elsevier.

Oggins, J., Veroff, J., & Leber, D. (1993). Perceptions of marital interaction among Black and White newlyweds. *Journal of Personality and Social Psychology, 65,* 494–511.

Orbe, M. P. (1995). African American communication research: Toward a deeper understanding of interethnic communication. *Western Journal of Communication, 59,* 61–78.

Rank, M. R., & Davis, L. E. (1996). Perceived happiness outside of marriage among Black and White spouses. *Family Relations, 45,* 435–441.

Rosenblatt, P. C., Karis, T. A., & Powell, R. D. (1995). *Multiracial couples: Black and White voices.* Thousand Oaks, CA: Sage.

Schuman, H., Steeh, C., & Bobo, L. (1985). *Racial attitudes in America.* Cambridge, MA: Harvard University Press.

Sillars, A. L., & Wilmot, W. W. (1989). Marital communication across the life span. In J. F. Nussbaum (Ed.), *Lifespan communication: Normative processes* (pp. 225–253). Hillsdale, NJ: Lawrence Erlbaum Associates.

Spanier, G. B. (1976). Measuring dyadic adjustment: New scales for assessing the quality of marriage and similar dyads. *Journal of Marriage and the Family, 38,* 15–28.

Staples, R. (1981). Race and marital status: An overview. In H. P. McAdoo (Ed.), *Black families* (pp. 173–175). Beverly Hills, CA: Sage.

Sudarkasa, N. (1981). Interpreting the African heritage in Afro-American family organization. In H. P. McAdoo (Ed.), *Black families* (pp. 37–53). Beverly Hills, CA: Sage.

Timmer, S. G., Veroff, J., & Hatchett, S. (1996). Family ties and marital happiness: The different marital experiences of Black and White newlywed couples. *Journal of Social and Personal Relationships, 13,* 335–359.

Tucker, M. B., & Mitchell-Kernan, C. (1995). Social structural and psychological correlates of interethnic dating. *Journal of Social and Personal Relationships, 12,* 341–362.

U.S. Bureau of Census. (1993). *Marital status and living arrangements.* (Current Population Rep., Series P-20, No. 478). Washington DC: U.S. Government Printing Office.

Veroff, J., Sutherland, L., Chadiha, L. A., & Ortega, R. M. (1993a). Newlyweds tell their stories: A narrative method for assessing marital experiences. *Journal of Social and Personal Relationships, 10,* 437–457.

Veroff, J., Sutherland, L., Chadiha, L. A., & Ortega, R. M. (1993b). Predicting marital quality with narrative assessments of the marriage experience. *Journal of Marriage and the Family, 55,* 326–337.

❧ 8 ❧

Communicating About "Race" in Interracial Families

Mark P. Orbe
Western Michigan University

On Saturday, July 20, 1996, the Multiracial Solidarity March drew thousands of multicultural persons to the Mall in Washington, DC in a display of pride, power, and unity (Marriott, 1996). In part, the march was intended to apply pressure to the federal government for the addition of a multiracial category in the next census. Coverage of this movement received widespread media attention across the nation, including front page coverage in the *New York Times*—the national paper of record (Hu-DeHart, 1996; Marriott, 1996). In the midst of several best-selling novels on multiethnic families (Delany & Delany, 1993; Haizlip, 1994; McBride, 1997) and the emergence of several multiethnic personalities, like Tiger Woods (Leland & Beals, 1997), it appeared that one could not escape discussions regarding race identity, interracial families, and politics.

The objective of this chapter is to examine the ways in which multiethnic families approach their communication about "race," racial identity, racism, and related issues. Specific attention is given to how parents approach their communication regarding such matters. Although presenting insight generally applicable to a variety of multiethnic families, the focus of the chapter is how families that are African American and European American communicate about issues related to "race."

Language choices play a crucial role in the treatment of research on culture, "race," and communication. According to Rosenblatt, Karis, and Powell (1995), "when we look at what has been written about interracial relationships, even things written recently by people who clearly want to support interracial relationships, we often see words that we consider to be prejudiced or stereotyping" (p. 7). Clearly, language choices are important in that they reveal much

167

about one's understanding of issues related to family cultural communication. Originally, the title of this chapter included the term *multiethnic families* instead of *interracial families*. This was done to recognize the importance of ethnic differences and dispute traditional thinking of "race" classifications as logical, scientific, and concrete (see Spickard, 1992). Throughout this chapter, "race" is placed in quotation marks for similar reasons. As this chapter on family communication about "race" began to take form, it became readily apparent that family members use a variety of different terms to describe themselves. In fact, this is one of the core issues of the chapter. My decision to prefer *multiethnic* over *interracial* reveals one particular approach to communicating about "race" (one of several that is discussed). In order to be true to the millions of families whose life experiences this chapter purports to describe (as well as the countless ways in which those life experiences are described), a variety of language is used throughout the chapter. Whenever possible, the language that is used within each approach to communicating about "race" is used when describing that specific approach. In this regard, readers should be made aware that the following terms will be used interchangeably: *Black/African American*, *White/European American*, *interracial/interethnic/multiethnic*, and *biracial/biethnic*. People of color is an inclusive term used to refer to non-Whites.

It is important to acknowledge that this chapter is written from the standpoint of a person who is a product of and participant in a multiethnic family. My father is second-generation Philippino American and my mother is European American (mostly Swiss). My wife has self-identified as African American most of her life but has grandparents who were European American (German) and Native American. Our three children, therefore, are multiethnic (the "official" designation of each of their birth records)—African/Asian/European/Native American. The insight generated herein is the result of reflection on my life experiences as well as countless other interactions with multiracial persons, families, and organizations during the past 30 or more years. Such an experiential/ethnographic approach aligns personal experience as evidence (Foss & Foss, 1994) and is valuable in providing a focus on the experiential in family communication research, not simply the experimental (Houston, 1989; Alexander & LeBlanc, chap. 9, this volume; Davilla, chap. 5, this volume). Much of what is included in this chapter is gleaned directly from my personal experiences and affirmed by the narratives of other multiethnic family members (shared with me personally or included in published accounts, biographies, or reports of scholarly research). Whenever possible, I have attempted to draw from all of these sources in advancing some fundamental ideas related to how multiethnic family members communicate about "race." Furthermore, the chapter is contextualized within a systems theory approach, specifically tapping into Kim and Rubin's (1988) work on intercultural transformation.

INTERRACIAL MARRIAGE AND FAMILY

On June 12, 1967, the U.S. Supreme Court decided the case of *Loving v. State of Virginia* and ruled that laws forbidding interracial marriage were unconstitutional (Brown, 1989–1990). At that time, 32 states had laws forbidding intermarriage between Blacks and Whites (Monahan, 1973). Substantial variation, however, existed on how each state applied its statute to specific groups. For instance, some state laws applied to a variety of interracial marriages between European Americans and African Americans/Asian Americans/Native Americans, whereas others only applied to marriages between Blacks (defined as having ½, ¼, or ⅛ amount of Black blood, depending on the statute) and Whites. Despite the punishment associated with these antimiscegenation laws—that often were drastically more serious for the person of color in the marriage—interracial marriages were not uncommon prior to the Supreme Court ruling.

However, since this landmark decision, the number of interracial marriages has continued to increase in great proportions. The most recent estimates reveal that the number of interracial married couples more than doubled between 1980 and 1995 (El Nasser, 1997). Statistics show that Hispanics and Asian Americans marry outside their race more often than African Americans (for instance, 60% of Japanese who marry in the United States wed someone from another racial group; Shepard, 1997). For the purposes of the focus of this chapter, data from the (1990) U.S. census (as cited in El Nasser, 1997) reveal that 6% of African-American men and 2% of African-American women are married to someone who is racially different. However, it appears that even this number is proportionally low and will show a drastic increase in the next census data. For instance, Holmes (1996) reported that out of all new 1993 marriages involving African Americans, over 12% were with a European-American partner (compared with only 2.6% in 1970).

In terms of existing literature, these statistics reflect a growing number of families whose multiethnic backgrounds make communicating about "race" an insightful point of analysis for those interested in intersections of culture, communication, and family. Whereas other chapters in this volume (e.g., see Dainton, chap 7, this volume; Ferguson, chap. 3, this volume; Daniel & Daniel chap. 2, this volume) focus on the communication of African-American or European-American families this chapter presumes to explore the communicative experiences of families that are both African American and European-American. Of particular interest to the author are the ways in which parents communicate about issues of "race" within their families, especially with their bi/multiracial children. Traditionally, interracial marriages were dissuaded by the ultimate questions of belonging and acceptance, especially regarding the experiences of (innocent) children who were destined to be alienated from/within both Black and White communities. For the first time in history, the number of bi/multiracial babies is increasing faster than the number of monoracial newborns (Root, 1996). How does the presence of such children affect how families communicate about "race?" The core of this chapter provides insight into the ways in which multiethnic families negotiate a unique social, cultural, and political positioning in a society in which racial boundaries are traditionally maintained.

The vast majority of research in the area of interracial relationships has focused on a number of issues related to Black and White couples. For instance, research has offered insight into a historical analysis of interracial marriages (Brown, 1989–1990; Porterfield, 1978; Washington, 1970), the acceptance of interracial marriages (Davidson & Schneider, 1992), comparisons of Black/White couples with other interracial couples (Monahan, 1973), as well as theories and motivations for such relationships (Alridge, 1978; Davidson, 1991–1992; 1992; see also Dainton, chap. 7, this volume).

Although not true for all research, a clear pattern can be seen within this body of literature: Black–White interracial relationships are fundamentally viewed as potentially problematic and pathologically based. Spaights and Dixon's (1984) article is the most vivid example of this line of research; their work focused on the "racially based pathology that allows partners in an interracial romance to view each other as sexual objects" (p. 132). In recent years, a number of scholars, many of whom are products of or participants in interethnic marriages, have treated the topic with greater sensitivity (Funderburg, 1994; Rosenblatt et al., 1995; Spickard, 1989). However, this work is primarily situated in the fields of sociology and psychology and does not readily address the ways in which multiethnic families communicate about issues related to "race" (although see Dainton, chap. 7, this volume).

DESCRIPTIONS OF INTERRACIAL FAMILY COMMUNICATION ABOUT "RACE"

The remainder of the chapter explicates different approaches that interracial families—biological, adoptive, and blended—assume in their communication about "race." Four specific orientations are discussed: (a) embracing the Black experience (i.e., H. Jones, 1996), (b) assuming a commonsense approach (i.e., Harris, 1997), (c) advocating a color blind society (i.e., Shirley, 1994), and (d) affirming the multiethnic experience (i.e., Wardle, 1991; 1996). Although these approaches are offered as general perspectives assumed by interracial families, it is important to note that the ways in which families negotiate their communication is largely informed by various factors, including the gender, age, spirituality, socioeconomic status of the parents, particular family structure, and situational contexts (i.e., geographical region, neighborhood, local community). Although the space limitations of this chapter do not allow for an in-depth treatment of these issues, they clearly represent implications for future research in the area of interracial family communication (see Conclusion).

Embracing the Black Experience

Traditionally, it has been African-American communities that have embraced interracial children as their own. Both European-Americans and African Americans have adopted the once legally, but still socially enforced "one-drop rule" that states that one drop of Black blood makes a person Black. In fact some states, such as Louisiana and North Carolina, literally followed the one-drop concept and defined being Black as having one Black great-great-grandparent (Spickard, 1992). Legal definitions notwithstanding, history demonstrates that children of Black–White heritage identified with and became part of larger African-American communities much more readily than they did European-American ones (Orbe & Strother, 1996). Davis (1991) estimated that two in three African Americans have mixed racial ancestry, much of which is visible in the great diversity of physical features among those of African descent (Morganthau, 1995). In fact, Davis (1991) asserted that "many of the nation's black leaders have been of predominately white ancestry" (p. 6) and cited formidable leaders such as Robert Puvis, W. E. B. Du Bois, Walter White, and A. Philip Randolph as examples.

Following this tradition, many parents of biracial children raise their children as Black with little or no attention to their White ancestry. The rationale behind interracial families embracing the Black experience can be summarized by three ideas. First, parents believe it is important to prepare their children for interactions in a society that will define them as Black regardless of their appearance. H. Jones (1996) simply stated, "My mixed-race children *were* Black—on their own and at their own peril, on the street, in school, in America" (p. 206). Although many interracial couples would prefer otherwise, the larger society still sees their children as Black and in order to assist in their survival/success, having a Black identity is seen as the only option (Rosenblatt et al. 1995).

Second, this approach allows biethnic children to benefit from the strength of African-American communities (Rosenblatt et al., 1995). In this regard, the identity of being Black provides an individual with a "large, identifiable, culturally defined group with which to affiliate" (p. 208). The same historically has not been true for those adopting a bi/multiethnic identity.

Third, interracial families see the Black experience in this country as positive, affirming, and inspiring (e.g., H. Jones, 1996). In this regard, parents seek to expose their families to the many historical and contemporary accomplishments of African Americans in politics, literature, business, education, and the arts. Giving children with African ancestry knowledge that they, in the words of one friend, "derive from African kings and queens" provides them with a strong sense of self that transcends the experiential boundaries of the United States. One White woman's response (H. Jones, 1996) to her daughter's question about the importance of being raised Black and not biracial best captures the essence of this approach: "I was not about to delude you guys into thinking you could be anything different in this country. And, frankly, I didn't think that being anything other than Black would be any more desirable" (p. 208).

The communication of the interracial family that embraces the Black experience revolves around their existence within larger African-American communities (extended family, church, etc.). However, even when interacting within predominately White settings, family members still maintain—and communicate from within—their African-American identities regardless of the White appearance (Scales-Trent, 1995; Williams, 1995). From this perspective, bi/multiethnic persons who seek to affirm their mixed ancestry are seen as attempting to identify with the privilege of the dominant culture and downplay their African heritage (Marriott, 1996). Although this charge may or may not have any validity, to those families who embrace the Black experience, there is no choice. The same could be true for the European-American parent; their direct connection/participation in a Black family positions them as "not quite White." In essence, their intimate relationships with African Americans typically prompt a transformation in the ways in which they are perceived by others and experience racial issues themselves; in this regard they see life "with new eyes" (Kim & Ruben, 1988, p. 308). H. Jones (1996) explained: "This transformation has stayed with me since [I first witnessed how my daughters were treated by others]. If White remains *how I'm seen* [emphasis added], what's changed, what I mean by 'not quite White,' is *how I see* [emphasis added]" (p. 205). According to Kim and Ruben's (1988) work on intercultural transformation, this mother, like some other European-American parents, experienced an "inner alchemy [where] ... intercultural knowledge, attitudes, and behavioral capacities construct[ed] a 'new' person" (p. 314).

Assuming a Commonsense Approach

Whereas the first approach to multiracial family communication about "race" was conditioned by historical conceptualizations of race, the second approach rejects these precepts and takes a more commonsense approach to communicating about issues regarding "race." The one-drop rule is viewed as antiquated; to behave as if one part of one's heritage does not exist based on this principle is seen as ludicrous.

This approach to how interracial families communicate about "race" is grounded in the following principle as articulated by a parent at a recent multicultural support group meeting: "We address issues of 'race' depending on what makes the most sense in that situation." One important consideration for those who adopt this approach is the presence or absence of both parents and the racial composition of their larger environment in which the family system resides. It makes sense, for instance, for children who are raised by their European-American mother in an all-White neighborhood to assume a White identity (see Davilla, chap. 5, this volume). This is especially true for those bi/multiracial persons whose physical identity is perceived by others as European. To raise a child as Black in these circumstances would not be logical, nor necessarily productive to the child's ability to fit in with other children. However, if the circumstances were to change, so might the racial identity of the child. Such is the case of a woman of Mexican and Irish-Catholic descent who explained the influence that her parents' divorce had on how "race" was addressed and experienced.

> Dana explained that her mother, with whom she lived in Florida until she was 13 years old, never really tried to teach her about her heritage ... Although she was aware of her Mexican heritage, her environment encouraged her to present herself as European-American like her school and neighborhood peers ... [This all changed when] she moved to Detroit to live with her Mexican father ... Her father took an active role in educating her about her Mexican culture. As a result, Dana has now come to identity herself as fully Mexican American. (Harris, 1997, p. 152)

For some members of interracial families, a commonsense approach to communicating about "race" can be met with a great deal of suspicion, disbelief, or awkwardness. Scales-Trent (1995) described herself as "a black American with white skin, an African American with both African and European ancestors" (p. 7). Raised as a Black American all her life, she is assumed to be European-American by most who do not know her. Her assertions about her Black racial identity are often times met with varying responses: "No, you're not," "No! You can't be," or "But you don't look black" (p. 73). One time, after being involved in a minor car accident,

> A policeman stopped to help. He took down the story. As he was taking down my name and address, I noticed that he had checked the "white" box. "Officer," I said politely, "you made an error on your form. I am not white. I am black." He gave me a long, bored look, decided not to discuss it, and said, "Sure, lady. If you say so." (p. 74)

Other examples of this are witnessed at the births of bi/multiracial babies. For instance, a friend's baby was categorized as White on birth records (based on his initial appearance), although his mother is African American and his father Latino American. Such a commonsense approach to "race" designations can also become quite argumentative, especially when individuals' communication is grounded in different conceptions of what constitutes sense making. Such was the case when my second daughter was born. Born with blond hair, blue eyes, and a very fair skin tone, she was categorized as Black by the nurse, White by her doctor, and multiethnic by her family. The conflict about what the birth records would show was based on the common sense of nurse ("Her mother is Black so that makes her Black"), doctor ("Just look at her! She's not Black, she's White"), and family ("She is African, European, Asian, and Native American and that's what her birth records should reflect").

Although some commonsense perspectives call for discussing "race" in static terms, others advocate a more fluid approach (Harris, 1997). Depending on circumstances, interracial families' communication regarding "race" changes. Such might be the case when visiting with different sides (Black or White) of the family and different relatives on each side. Or, in some instances, this may occur when some advantage might be gained by identifying with one group rather than the other. Such was the case for one African-American man who wanted to get his daughter into a magnet school. Knowing that the "White spaces fill up quicker," he checked off African American on the form. "Are you going to feel guilty?" he reflects. "No. She is African American" (quoted in Rosenblatt et al., 1995, p. 196). This type of scenario has been repeated to me several times over the years; in many instances it is told by those who want to point out how biracial family members often learn how to "play the game" and "use the system." However, according to those who assume a commonsense approach to the ways in which they communicate about "race," it makes sense to take advantage of such benefits. This is especially true because interracial families often have to face a great deal of discrimination from European Americans who perceive them as "too Black" and African Americans who think they "aren't Black enough." Although not necessarily the norm for all interracial families, such a marginalized societal positioning has direct consequences in the routine decisions of everyday life within a society that maintains racial divisions (i.e., where to live, whom to socialize with, where to attend church, whom to date, etc).

Advocating a Color-Blind Society

The third approach to communicating about "race" advocates a color-blind society, one in which individuals are seen, treated, and embraced as human beings regardless of any cultural differences. Conversations around issues of "race" are situated in the premise that the concept of "race" is illogical, unscientific, and a "man-made tool to divide and conquer others." When asked about the "race" of family members, those with this approach simply reply: "Why human of course!" Children, it is reasoned, are not born with specific ideas about human features such as race, so why should parents teach them?

In some instances, those families whose communication is grounded in this approach draw from their spiritual backgrounds for guidance and strength. Such was the case for Brenda Mahin's daughter. When school officials, prompted by the U.S. Department of Education's Office of Civil Rights, required that her daughter specify her race, she refused. Followers of the Baha'i religious faith, they asserted that "our family believes very strongly in the oneness of mankind [sic]. There is but one race—the human race" ("No Place for Mankind," 1989, p. 17). Although many regard Sunday mornings as the most segregated time in the United States, some multiracial families have found ministries that embrace interracial worship (Williamson, 1995). In fact, many see their participation in such services as consistent with the primary teachings of spirituality. As heard in the testimony of one European-American woman in a recent city-wide [interracial] religious celebration, "God's love is color blind; following his examples allows me to see others with no regard to issues of race."

"Love has no color" is a phrase embraced by thousands who strongly support the process of transracial adoption (e.g., Shirley, 1994). Advocates of this growing trend focus on the idea that European-American parents who can provide "loving, quality homes" to children of African descent are a much better option than leaving the children in foster care. Opponents argue that African Americans are best equipped to raise African-American children who must survive in a racist society. Instead, some multiracial families—including adoptive and biological households—promote the idea of advocating a "transracial family," one that symbolizes their ability to transcend the limiting notion of "race" in their communication within and beyond the family (Shirley, 1994). Rosenblatt et al.'s (1995) work on multiracial couples indicated that most often it is the European-American parent whose place of privilege allows him or her to "not see race" or "want to raise their children colorblind" (p. 197, and see Davilla, chap. 5, this volume). Such was the case in 1995 when I was called upon to speak to a multiracial alliance on the topic of raising bi/multiracial children. Although the participants of the group were quite diverse (various ethnic groups, different ages, and biological, adoptive, and blended families), I was specifically asked to provide insight contrary to the parental strategy used by many in the group to raise their children with no regard to "color." For some in the group—particularly some of the people of color—this option was not realistic in a society that is fixated on issues of "race."

However, the advocates of this approach see otherwise. Although they may acknowledge the historical ramifications of "race," they are determined not to continue promoting "an idea whose time has passed" (phrase borrowed from a popular T-shirt). Instead, they consciously attempt to avoid the use of "race," opting for different descriptors for themselves and others: bi/multiethnic identity, interethnic marriage, or multicultural couples. As one man told me a couple of years ago, "the only time I use 'race' is when I'm talking about cheering someone to the finish line!" Whereas some see this approach to communicating about "race" as idealistic and naïve, others see it as a perspective whose time has come. In the words of one parent "If now isn't the time to start advocating a color-blind society, when is it?"

Affirming the Multiethnic Experience

"Your diverse heritage makes you special" is a common message used by families assuming the fourth approach of communicating about "race." This final perspective focuses on multiethnic families affirming the uniqueness of each of the cultures that they represent. Wardle (1991), the father of four biracial children and director of the Center for the Study of Biracial Children, believed that children "should be raised with the identity of the totality of both birth parents' heritages" (p. 5). In response to this approach, other African Americans (including those with European ancestry who define themselves as Black) may regard this approach as nothing less than cultural disloyalty (Wardle, 1996). However, Wardle (1996; 1991) and others described a key component of this approach as having a commitment to Black history, social consciousness, and cultural affirmation—but not at the expense of denying the presence of other parts on one's cultural heritage.

For many multiracial families, part of this approach toward affirming a multiethnic experience includes allowing children to make their own self-designations about "race" and racial identity. Root's (1996) "Bill of Rights for Racially Mixed People" included a number of value statements that represent this approach. Included in this list are rights to "not justify my existence in this world," "not to keep the races separate within me," "change my identity over my lifetime," and "identify myself differently" than strangers/parents/siblings do (p. 7). Affirming the multiethnic experience also means that family members must learn various communication strategies for instances when others challenge or refute their assertions as bi/multiethnic persons. Communication also involves lessons about prejudice, discrimination and racism (see Daniel & Daniel, chap. 2, this volume; Ferguson, chap. 3, this volume). "Some of the racism that a child must learn to deal with is identical to the racism directed at any black child, but there are also racist words and actions directed specifically at a black–white biracial child" (Rosenblatt et al., 1995, p. 193).

Central to this approach to communicating about "race" is the refutation of dualistic thinking that forces families to choose between being Black or being White. Proponents, such as Harris (1997), contend that "America must identify bi-racial individuals ... [as] neither one nor the other but a combination of the two" (p. 154). Such a perspective forces others to question the existence of traditional thinking about racial classifications/differences. In fact, raising children to recognize their bi/multiracial heritages symbolizes the "epitome of a racist-free society" (Wardle, 1996, p. 197). Tav Nyong, as quoted in Wardle's (1996) work, captures the essence of this idea:

> Interracial people, bi-racial people, non-racial people, whatever we call ourselves, are the wave of the future. Our growing numbers are the inevitable result of racial integration. The stubborn impasse America has reached by polarizing along Black–White lines will eventually be overcome by the increasing numbers of people who refuse to align themselves on either side. We are living arguments that a reconciliation is possible, inescapable reminders that humanity shares a common heritage, as well as a common future. (p. 199)

In 1992, my wife and I were interviewed for an article on interracial relationships on college campuses, and a debate on similar ideas was explored. In the article, well known African-American psychologist Dr. Gwen Goldsberry-Grant contended that interracial dating often ignored issues of race and was comparable to "trying to use band-aids to cure a cancer" (A. Jones, 1992, p. 16). Furthermore, Grant saw multiracial families' attempts to affirm each aspect of their cultural heritages as ineffective in dealing with the larger problem of societal racism. However, the author of the article ended with a thought-provoking idea that captures the power of affirming the multiracial experience: " ... isn't it ironic that the children who are the end-result of relationships that can splinter cultural groups could also be the glue that binds them together?" (A. Jones, 1992, p. 16).

CONCLUSION

Based on its experiential/ethnographic grounding, this chapter is meant to be descriptive rather than theoretical or evaluative. No one approach to how multiracial families communicate about "race" is ideal or necessarily correct; much depends on the particular circumstances and daily life experiences of the specific family. At one point, my wife and I—and the quite large network of extended multiethnic families that we are part of—have approached the issue of "race" and racial/ethnic identity using each of the four perspectives described in this chapter. Clearly, the choice of communication strategies regarding issues of "race" involves a dynamic process by which individuals (and the families) constantly negotiate their past, present, and future course(s) of action. Although the classification scheme of interracial family communication presented here may appear straightforward and clear, the ways in which they are negotiated in the daily lives of families across the United States can be quite complex. In addition to how their approaches to communicating about "race" may change over time, changes or adaptations may occur within or between different settings. It is also possible that different approaches might be taken simultaneously by different persons within the same family (i.e., African-American mother seeks for the family to embrace the Black experience, whereas a European-American father focuses on advocating a colorblind society). Within this context, one can see how the four approaches are complicated by other factors such as family structure (single parent, traditional, blended, or adoptive family), gender/race of particular parents, and situational context (geographical region, neighborhood, local communities).

Given the large increases in families representing diverse cultural backgrounds, research that focuses on the communication of multicultural families appears to be a fruitful source for those scholars and practitioners interested in the intersections of family, communication, and culture. The number of research areas within this genre is countless. However, specific to the descriptions included in this chapter are several directions for future scholarly inquiry. First, additional research can further explore the four approaches of interracial family communication. Do additional approaches exist? Will future research reveal that some approaches are more evident among certain interracial families (based on such factors as age, gender, region, or socioeconomic status)? Can empirical research help support, refute, or extend these approaches? What value do such lines of inquiry possess?

Second, scholars interested in how multiracial families communicate about "race" may explore specific strategies that are used within each approach. Existing communication research on self-disclosure, conflict, and family communication more generally provides a foundation from which to draw. Additional inquiries can explore questions specific to multiracial families. For instance, do African-American and European-American parents have different roles in the identity formation of their child as some suggest (Rosenblatt et al., 1995)?

Finally, research on multiethnic family communication can generate inquiries into the various ways in which monoracial families communicate about "race." Although some existing work suggests that African-American families address the topic more readily than their European-American counterparts (Daniel & Daniel, chap.2, this volume; Hale-Benson, 1986), future research can create a greater awareness of the differences and similarities between various family types (e.g., see Socha & Beigle, chap. 10, this volume). How do other families of color (i.e., Latino or Asian American families) describe their communication about "race?"

The approaches that multiracial families and individuals take in communicating about "race" are linked (albeit consciously or unconsciously) to a distinct social consciousness. In this regard, personal choices are political in nature. The various perspectives that all family units assume when communicating about "race" are insightful in that they represent contemporary societal thought on racial issues. "Ultimately, the intercultural communication experiences of individuals contribute to the evolution of the social systems of which they are a part" (Kim & Ruben, 1988, p. 311). Clearly, from a intercultural transformation perspective the ways in which family units communicate about "race" affect and are affected by societal beliefs and values. This is certainly evident by the events referred to in the opening paragraphs of this chapter. Family communication scholars versed in the complexities of culture are well equipped to explore the intricate linkages between individual expression, family communication, and the larger sociopolitical society.

REFERENCES

Alridge, D. P. (1978). Interracial marriages: Empirical and theoretical considerations. *Journal of Black Studies, 8*, 55– 68.

Brown, P. (1989–1990). Black–White interracial marriages: A historical analysis. *Journal of Intergroup Relations, 26*(3 & 4), 27–36.

Davidson, J. R. (1991–1992). Black–White interracial marriage: A critical look at theories about motivations of the partners. *Journal of Intergroup Relations, 28*(4), 14–20.

Davidson, J. R. (1992). Theories about Black–White interracial marriage: A clinical perspective. *Journal of Multicultural Counseling and Development, 20*, 150–157.

Davidson, J. R., & Schneider, L. J. (1992). Acceptance of Black–White interracial marriage. *Journal of Intergroup Relations, 19*(3), 47–52.

Davis, F. J. (1991). *Who is Black: One nation's definition.* University Park: The Pennsylvania State University Press.

Delany, S., & Delany, A. E. (with A. H. Hearth). (1993). *Having our say: The Delany sisters' first 100 years.* New York: Kodansha International.

El Nasser, H. (1997, May 9). Millions in America claim a varied racial heritage. *The Louisville Courier-Journal,* p. A7.

Foss, K. A., & Foss, S. K. (1994). Personal experience as evidence in feminist scholarship. *Western Journal of Communication, 58,* 39–43.

Funderberg, E. (1994). *Black, white, other: Biracial Americans talk about race and identity.* New York: William Morrow.

Haizlip, S. T. (1994). *The sweeter the juice: A family memoir in black and white.* New York: Simon & Schuster.

Hale-Benson, J. E. (1986). *Black children: Their roots, culture, and learning style.* Baltimore: John Hopkins University Press.

Harris, T. M. (1997). "I know it was the blood": Defining the biracial self. In A. Gonzalez, M. Houston, & V. Chen (Eds.), *Our voices: Essays in culture, ethnicity, and communication* (pp. 149–156). Los Angeles: Roxbury.

Holmes, S. A. (1996, July 5). Study finds number of interracial couples is increasing sharply. *The Louisville Courier-Journal,* p. A4.

Houston, M. (1989). Feminist theory and black women's talk. *Howard Journal of Communication, 1,* 187–194.

Hu-DeHart, E. (1996, August 22). To be (a multiracial statistic) or not to be (that is the question). *Black Issues in Higher Education,* pp. 44–45.

Jones, A. (1992, Summer). What color is love? *Inside/Out, 1*(1), pp. 14–16.

Jones, H. (1996). Children of mixed-race unions should not be raised biracially. In D. Bender & B. Leone (Eds.), *Interracial America: Opposing viewpoints* (pp. 204–209). San Diego, CA: Greenhaven.

Kim, Y. Y., & Ruben, B. D. (1988). Intercultural transformation: A systems theory. In Y. Y. Kim & W. B. Gudykunst (Eds.), *Theories in intercultural communication* (pp. 299–321). Newbury Park, CA: Sage.

Leland, J., & Beals, G. (1997, May 5). In living colors. *Newsweek,* pp. 58–59.

Marriott, M. (1996, July 20). Multiracial Americans ready to claim their own identity. *The New York Times,* pp. 1, 7.

McBride, J. (1997). *The color of water: A black man's tribute to his white mother.* New York: Riverhead Books.

Monahan, T. P. (1973). Marriage across racial lines in Indiana. *Journal of Marriage and the Family, 35,* 632–640.

Morganthau, T. (1995, February 13). What color is Black? *Newsweek,* pp. 63–65.

No place for mankind. (1989, September 4). *Newsweek,* p. 17.

Orbe, M., & Strother, K. (1996). Signifying the tragic mulatto: A semiotic analysis of Alex Haley's *Queen. Howard Journal of Communication, 7*(2), 113–126.

Porterfield, E. (1978). *Black and white mixed marriages.* Chicago: Nelson-Hall.

Root, M. P. (1996). *The multicultural experience: Racial borders as the new frontier.* Thousand Oaks, CA: Sage.

Rosenblatt, P. C., Karis, T. A., & Powell, R. D. (1995). *Multiracial couples: Black and white voices.* Thousand Oaks, CA: Sage.

Scales-Trent, J. (1995). *Notes of a white black woman: Race, color, community.* University Park: The Pennsylvania State University Press.

Shepard, P. (1997, April 3). Possible mixed-race category in U.S. census stirs debate. *The Louisville Courier-Journal,* A7.

Shirley, J. (1994). Do transracial placements work? A personal view. *New People: The Journal for the Human Race, 5*(1), pp. 18–19.

Spaights, E., & Dixon, H. E. (1984). Socio-psychological dynamics in pathological Black–White romantic alliances. *Journal of Instructional Psychology, 11*(3), 133–138.

Spickard, P. R. (1989). *Mixed blood: Intermarriage and ethnic identity in 20th century America.* Madison: University of Wisconsin Press.

Spickard, P. R. (1992). The illogic of American racial categories. In M. P. P. Root (Ed.), *Racially mixed people in America* (pp. 12–23). Newbury Park, CA: Sage.

Wardle, F. (1991). Tomorrow's children. *New People: The Journal for the Human Race, 2*(1), p. 5.

Wardle, F. (1996), Children of mixed-race unions should be raised biracially. In D. Bender & B. Leone (Eds.), *Interracial America: Opposing viewpoints* (pp. 197–203). San Diego, CA: Greenhaven.

Washington, J. R. (1970). *Marriage in Black and White*. Boston: Beacon Press.

Williams, G. H. (1995). *Life on the color line: The true story of a White boy who discovered he was Black*. New York: Dutton.

Williamson, B. (1995). New faith: Is God colorblind? *New People: The Journal for the Human Race, 5*(3), pp. 10–11.

9

Cooking Gumbo— Examining Cultural Dialogue About Family: A Black-White Narrativization of Lived Experience in Southern Louisiana

Bryant K. Alexander
California State University, Los Angeles

H. Paul LeBlanc III
Southern Illinois University at Carbondale

Only recently have family scholars begun to consider the relationship between ethnicity and family functioning (e.g., see Galvin & Brommel, 1996). As McGoldrick (1993) suggested, ethnic values and identification with a cultural group are transmitted through communication in everyday family life. In this volume, Socha and Diggs (chap. 1) contend that family communication plays a foundational role in the formation and maintenance of societal ethnic culture and the management of ethnic cultural relations. Thus, there exists a symbiosis between family life and membership in a culture.

The symbiosis suggests a distinction between families and their communication along ethnic lines. Some chapters in this volume demonstrate the variations in family relationship maintenance and negotiation associated with cultural differences (e.g., see Dainton, chap. 7, this volume; Davilla, chap. 5, this volume). These distinctions can assist us in understanding the differences and help us to manage the distances between cultural and ethnic groups. However, understanding the commonalties that make us human in our experience of familial life is equally important and can positively influence our interactions with each other (e.g., see Dainton, chap. 7, this volume). According to Kim and Ruben (1988), a transformation occurs within individuals through their intercultural interactions and allows them to understand such commonalities. In this vein, we see a particular need to contribute scholarship that blurs the demarcation between Black and White family communication.

The purpose of our chapter is to examine the transformation of racial and ethnic difference into shared cultural truths, or the assumptions about family that are deemed "to be true" based on experience and tradition. Capitalizing on our common geographical and cultural background as males "born and reared" in southern Louisiana, we ground our research and theorizing in lived experience. Specifically, the depth and scope of our interest is reflected in the following four chapter goals: (a) describe the cultural history of White Acadian culture and Black culture in southern Louisiana, which moves us toward the development of a joint definition of family in the region; (b) demonstrate commonality in cultural experiences centered in the dissemination of family cultural values; (c) examine how the common cultural mix of southern Louisiana is demonstrated within family through family rituals, myths, and storytelling; and (d) develop a recipe for examining cultural family dialogue.

The clarion call for increased multiculturalism and intercultural communication resonates throughout the communication discipline and permeates both public and private sectors (see Infante, Rancer, & Womack, 1993). In response to this call, we—bluntly described as a Black man and a White man—join together in an intercultural dialogue to chart cultural evolutions, practices, and beliefs of our shared cultural upbringing in southern Louisiana. We use a method that is historical yet is grounded in autobiographical and ethnographic narratives of both ourselves and representative others. We do not deny difference as a racial and ethnic determinant, but we rearticulate the nature of difference that casts Blacks or Whites as "other." The chapter speaks to and about commonalties that cross racial lines to blend into the cultural milieu of the region.

The chapter is grounded in the emerging cultural theory that maintains that races interact such that the resultant combination produces a political and cultural terrain that is unique to a specified cultural region (see Hecht, Collier, & Ribeau, 1993; Orbe, chap. 8, this volume). Also, the chapter is grounded in the metaphor of "gumbo," a hot, spicy, dark, soup-stew mixture of southern Louisiana. The historical origin of gumbo is found in the mixed cultural offering of Africans, Acadians, and Native Americans in Louisiana (Brasseaux, 1987). The sharing of recipes and of the meal, practices not unique to southern Louisiana, are central or core to the experience of family for the people of this region. The mixture of ingredients, the food, and the culture itself offers a unique cultural flavor of family indicative of the region and its people.

Although we emphasize cultural similarities, we contend that the need to validate individual cultural values is the hallmark of establishing social significance. Acknowledging uniqueness and articulating significance is not equated with difference, the process of "otherizing," or perpetuating the binary oppositions of Black and White. Rather, the process of establishing social significance is embedded in the ideal of identifying relationship to others within the social environment and of discovering the recipe for engaging in a cultural dialogue. It is through the examination of the commonalties of the cross-cultural experience of family that a recipe for examining cultural dialogue can evolve.

CULTURAL COOKBOOKS

Defining Culture

A *culture* is a way of life, a series of recipes, for a group of people and includes shared values, customs, rituals, and beliefs, similar to what might be found in ordinary cookbooks (Cohen & Eames, 1982; Ember & Ember, 1993). The group of people that comprise a culture can be identified by observing participation in shared activities such as cooking meals. Families are small groups that share activities that can be unique or idiosyncratic to the members of the family (each family reinterprets recipes). Indeed, Wood (1995) argued that families assign meaning to shared events, rituals, activities, and interactions that comprise family life.

Wood (1982) proposed that a relational culture exists when persons create and sustain personal relationships. Many family communication scholars assume that families create and maintain their own unique family minicultures (Socha, in press; Whitchurch & Dickson, 1999). However, families are situated within larger cultural contexts by the membership they share in other groups such as ethnic and religious groups (see Putnam & Stohl, 1990, for a discussion of bona fide groups that emphasize this point). Particular regions of the country also share common languages and dialects that help characterize a cultural grouping. Louisiana is such a region. The next section describes some general cultural features of southern Louisiana as a backdrop for the study.

Early Cultural "Cookbooks" of Southern Louisiana

Louisiana has a unique cultural history. As with other regions of the United States, it was peopled by Native American tribes before the first European settlers arrived. Also, as with many other states, particularly in the South, Africans were forcibly settled there by the slave trade. However, unlike many other regions of the United States, Louisiana was settled first by Europeans of French and Spanish descent. In particular, Acadians (i.e., French people who originally settled in Acadia, now known as Nova Scotia, Canada) settled along the Mississippi corridor beginning in the 1750s (Rushton, 1990).

The Louisiana settlement of Acadians differed from the settlement of other people of European descent in the New World in a significant way: it occurred as a result of forced deportation, called the "dispersion" or "le Grand Dérangement," from a region in the New World. For more than 100 years, the Acadians developed their own culture and sense of community in the new world, but were deported following the onset of the French and Indian War, also known as the Seven Years War (Rushton, 1990). Historians (e.g., Brasseaux, 1987; Dormon, 1983; Rushton, 1990) refer to this as the "dispersion" because of the British intent to disperse the Acadian culture and thus neutralize any threat against their colonialists' claims in the New World. The dispersion took the form of breaking up families and extended families and shipping them in different directions. Many Acadians were imprisoned, kidnapped, or sold into indentured servitude or slavery (Rushton, 1990). As a result, only a portion of Acadians made their way to Louisiana for final settlement after the 8- to 10-year period of the dispersion (see Daigle, 1984; Dormon, 1983).

The dispersion of the Acadians shares a particular similarity with the American slave trade of Africans: the methodical removal and re-collection of oppressed people. In the same region, freed displaced slaves also sought to create a life in a geographical and political climate that forced a large scale acculturation of new traditions and ways of living. Both groups experienced the diaspora: settlement in a region far from their ancestral homeland.

When the Acadians and newly freed African slaves settled in Louisiana, they developed, separately, very tight-knit communities (Dormon, 1983). This was in part because of their previous cultural practice of maintaining extended families within the same village, often on the same plot of land, and their common experience with the dispersion of their culture (see Dormon, 1983; Owens, 1981). Between 1760 and the early 1900s, the Acadians and African Americans of southern Louisiana tended toward group isolation and endogamy (Dormon, 1983). Both groups developed identity by strong kinship-dominated social grouping. According to Dormon (1983), characteristics ascribed to Acadians, and likewise to Blacks (by persons outside of the culture) included: (a) material poverty, (b) lack of ambition or enterprise, (c) lack of a desire to adopt the values of the Anglo-American majority, and (d) ignorance, illiteracy, and lack of any inclination toward acquiring formal education. These ascribed qualities coincided with the development of the pejorative meaning of the term *coonass* (see Brasseaux, 1987) and the extenuating and equally pejorative term *nigger.*

Although Acadians and African Americans tended toward isolation, which was both self and other imposed, they did assimilate. For example, vocabulary, language, and cuisine were utilized from Native Americans, Spanish Creoles, and from each other (Ancelet, Edwards, & Pitre, 1991; Brasseaux, 1987). For example, gumbo is a type of okra stew associated with Acadian culture. The term *gumbo* has its origins in the Bantu (African) language and means okra (Daigle, 1984). Gumbo is often prepared with filé, a spice made from ground sassafras leaves, which was introduced by the native Houma tribe (Daigle, 1984). Many persons of southern Louisiana, not of direct Acadian descent, also assimilated characteristics of the Acadian culture. The primary example of this is the Cajun language, spoken by many people in southern Louisiana, including Native Americans, freed slaves, and Spanish Creoles.

The purpose of this description of the culture of southern Louisiana is two-fold. First, family and relational culture is situated within a larger culture. Families learn about what it means to be a family both within the family through interactions, shared rituals, meanings and outside the family through contact with the larger community. Second, this brief overview of southern Louisiana culture demonstrates the commonalties of experience for persons of different ethnic groups, including the authors, who grew up there; in particular, the experience of "otherness," or unity in opposition to the dominant mainstream shared culture. In the next section, we describe the method used to access narratives of lived experiences of family within this cultural backdrop.

THE RECIPE: METHODOLOGICAL APPROACH

This study braids two methodological procedures: ethnography and autoethnography. The combined approach features the expressed ideas, feelings, and experiences of members of Black families and White families, which include the authors, in southern Louisiana. First, ethnography employs participant-observation and interviews to narrate the lived expressions of the participants and the observer. Second, autoethnography combines the process of ethnography with the self-reflection of autobiography to explore lived experience within a specified context such as family. Next, we offer a more detailed description of how these approaches were followed in this study.

Ethnography and the Ethnographic Interview

Ethnography is both a process and a product of describing culture. It is grounded in a phenomenological perspective that holds phenomena are socially constructed through individual or collective definition of the situation (Taylor & Bogdan, 1984). Spradley (1979) argued that "[the] essential core of this activity aims to understand another way of life from the native point of view" (p. iii). It is a process in which the observer/researcher attempts to engage "participant observation as a strategy for both listening to people and watching them in natural settings" (p. 32). Spradley suggested three ways to initiate or discover questions in the ethnographic interview: (a) record the questions that naturally emerge within the cultural community about the specified phenomenon, (b) inquire directly about questions used by participants in a cultural scene, and (c) pose descriptive questions that ask informants to talk about particular cultural scenes. Spradley also advocated the descriptive questioning approach, which is "less likely to reflect the ethnographer's culture" or research agenda (p. 85).

Within this study, we used descriptive questions that asked informants to talk about particular cultural scenes. The interview protocol was applied consistently throughout the interviews. The protocol was structured around four primary questions: (a) What does family mean to you? (b) What are some of the family stories (myths, rituals) that your family tells (or engages)? (c) What are your family values? and (d) How do you feel (think) about family values in your larger community? A series of follow-up questions were included in the formal protocol as a means of clarifying the primary intent of the question or to probe for further elaboration.

Ten informants were interviewed, five Black and five White. Each informant was chosen according to the following criteria: (a) adults engaged in creating their own family, and (b) adults who are a primary family storyteller or serve as family historian. The sample included one member of each author's family of origin, one member of each author's extended family, and two nonfamily individuals acquainted with an author. Each interview was conducted at the informant's home or by telephone and took 45 to 90 minutes. The interviews were recorded on tape and the manifest content was transcribed. The authors individually analyzed the transcripts utilizing phenomenological explication (see van Manen, 1990), then compared results to determine common themes among all interviewees.

Ethnographic data analysis involves three distinct phases: (a) discovery, which refers to identifying themes; (b) coding, which refers to a system of categorizing the data; and (c) understanding the data or coming to understand the meaningfulness of the data as collected in a specified manner. During the analysis, the researcher looks for connections and/or relationships between spoken utterances that "remain tacit, outside of their awareness" and aspects of cultural relationships that are being signaled (Spradely, 1979, p. 93). In this study, the shared cultural and racial membership between the interviewee and the interviewer allowed for an understanding that emerged within the broader interaction that gave a fuller meaning to the specified language.

This study concentrated on the discovery phase of data analysis by identifying specific emerging cultural themes concerning race and family. Spradely (1979) defined a cultural theme as "any cognitive principle, tacit to explicit, recurrent in a number of domains and serving as a relationship among subsystems of cultural meanings" (p. 186). Ultimately, he suggests that culture and every cultural scene is more than a jumble of parts. It consists of a system of meaning that is integrated into some kind of larger pattern. For our purposes, theme analysis seemed a most appropriate method, given our research goal of uncovering and comparing cultural themes of Black and White families. We transcribed our interviews and read them carefully with the goal of identifying cultural themes or recurrent referents that linked (tacitly or explicitly) issues of "family" and "cultural truths." Such a method maximizes ecological validity, but does raise reliability issues. A team approach helped to manage these concerns.

Narrative

The "personal narrative has been used at the intersection of private and public spheres where the telling of a personal experience is part of a social process of coping" (Langellier, 1989, p. 260). The ethnographic interview taps into the notion of personal narrative by allowing participants to articulate lived experience. Before telling our own stories, we review past work on narration, and then examine the varying uses of story.

Fisher (1984) argued for using narration as the paradigmatic frame in which to view the nature of human beings. He offers a metaphor to describe the root nature of human beings: *homo narans*. This metaphor is designed to subsume other human metaphors: *homo faber, homo economous, homo politicus, homo sociologicus, psychological man, ecclesiastical man,* and *homo sapiens.* In subsuming all other metaphors, it views humankind as narrators who use stories to "assume, account and recount" for the past, the present, and the future. According to Fisher, we "tell stories to ourselves and to each other to establish a meaningful life-world" (p. 6).

In Fisher's (1984) paradigm, there are five basic assumptions:

(a) humans are essentially story tellers; (b) the paradigmatic mode of human decision-making and communication is 'good reasons' which vary in form among communication situations, genres, and media; (c) the production and practice of good reasons is ruled by matters of history, biography, culture, and character; (d) rationality is determined by the nature of persons as narrative beings—their inherent awareness of narrative probability; and (e) the world is a set of stories that must be chosen among to live the good life in a process of continual recreation. (p. 8)

Underlying these assumptions is an ontological view that includes narration and the process of telling stories as a primary means of offering varying ways of being or options for living.

The idea of human beings as storytellers indicates the generic form of all symbol composition, it holds that symbols are created and communicated ultimately as stories meant to give order to human experiences and to induce to others to dwell in them to establish ways of living in common, in communities in which there is sanction for the story that constitutes one's life. One's life is, as suggested by Burke, a story that participates in the stories of those who have lived, who live now, and who will live in the future. (Fisher, 1984, p. 7)

Fisher suggests we live life through story and by story. Storytelling then becomes agency; how we become and how we maintain.

Storytelling as a method to maintain and or build cultural communities is not new. For example, Kirkwood (1983) analyzed the use of parables within the Jewish community. He stated that rhetoric has long been seen as "a human potentiality to understand the human condition. Parables, especially those designed to move listeners to acts of self-confrontation, are exemplars of this function" (p. 58). Garner (1983) also analyzed the "folkloric speech event popularly known in the Black community as 'playing the dozens.'" According to Garner (1983), "The game is an important rhetorical device which promotes community stability and cooperation by regulating social and personal conflict. This expressive game influences, controls, guides or directs human actions in ways consistent with community norms" (p. 47).

Finally, Labov and Waletsky (1967) examined personal narratives as a part of research on Black English Vernacular and to explain reading failure in inner-city school children. They recorded and observed children and adolescents telling personal narratives in response to specified "Danger of Death" questions, such as, "Were you ever in a situation where you thought you were in serious danger of getting killed?" (see also Labov, 1972).

The term *narrative* suggests that a referential and evaluative function exists in which the story is presented in a sequential order, present to past, in the order it happened from the point of view of the narrator who experienced the story (Langellier, 1989). Yet, assumptions about narrative primarily focus on the relation among clauses and sequences of story elements and do not comment on the context from which the story emerges or on the specific content and audience of the story. Thus "the primary purpose in telling personal narrative is self-presentation" (p. 248).

Within this study, we proposed that when races interact within a specified geographical region, the result is the formulation of cultural ideals that resonant within the common lived experiences of both groups. The study is specified within the cultural mix of Blacks and Whites in southern Louisiana. We proposed that, through storytelling and family rituals, they share and refer to common values and ideals that result from both the commonality of the shared cultural community and the inevitable resistance that is integral to any community. The study does not seek to reduce difference but to focus on commonality.

This study was grounded in a number of theoretical perspectives previously stated. It was also grounded in the shifting borders and boundaries of cultural studies. Grossberg (1994) outlined four approaches to locating and defining the project of cultural studies.

> [T]he main lesson of cultural studies is that in order to understand ourselves, the discourse of the Other—of all the others—is that which we most urgently need to know. Second, for cultural studies, the very nature of the relation between culture and power depends upon the particular context site into which it is attempting to intervene. Third, the very concept of culture itself is contextual or at least polysemic. It is caught between social formations, everyday life, and representational practices. Fourth, in cultural studies, the practice (or text) itself and its effects are also contextual. (p. 67)

Autoethnography

According to Lionnet (1989), autoethnography is a method of "defining of one's subjective ethnicity as mediated through language, history, and ethnographical analysis; in short ... a kind of 'figural anthropology' of the self" (p. 99). The method is an explication of lived experiences and encounters within a specified cultural context and combines self-reflection of autobiography and the intense scrutiny of "other" as found in ethnography. We used this method as a means of positioning ourselves both as researchers and members of the cultural groups we studied. Autoethnography positions us in our own study, in a role that Hooks (1990) labeled "indigenous ethnographer," or one "who enters culture where they resemble the people they are studying and writing about" (p. 126). This includes, for example, Black writers writing and theorizing about the Black experience. The authors' individual autoethnographic narratives were constructed before the interviews were conducted in order to reflect on how their articulated lived experiences compared to the themes that emerged in the data analysis.

This project braids the methods of ethnography and autoethnography, and deliberately rejects a linear ethnographic process that may objectify if not deny our lived experience. It is our intent to join our voices with our participants in what Conquergood (1985) called a "dialogic performance" in which "different voices, world views, value systems, and belief ... can have a conversation with one another" (p. 9). We seek to mark those points of intersection and divergence between what Lionnet calls the "individual (auto-) and the collective (ethno-) where the writing (-graphy) of singularity [can and] cannot be foreclosed" (p. 108). Consequently, this project is dialogic in its intent "bring[ing] self and other together so that they can question, debate, and challenge one another" (p. 9).

In the next section we use aspects of our articulated lived experiences as a Black man and as a White man who both grew up in southern Louisiana. Within our narratives and the following analysis of data, we seek to demonstrate how an understanding of race, culture, and family values are disseminated through narratives. The narratives also display how the notion of family is also an oppositional term that is defined in relationship to other or how we come to know self by comparing ourselves to experiences with others. The family narratives of each of the authors were constructed prior to interviewing coparticipants as points of entry into the research project. Following transcription of the interviews, the narratives were consulted as part of the data analysis.

PREPARATION:
LIVED EXPERIENCES OF BEING BLACK AND WHITE
IN SOUTHERN LOUISIANA

Bryant Alexander (Black Male): Lafayette, Louisiana

I am the fifth child of seven children and the fourth boy of five boys in my family. In many ways, my experience growing up as a Black man has been highly influenced by my parents and their culturally imbued methods of raising their children and rearing a family. As I reflect on my growing up and issues related to the notion of family and family values, I find that those memories are intricately inter-woven within narratives: strategically crafted stories, lived experiences, and artic-ulated and directed recollections. These stories were told with the intent and purpose to inform, to persuade, to educate, and to acculturate. They were meant to harden the body, soften the heart, and expand the soul. The stories that my parents told were rich in the cultural milieu of the South and were steeped in their lived experience as Black people. Their stories constructed the image of the Black family as (necessarily) the primary source of nurturance, support, information, and education for Black children. My Black family was the center of sociocultural training for both the public and private spheres, within the presence of others (Whites) and within the company of the extended Black community.

Like craftspersons, artisans, and master storytellers, they would extrapolate lived experiences, shaping and applying them to a given situation—a parenting moment was in essence a teachable moment. Their stories were thematically linked, yet distinctly based on gender (who told the story), the specified behav-ior (what the story was about), or the responsibility they were redirecting (why they were telling the story). The stories translated into hard and fast rules, defi-nitions of family, and the mandatory relational dynamics that were going to ex-ist within our household. They were rules for living inside and rules for behaving outside of the household, survival skills, and public behaviors—all of which were extensions and reflections of the family. My parents both had separate sto-ries that reflected their parental role.

My mother's stories (with mother as the primary caregiver and nurturer) pri-marily marked her lived experience. She was the eldest of two children (daugh-ters) born to a sharecropper and a domestic laborer in Lafayette, Louisiana in the late 1930s. Bilingual from an early age in order to speak to her French-speaking parents, their peers, and associates, she told stories both in English and French of their economic poverty.

Yet, the riches present in her love and respect for her parents, her sister, and their close-knit family unit far outweighed any hardships. Her family was a haven away from mistrust and fear; a place where Black human dignity was celebrated. Her desire to have a large family stemmed from her loneliness as a child, being 15 years older than her only sister. Later, mother married and had seven children: the first five within close succession to each other followed by a 5-year gap between the fifth and sixth and a 3-year gap between the sixth and seventh children. With her strong Catholic upbringing, she instilled in us the necessity to value, respect, love and support our brothers and sisters—no matter what. Our biggest sin as children, and consequently my mother's biggest heartbreak, was to see us fighting or arguing among ourselves. Those were the moments—beyond lying, stealing and other mischief—that were deemed cardinal sins against family. For my mother, family meant "unity, (emotional) support, respect and love for each other and God." She would often say, "When Ma'me and Da'de are gone, all you will have is your brothers and sisters. All you will have is family."

My father's stories were (primarily) stories of cultural negotiation. He often told us stories of what it meant to be Black men. Born in the early 1930s to a father who worked for the Southern Pacific Railroad laying tracks throughout the South (consequently, spending little time at home), and a mother who worked as a domestic, my father was the youngest of three children. He had an older sister and brother. His stories spoke of marginalized citizenship, of "back doors," of "side paths," and of limited opportunities. As a Black with no education trying to raise a family in the 1950s, he spoke of having to compromise his dignity in working odd jobs and providing public services as he sacrificed for his family. For my father, "family" meant "sacrifice, (financial) support, commitment and dedication." His primary role as a father was to provide for his family, discipline his children—teaching them the difference between right and wrong and how to stand up for themselves, and helping them to learn from his mistakes and triumphs. In the end, I think my father—more so than my mother—sought public and social validation of having a good family, one based on the disposition, character and success of his children. It took me many years to realize his logic: that the notion of family is not exclusively a private concept or endeavor—it is a private project enacted in the public space of the community. It is a project that is evaluated and assessed based on products produced and decorum maintained; it both accommodates and expands the social sphere.

Both of my parents used their lived experiences as a foundation to build models for their own families. Yet, in spite of the variations of their approaches, my parents did share common stories. These were the stories that focused on racial differences between Blacks and Whites, particularly in terms of access and privilege. These were the stories of oppression and the subjugation of Blacks to Whites. These were the stories that marked difference. My mother told stories of when she worked as a maid and how she was treated inhumanely. My father spoke of having to sublimate his own pride under Jim Crow laws that denied him access to public services and denied him rights that should have been granted any man. My parents told stories of the assumed rights of Whites, but these stories were told not necessarily to reify the problematic relational dynamics between Blacks and Whites, but as a means of not forgetting.

These stories were always told in a context of learning. They were often prefaced with phrases like "Everything changes, but some things never change," or "You have more opportunities than we had, but don't allow that to cloud your judgment." Their stories were lessons about the other; to offer respect and kindness, but not at the sacrifice of your own humanity. Their stories were warnings about difference, class, and privilege. They emphasized education as a means of gaining access, religion for spiritual guidance, and the black community as a source of support.

My parents' definition of family went beyond typical definitions such as "a fundamental social group" or a "group of persons sharing a common ancestry," to a community of people linked biologically, socially, and culturally. A *family* is a group of people who influence each other in ways that seek to nurture each individual and with an eye on the collective whole. It is an aggregate of social and cultural influences that shapes worldviews, and cultural and intercultural perceptions. It is an enclave of shared experiences, narratives, and stories that are told with the intent to extend and capitalize on individual experience. It is a generational proliferation of lived experience that is critical without being reductive and additive without being suppressive. That is, my family has always been the source of my greatest joys and of my greatest pains. It is within that unit that the seeds of my past were sewn. All of my joys and pains, failures and success, hopes and desires return to this place for acknowledgment and affirmation.

My mother and father continue to parent their adult children, but it is within their role as grandparents that the proliferation of family values becomes most evident. The evidence is clear when my younger brother says to his 18-month-old twin children, born of a White woman, "Nicholas, don't pick at your sister. When Mama and Daddy are gone ... all you will have is each other. All you will have is family." My mother smiles as she listens to this in the background and nods her head.

Paul LeBlanc (White Male): Baton Rouge, Louisiana

I am the fifth child of seven children, the first boy following four girls. I remember most the shared activities of my family. For example, we often went on trips together as a regular Sunday activity. The family would pile into the car and take a Sunday drive. Sometimes as we drove around we would sing songs.

We went to church together and also participated as a family in church-related family retreats. My parents were often involved in (Catholic) church-related activities such as Marriage Encounter. Many of those activities were couple related, but my parents would involve us children in their couple activities by telling us about what they did in Marriage Encounter. They made many friends through their activities who also became friends of the family. Those families had children who became our friends as well.

We also shared meals together. At supper-time, family members told about their day's events. Storytelling in my family, until the time I was an adult, most often was about current events. As children, my parents told us very little about their childhood. What we gained in knowledge about their childhood primarily occurred as a result of extended family get-togethers. Often we would visit our cousins or grandparents and have family reunions. I remember my mother's side of the family having two extended family reunions in the past 30 years. However, on my father's side, the extended family met once a year. Those family reunions entailed all descendants of my great-grandfather. At those family reunions, we would often hear stories about our ancestors.

I began hearing stories about my parents' childhood when I was an adult. The first major storytelling event followed my maternal grandmother's funeral. Our family went to my mother's sister's house. My aunt and uncle, who were both older than my mother, began to tell family secrets about their growing up. It was there that I first became aware of my maternal grandmother's life and, consequently, my mother's childhood. It became evident during that event that my mother's childhood was very painful and, perhaps, she had tried to forget it by not talking about it. Or, perhaps, she did not know or understand what occurred because she was too young when many of these events took place.

It was after my grandmother's funeral that we began to hear more stories about our parents' childhoods. The details came in small doses, but they nevertheless were cherished because they helped us understand more about who we were as a family and helped me understand who I was as an individual. Storytelling became a family ritual: the taboo of talking about the past had been broken. Over the past several years, storytelling has become a regular event when my family of origin gets together for holidays or when we converse with each other interpersonally.

Following my mother's funeral a few years ago, significant events that occurred in my mother's childhood came to light through stories she had shared with my father and through a journal that she kept. The stories about my mother were a source of catharsis during our time of grieving. The storytelling did not end after the event of the funeral but continues as we self-reflect. Still, the introduction of family storytelling only recently in my family's lived experience required the unveiling of long-held family secrets.

Through my observation, as a participant in my own family and as an individual seeking to understand both personally and academically these family processes, I hypothesize that family secrecy occurs because of (a) an inability to cope with traumatic experiences, (b) a desire to avoid pain or talk that might elicit pain, (c) a desire to maintain the status quo in familial relationships, thus gaining a "false" sense of stability, or (d) a fear of destroying trust. However, in the long run, family secrecy has a negative effect on intimacy and trust. Secrecy affects intimacy by disallowing the telling of stories that contribute to understanding. Secrecy affects trust by disallowing communicating the fear of loss.

My family's storytelling served the purpose of creating a sense of identity. For example, my father has engaged in genealogical research; a project to trace the LeBlanc family tree has expanded to include both maternal and paternal ancestors. My father has engaged in the process of telling the family history. This learning and telling of history has become an important aspect of developing identity.

For myself, I have found this gaining of awareness about my heritage important for understanding the values that I hold and the source of those values. Often times my father and I have discussed how not knowing our history has affected us. Talking about our Acadian heritage, in particular, was something that had been avoided in immediate and extended family get-togethers and family reunions. I understood this to be a result of some embarrassment that my father's family had about their heritage because of the negative connotations associated with being of "French" descent, such as being uneducated. As I was growing up, being a "coonass" was not something of which to be proud. There seemed to be a concerted effort to look only to the future and to progress. However, that attitude seemed to be imposed from outside of ourselves.

With that concern about our heritage came the value for respectfulness toward others. Demeaning or pejorative terms were not allowed in our family. When others came into our home, they were to be treated as guests. There was no talk of differences, perhaps hiding shame of our ancestry, our past, or our unwitting and unintended participation in a culture of oppression. We learned the importance of justice and compassion within the rubric of secrecy.

Like the secrecy of my parent's childhood, our ancestry and heritage only became important to us later in our family's life. The ritual of storytelling of our current events, our past, and our heritage became an important binding force for our family. As our heritage was not an issue discussed, neither was the differences between ourselves and others. Our family's process ignored differences in order to overlook our own, particularly during a time of civil and racial unrest. To exemplify this, the stories of my family and those of my coauthor have been included. In the next section, we describe and analyze interviews of family members and friends of our families living in southern Louisiana.

SERVING IT UP: EXPANDING THE CIRCLE OF REGIONAL FAMILY STORIES

We conducted interviews with our own respective Black and White families and friends in southern Louisiana. In particular, each author interviewed one parent, an aunt, an uncle or grandparent, and two friends of the author's family. The data were gathered in response to four main questions. Using narrative analysis, outlined earlier in this chapter, responses were analyzed inductively to identify themes that were common across the interviews. Many themes that emerged throughout the interviews are intermingled. For example, defining "family" was intricately interrelated with "family values." For purposes of clarity, however, we use the four main questions to structure our data analysis.

What Does Family Mean to You?

For both Black and White families, primary themes of support, love, comfort, connection, and direction emerged. The respondents described "family" as a place, sometimes spatially designated like southern Louisiana, but most often as a reservoir of heart-filled emotions and lived experiences. These experiences are shared by a group of individuals who offer comfort and guidance to each other. For example, a White male respondent noted:

A family is supportive of each individual allowing them space to discover their direction, supporting them in it as they find it, and to point out or to save them from some of the errors that they make, some of the misinterpretations of life as it is for them. It's a place where you can feel comfortable and secure where you know that you're loved regardless of the negative things that may be part of your being; [and] don't always bring condemnation down. It's a place where memories can be built. Family represents a place where you can go and be yourself and loved in spite of yourself. It is a place where values can be learned.

For these individuals (both Black and White) the notion of family is not only relegated to those who share a biological link, but it is a heartfelt and socially imbued experience of connection and respect. For instance, a Black respondent noted that her sense of family extended not only to her biological family but also to her sorority.

A family is a group of people with the same interests and love for one another, [and] a relationship with one another. That family can be the ones living in a house, [and] support of people out in the community, like my sorority. When I was on campus, my sorority was my family. Anything that I could do to help them I would do, and vice versa. I would think that would be a family. [A family is] the group of people living, or not only living together but associated, who love and have affection for one another: The relationship of love and understanding, and giving and taking.

Collectively, the responses describe "family" as including reciprocity of respect between people who share common links—whether through a biological connection, a social organization and affiliation, or a broader based cultural affiliation. The reference to the sorority alludes to a racial and cultural link of "sisterhood" because the sorority is a service-based organization comprised of Black women and is developed and maintained through social support and respect.

The sorority (and fraternities) becomes a surrogate or extended family where social support, love, and connectedness are built-in components to the social structure. Yet, within this structure another Black (male) respondent suggested that dependency and interdependency seem to be different familial characteristics. He suggested:

In some families, you don't have to depend on others. It is an understood thing. It is family, and we love our family. In some families there is a need. You have to depend on each other. It all boils down to loving; having this deep relationship. It is just different. It is beautiful.

In his response, dependency refers not only to the necessity to rely on others to fulfill your needs, but also and more important to an indescribable place of feeling comfort, where one does not weigh thoughts or measure words. In this sense, the family is constructed based on the notion of interdependency. In general, *interdependency* means "that change in one part of the [family] system affects all the other parts of the system, but no one part controls or determines an other" (Stewart & Logan, 1993, p. 46).

This respondent echoes the notion of other Black and White respondents who suggested that the interactions and relational dynamics within family systems (within their lived experiences) are based less in a contractual agreement of membership and fidelity as much as they are based in a reciprocal responsibility to self and other. A Black female respondent articulated this notion as a basic family value as well as a commentary on the larger cultural community.

> Maybe there was [or should be] a course in high school where the teacher [like parents] would say, "Whatever decision you make, think about how it affects the entire system." I think that was strived for in my day when you had to make decisions. You wouldn't just think of yourself. For example, the girl when she had to make the decision of whether or not to have sexual relations with a guy, she wouldn't just think about herself. She would have to think about the effect it would have on the entire family.

In the words of another Black female respondent, ultimately "the family is a group of persons with certain ties, a bonding, a group relationship in which we feel connected to one another; to know that you have family you can fall back on—and ultimately people who can fall back on you."

What Are Your Family Values?

Family values are disseminated through storytelling and concretized by example. The respondents collectively articulated our common family values: respect (for self and other), hard work, honesty, and education, all of which were concretized and reinforced through strong religious practices—and the value of going to church. One White female offers a typical response to the question.

> We were raised to do well. We had to work. Laziness was not a value. I can remember people talking about or criticizing others for being lazy. There was something wrong with being lazy. [Also] when you live down the block from the church in the 1940s and 1950s, you were certainly brought up with the Church as the authority figure, with the father figure and the mother figure in the family. Going to church and all the rituals were paramount. That wasn't a freedom, you either had to do it or you were going to hell.

The response refers to the strength of family rituals, that of going to church as a form of unnegotiated participation. It also speaks to a governing body of rules that served as a guideline for living. The response alludes to the relationship between church and family, with the church providing broad-based guidelines for the family, under the authority of the parents who provided a daily structure for life.

Between church and family, values or the fundamental equipment for living are disseminated and nurtured. A Black female respondent echoes this notion, but also makes the link between church and education.

An example was we had to go to church on Sunday. It wasn't a thing of what you are or not going to do, it was a must. I tried to take my kids to church every Sunday. That was handed down as a value. And another value was education; my mother and father attempted to educate us. That was a priority in our family. I ended up educating my kids. That was a value that you accepted and carried on. Besides education and religion, a value was being all that you could be: wanting to be something. Having the desire to live a full and good life, and to be a good person was something else that was of value. Be the best you can be. I think our values carried over.

Both White and Black respondents saw church and education as the primary values that were present before them as children within their family of origin and later what they extended as values to their family of creation. Mncwabe (1988; who writes about education in South African) suggested that Black and White parents in southern Louisiana saw that "education should remedy its past inefficiencies and inadequacies" (p. 61). These inefficiencies reflected both racial/cultural variables as well as class/economic issues that oppressed them in their own lived experiences in southern Louisiana.

Black and White respondents articulated a desire for a (re)generation of family values. They spoke about the need for their children to not only embody, perform or enact the prescribed family values as a display of what they had learned, but also to pass those same values to their children. Included within the personal teaching of both Whites and Blacks was the hope that their children would desire to transform their social communities, often filled with racial strife and dissension, into places of trust and comfort. Their hopes are designed on modeling community based on their notions of family.

What Are Some of the Family Stories That Your Family Tells?

Responses to this question varied from specific stories repeated throughout their childhood to the daily activities of family life, like the Sunday dinner. However, a major theme was family as a context for telling stories, which seemed to be more significant to the respondents than the stories themselves. In most cases, they spoke less about individual stories told within the family and more about the context in which stories emerged.

One White female respondent spoke of sitting around the dinner table, like a campfire, and listening to the adults talk.

Meals [were] very important to us as we grew up, that's the thing I can remember. Sitting around the dinner table as a young child with my brothers. They were ten, twelve and fifteen years older than me. I was like a kid listening to the adults talk. I can just remember we all had a place to sit. I can still remember who sits where. We had meals together, evening meals, certainly six days a week. On Sundays we just had a big meal, which was a special occasion. We usually had other people there, like cousins. The evening meals were usually where we dealt with business. We lived on a farm, and we talked about what needed to be done in the barn and what's got to be done in the gar-

den. And with my children we even have meals together. My older brother went into
the service, where he was for three years, and when he got back he took a leadership
role in the family. He started saying grace before the meal, this was about twenty-five
years ago, and we've been saying grace ever since.

In response to the prototypical image of families sharing their day at the dinner table and what the respondent casually refers to as "dealing with business"
and "what needed to get done," we buttress the voice of Langellier (1989) when
she says that:

> [I]n everyday talk we tell stories, or personal narratives, about our experiences [and]
> the mundane happenings of an ordinary day and the extraordinary events that mark
> our lives. One of the first structures of discourse acquired by children, personal narra-
> tives continue to be told throughout the life span by a wide variety of people from di-
> verse social classes in a far-ranging array of situations. Called the prototypical
> discourse unit, the personal narrative is part of the study of everyday life and the cul-
> ture of everyday talk. (p. 243)

It is through this kind of talk—the informal storytelling, the talk that narrates
our lives—that, ultimately, families come to know each other. It is through this
kind of talk—the talk of "dealing with business" and "what needs to get
done"—that values are shared and the character of a family is displayed.

A Black male responded to the question of storytelling by describing it as lay-
ered with multiple levels of meaning. He used a personal narrative to concretize
a narrative trope (a type of story) that was shared within his own family and with
families of many Black homes. The trope of this narrative is alluded to in Bryant
Alexander's opening narrative in regards to his father. The respondent tells the
story of a race-related incident. The story is told both as a lesson and an articulated experience in which different family values clashed.

> I was working up the street, and I had gone in there [a café] to get sandwiches for me
> and the fellow who was my boss. For some reason I felt like keeping my cap on my head.
> I didn't really need it. I walked through the area where they were playing a pool game
> and drinking beer. I walked in straight to the kitchen and a guy yelled at me, "Take your
> hat off." I probably did; I don't remember, but I got my food and started walking back
> out. I put my hat on. The guy came up to me, I was a puny kid, [and] he slugged me. Of
> course, there was nothing that I could do. He was larger than I was. There was no ques-
> tion of me getting into a fight with him or any other White person in that café. You
> have to wonder what kind of values his family taught him.

Langellier (1989) stated that "narratives are used not only in talk to talk, not
only to recapitulate past events, but to negotiate present and future events" (p.
261). This narrative of "going into a café to get a sandwich" unearths a family-
and community-based dynamic in which narrative serves as the tool for instruction. The elements of the lesson are concretized within the narrative, then
fleshed out and applied to a current phenomenon. Bauman (1989) suggested

that "telling stories is literally a means of remembering a dismembered way of life by insisting on the personalization of place, revivifying the ruins with direct social and contextual meaning" (p. 179).

These ideas are further concretized within the narrative of a White female responding to the same question. Buttressed against the memories of parents reading and singing to children she offered a story that unearths how issues of racial and cultural differences are disseminated within families.

> [Parents] would read to [children], sing to them, play pretend, sit outside and look at lightening bugs. One thing that was very big when I was growing up and affected me greatly was the whole aspect of racism, because we lived on one block and across the street were Blacks. We lived side-by-side on the same street. So, I saw Black people every day. We had a definite separation. And so that was an ongoing thing as far as learning the roles and the rules. One time when I got a little doll for Christmas, one of my aunts laughed and said it looked like a "nigger" doll. That really hurt my feelings because for some reason it must have been wrong to look that way and I couldn't understand why. All those prejudices helped formulate things, yet my parents were very kind to one another. My parents were very generous with anybody. I don't think I grew up any more prejudiced than anybody else at that time.

Her response explains that family narratives are not only articulated utterances foregrounded as a story. The lived experiences of people within families, felt contact, modeling, and behaviors all reference sociocultural perceptions and the accompanying values that are taught and learned through embodied living.

How Do You Feel About Family Values in Your Larger Community?

This question engendered a wide variety of themes that ranged from specific examples of dealing with difference and indifference in the community to how family and community values were shared. The closing line of the "going into a café to get a sandwich" narrative clearly asks the question of how differing family values come in contact within a specified context. Yet, two of the White respondents and two of the Black respondents also mentioned that prejudice was not specifically taught within their homes, and they attempted to protect and insulate their children from it. However, the virulent racial times of the 1940s through the 1960s (which is the time period most cited) inevitably influenced the nature of community life. A White female offers her response to the question.

> At that time there was such a definite unspoken tradition of Blacks and Whites and their place and their interaction with each other: it was a given. I used to resent—we used to think the Blacks were so lucky to be able to sit in the balcony at the theater. We had to sit downstairs. I used to get mad at that. We didn't see them as being treated badly. But, when we grew up [during the 1950s], in Morgan City especially, [it was] very anti-Jewish. There was a lot of that type of bigotry which wasn't directed at the Blacks … It wasn't overt with Blacks: it was more indifference.

This narrative response taps into a tumultuous time of racial strife in the South, yet it does so in interesting ways. The difference that is marked is a weird configuration of pride and prejudice, limited access and positionality. In this narrative, the balcony—a place in which Blacks were relegated in the ultimate enactment of the separate but equal ideology that governed the day—becomes the place of envy. Issues of family difference were not mentioned, although the assumptions about family values were articulated in phrases such as "I guess their parents were teaching them right from wrong too."

The themes of shared family and community values were articulated by both White and Black respondents, but this notion was concretized not in the mixed (Black and White) community, but divided across racial lines. The stronger articulations of this notion came from a Black female respondent.

> When I grew up, whatever that neighbor or the older person said or told you was what was done. And if you got a whipping from somebody else or at school, well then when you got home you got another one. The people that lived around me, I got a lot of help. So the community really helps you with your family. And there is a relationship of respect that they have to show. You took care of what adults said. Now I won't ask you if my child said something, but then it wasn't like that. Whatever an adult said in the community was important.

Within this response, she, as did others, spoke about a form of in loco parentis. In loco parentis as they speak of it, was not a typical response to the power-laden academic version that operated at that time within the schools—which inevitably superseded family values for some culturally enriched master plan of democratic life. In the Black community and others, in loco parentis was constructed to affirm community and family values. Literally stated, in the absence of your parents and in the presence of another adult Black person in the community—that person stood in the place of your parents.

The assumption of parental status was based in a shared value system. Any Black adult had the right to "correct" you. The term *correct* in its denotative and culturally connotative sense carries the same meaning. The notion embodies both the righting of wrongs and the teaching of lessons. In many cases that could be a gentle whipping or the articulation of family- and community-shared value through a narrative.

In the previous articulations of lived experiences, all respondents spoke of individual family traditions that reinforced family values within the specified site of the household. Yet, here they spoke of a social system called a community that helped reinforce the practice and theory of family and family values. Family was practiced throughout the community and not just within the close confines of the home. Both Black and White families spoke of this tradition within their specified cultural communities. Both Black and White families seem to long for a nostalgic period when community was a synonym for family and family was a refuge.

What constituted community for Black and White families differed in scope, although it contained common elements. Our autobiographical narratives spoke of church and religion as important binding forces for ourselves and our families. Our interviewees expressed the same sentiments, and it is interesting that we were all raised as Roman Catholics. The stories of our interviewees rang true in our own experience, as Bryant Alexander expressed an understanding about the stories he was told by his "parents." Those stories were intended to teach about the importance of identity as a method of survival in a hostile world.

That identity manifested itself through the definition of family and community. Identity was important to all of us at different times or stages in our development. Identity was gained through our associations with family, community, and culture. In the LeBlanc family, identity became a process of regrouping after unsatisfying attempts at assimilation. This regrouping manifested itself with two interviewees who moved their family back to Louisiana after living in another state.

DISCUSSION: COOKING GUMBO— THE PROCESS AND THE PRODUCT

Southern Louisiana is a place of rich heritage. One of the central themes of the region is the cuisine. Gumbo is a thick stew made from many diverse ingredients and is relished and eaten with great delight by families of the region.[1] However, the importance of gumbo is not only the ingredients that make up the stew but also its preparation. The mixing of ingredients in a time-honored way, embellished by each new generation, creates the foundation for connectedness.

The experience of "family" is, for both Blacks and Whites in this region and elsewhere, much like cooking gumbo. Despite differences in experiences between Black and White families, there are common elements. As a Black respondent observed, "they (White people) probably desired for [sic] the same things that our families desired for [sic]." It is the commonality that promotes and influences our connectedness.

Baxter (1993) described the relational phenomena of dialectical tensions that individuals feel as they develop, maintain, and negotiate their relationships. One such tension is the desire for integration or connectedness with others in the form of relational intimacy and is countered by the desire for separateness from others to maintain self-identity. Yet, this dialectical tension could exist at different levels of context, from the intrapersonal to the dyadic to the familial to even the interactions between social and cultural groups.

As Ruesch and Bateson (1987) proposed, the individual is defined through communication at four levels: (a) the intrapersonal, (b) the interpersonal, (c) the social, and (d) the cultural. Each of these levels influences who the person becomes. The person is not isolated from the context but rather is situated

---

[1] See appendix for two of many culinary recipes for gumbo.

within several concurrent contexts. As our own experience and interviews have shown, we could bracket out the elements for discussion, but we realized that all of the ingredients were needed to make the gumbo.

At the cultural level, the experience of each group paralleled the other. Although slavery for hundreds of years and deportation are not equivalent, the outcome of self- and other-imposed isolation may have influenced greatly a reliance upon community, neighbor, and family in both groups. Both groups talked about the desire for connection with community.

Community can be defined in different ways to include not only extended family or neighbors but also those within a cultural group or region. We only seem to be aware of the influences of culture we experienced through direct interaction. Therefore, attributions of origin for values remained within the family or community. The construction of identity occurred within that family/community context.

It was upon definitions of community that divergencies in experience were described. For the articulated Black experience, there was a reliance upon community and the culture derived from within. Parents relied upon their Black neighbors to assist in the raising of children. The raising of children included protection from the ugliness of the world outside of the group. The group was defined by opposition to the other. The Black community therefore was self-defined as a subgroup within the larger White majority, but with qualities that kept them separate.

In the articulated Black experience, there was a desire for separateness from Whites. Despite cultural pressures to mainstream, the Black community experience was to maintain strong bonds to extended family and the Black neighborhood. However, external pressure did have the effect of loosening the tight-knit communities. The Black people interviewed expressed lamentations over a separateness within the immediate community and a distance between the generations.

In the articulated White experience, there was an experience of separateness from their larger and more immediate community. Although family was defined as including extended family members, it was less common to include neighbors in the definition. Pressure existed to limit definitions to the nuclear family. But with the separateness came a desire for connectedness to the immediate community of neighbors. There was movement toward regaining identification with the cultural group by connecting with extended family. At the same time, there was experienced the tension of trying to gain entry into the mainstream. Among White families and Black families as well, there was a sense of otherness and separateness from the larger community.

The South historically has been perceived as a hotbed of racial unrest. The struggle has been situated at the intersection of Whiteness and Blackness and a hierarchy of value constructed to and against the other. "Otherness" is a construction of difference between specified populations, whether projected or self-imposed, which leads to the development of social hierarchies and ways in which people define themselves in oppositional terms. Ricoeur (1992) suggested that self is based on the dialectic between selfhood and otherness. It is this dialectic between self and other, between Black and White, that is characteristic of the climate of southern Louisiana. Identity, as it was experienced by ourselves and our families, involves meanings of sameness shared within a specified community, which helps to constitute character and selfhood. The identity of family, thus, is based in the shared notions of those who constitute that aggregate of beings.

Concurrently, the notion of what constitutes the Black family or the White family is based not only in internal definitions of "family" but also in how the specified family orients itself to outside variables. The Black definitions of family constructed in this chapter refer to relational bonds manifested in love, but reinforced in protection. It is a result of being otherized by Whites as well as the act of otherizing Whites by Blacks. The White definitions of family refer to a struggle for identity at a border crossing of White privilege and the cultural stigma of being Cajun. The struggle against otherness becomes a galvanizing agent in community building.

However, despite the divergencies of experience between the Black and White communities of southern Louisiana, belongingness was constructed from social interaction with those defined as community. Interpersonal interactions that helped define self occurred within the context of family. Commonalities of values between Black and White families could be explained by the similar ways in which values were taught: by example, by problem solving, and by addressing of wrongdoing.

It has been the process of raising children from one generation to the next, much like cooking gumbo, which has led to our commonalities. Black and White families in southern Louisiana cook with similar ingredients and all partake of the stew. By examining the commonalities we may gain a better appreciation of each others experience of "family."

We conclude that similarities exist in the lived experience of Black and White families of southern Louisiana. Those similarities include both topic and method of communication. As Socha, Sanchez-Hucles, Bromley, and Kelly (1995) pointed out, very few studies of Black family communication have been conducted. Furthermore, family communication research may overlook the similarities between Black and White families and their communication, just as it may overlook differences that are based on larger cultural contexts. However, we believe that the similarity of cultural experience between Acadian and African-American families of southern Louisiana may contribute to the dialogue about family.

The study suggested that common elements, such as values and rituals, may exist across racial groups. Although this study had a small sample size and only addressed families within a specific cultural region, it suggests several directions for future study. Future studies might examine (a) the interplay between ethnic history and current practices within the family, (b) the relationship between narrative, self-identity, and definitions of family among different cultural groups, and (c) commonalities of the experience of families among U.S. cultural groups. To study family communication among different cultural groups, researchers should not simply assume that commonalities exist, but rather should describe characteristics that can be demonstrated as common to those groups. Demonstrating commonalities could assist in, as Socha and Diggs suggested, the development of positive ethnic relations.

APPENDIX

The LeBlanc Southern Louisiana Gumbo

Ingredients:

½ lb. sausage	2 minced cloves of garlic
1 fryer chicken	2 cups of cut okra
1 cup of roux	2 quarts of water
2 medium chopped onions	¾ tsp. of cayenne pepper
1 cup chopped shallots	2 tsp. of salt
2 tbls. chopped parsley	2 tsp. of gumbo filé

1. Boil chicken: Place whole chicken in a pot of water and allow to boil until chicken is cooked. When chicken is done, save chicken broth. Pour cold water over chicken to cool the chicken. Debone the chicken. To help in this step, either quarter the chicken before boiling or use boneless chicken. Cut the chicken and sausage to bite-sized pieces.

For seafood gumbo, the chicken and sausage can be replaced by a mixture of precooked shrimp tails, crab meat, oysters, or crawfish tails. The best way to cook the seafood, before adding to the gumbo, is to boil in a mixture of water and spices. Try Zatarain's crab boil, which comes in a bottle. If the crab boil cannot be found, then try a tablespoon of salt, ¼ teaspoon of cayenne pepper, and a dash of Tabasco or Louisiana Hot Sauce. Remove seafood shells before placing seafood in the gumbo.

2. Make roux: Place equal parts of oil and flour in an iron pot. Stir mixture until mixture becomes a paste with no lumps. Turn heat to medium to medium-low. Stir mixture constantly until roux is golden brown. It is very important not to burn the roux! Therefore, stir constantly. Do not stop! This step can take 45 minutes. For that reason, you may want to make several cups of roux and save the extra in the freezer for later use.

3. Add onions, parsley, and garlic to the roux. Sauté onions, parsley, and garlic, stirring constantly until soft.

4. Add other ingredients, except filé. If using chicken stock, add only enough water to the mixture to make approximately 2 quarts of gumbo. Bring mixture to a boil. Stir.

5. Lower heat to low, cover tightly, and cook for 30 minutes.

6. While gumbo is cooking, make rice as usual.

7. Add gumbo filé, if necessary, to thicken the gumbo. Okra thickens the gumbo, so adding filé may not be important.

8. Turn off the stove, fix a bowl by pouring gumbo over a serving of rice, and enjoy.

The Alexander Southern Louisiana Gumbo

Ingredients:

½ lb. sausage	2 cups of okra (optional)
1 hen	1 gallon of water
1 cup of roux	red pepper
2 medium onions	salt
fresh parsley	gumbo filé
cooking oil	dried shrimp
garlic (optional)	

The basic southern Louisiana gumbo often refers to the dark and spicy soup-like mixture. Okra, seafood, and chicken are three types of gumbo based upon what the primary meat or flavoring agent is used. The three elements are not automatically added, although they may be added in equal portions to make a Chicken and Okra Gumbo or a Seafood and Okra Gumbo. This is a recipe for Chicken Filé Gumbo, yet the variations are simple and will be noted along the way. There are three stages in making any gumbo.

1. Make a roux: a roux is a flour-based thickening agent. Some cooks choose to use a mixture of floor and oil (or butter) cooked open in a cast iron pot, but to cut down on the fat content use just plain flour. It has the same effect without adding additional fat, and it does not add a greasy flavor to the gumbo. The roux can be prepared over the stove in the cast iron pot by bringing up the heat and stirring the flour constantly. The flour is cooked, when it begins to turn brown. Continue cooking and stirring until the flour mixture is an even light brown color. Now it is considered a roux.

Roux can also be made in the oven by baking the flour in a cake or roasting pan at 400°F. The consistent heat of the oven matches the consistent heat of the cast iron pot when cooked on the stove. Periodically, open the oven and stir the mixture in order to insure an even browning. As with the stove top method, this should take about 45 minutes.

The advantage of a dry roux (without oil or butter) is that it can be prepared in advance and stored in the cabinet (in a glass jar or Tupperware because no refrigeration is needed). Each pot of gumbo uses about 1 cup of roux.

2. On the stove, lightly cover the bottom of a large pot (2 gallon or 10 quart) with your favorite cooking oil. To the pot, add 2 finely chopped medium-sized onions, 1 finely chopped green bell pepper, and a 1 stalk of celery. Add a clove or two of garlic, to taste. After these are simmering and the onions are slightly translucent, add the parts of

chicken. Choose a hen, which is a little tougher and will withstand the boiling of the gumbo without having the meat fall off the bones. (Deboning the chicken is not recommended unless the meal is served to large groups of people in small portions, or if fumbling with chicken bones is to be avoided.) For a large southern Louisiana family, each person could have a whole chicken part in their serving.

For a seafood gumbo made with crabs, shrimps, and/or crawfish, the seafood could be prepare separately with a seafood boil. A popular brand is Zatarain's, produced in New Orleans.

3. After the chicken is smothered, or slightly browned in the oil mixture, remove the chicken from the pot and add the roux. The roux should be stirred into the mixture of oil, onions, peppers, and the fat or chicken broth. After the roux is thoroughly mixed, add a gallon of water. Then return the smothered chicken (or seafood) to the pot. Lower the heat and allow the gumbo to cook and simmer for about one hour, stirring occasionally.

It is at this time that seasonings such as black pepper, red pepper, and salt (all to taste) might be added. This is also the time to add flavorings such as a packet of dried shrimps, which can be purchase in most southern Louisiana stores. You may also add a couple links of hot smoked sausage. These are cut into small (¼ inch) chunks and added to the gumbo. You may also want to add some freshly cut parsley, about 2 to 3 tablespoons. Parsley flakes work fine also.

(In making an Okra Gumbo or adding okra to any combination of chicken or seafood, the precooked okra is added as the last ingredient after the gumbo has cooked and is simmering. Add okra to taste; 3 to 5 cups of cooked okra is usually fine. The okra is added to the gumbo along with 1 can of tomato paste. The mixture is simmered 15 to 20 minutes, then served. Gumbo filé is usually not added to an okra gumbo.)

While your gumbo is cooking, make a pot of steamed rice. The gumbo should be done after about 45 minutes. All the meat in the gumbo should be thoroughly cooked, and the gumbo should be dark and rich in coloring. The final addition to the gumbo is the gumbo filé, a southern Louisiana seasoning made with ground sassafras leaves. Zatarain's also makes a gumbo filé. You can add 1 to 2 tablespoons of gumbo filé to the entire gumbo or ½ teaspoon to each individual serving. Adding it to the large pot ensures an even distribution through the pot and negates the need to continually add filé on second and third servings. In leftovers, the rich mixtures of sassafras leaves joins with the other seasoning of the gumbo to create one of the best southern Louisiana leftover meals.

Whether adding the gumbo filé to the entire pot or not, remember to stir the entire mixture in order to circulate the seasonings. Then, in a deep dish bowl, place 1 to 3 large tablespoons of rice. Using a ladle or a coffee cup to scoop some gumbo, pour the gumbo over the rice. Try to ensure that each bowl gets a piece of chicken and some of the sausages that were added to the pot. Enjoy.

REFERENCES

Ancelet, B. J., Edwards, J., & Pitre, G. (1991). *Cajun country.* Jackson: University Press of Mississippi.
Bauman, R. (1989). American folklore studies and social transformation: A performance-centered perspective. *Text and Performance Quarterly, 9,* 175–184.

Baxter, L. A. (1993). The social side of personal relationships: A dialectical perspective. In S. Duck (Ed.), *Understanding relationship processes 3: Social context and relationships* (pp. 139–165). Newbury Park, CA: Sage.

Brasseaux, C. A. (1987). *The founding of New Acadia: The beginnings of Acadian life in Louisiana, 1765–1803.* Baton Rouge: Louisiana State University.

Cohen, E. N., & Eames, E. (1982). *Cultural anthropology.* Boston: Little, Brown.

Conquergood, D. (1985). Performing as a moral act: Ethical dimensions of the ethnography of performance. *Literature in Performance, 5*(2), 1–13.

Daigle, J. O. (1984). *A dictionary of the Cajun language.* Ann Arbor, MI: Edwards Brothers.

Dormon, J. H. (1983). *The people called Cajuns: An introduction to an ethnohistory.* Lafayette: University of Southwestern Louisiana, The Center for Louisiana Studies.

Ember, C. R., & Ember, M. (1993). *Anthropology* (7th ed.). Englewood Cliffs, NJ: Prentice-Hall.

Fisher, W. (1984). Narration as a human communication paradigm: The case of public moral argument. *Communication Monographs, 51,* 1–22.

Galvin, K. M., & Brommel, B. J. (1996). *Family communication: Cohesion and change* (4th ed.). New York: HarperCollins.

Garner, T. (1983). Playing the dozen: Folklore as strategies for living. *Quarterly Journal of Speech, 69,* 47–57.

Grossberg, L. (1994). Introduction. In H. A. Giroux, & P. McLaren (Eds.), *Between borders: Pedagogy and the politics of cultural studies.* New York: Routledge.

Hecht, M., Collier, M. J., & Ribeau, S. A. (1993). *African American communication: Ethnic identity and cultural interpretation.* Newbury Park, CA: Sage.

Hooks, b. (1990). *Yearning: Race, gender, and cultural politics.* Boston: South End.

Infante, D. A., Rancer, A. S., & Womack, D. F. (1993). *Building communication theory* (2nd ed.). Prospect Heights, IL: Waveland.

Kim, Y. Y., & Ruben, B. D. (1988). Intercultural transformation: A systems theory. In Y. Y. Kim & W. B. Gudykunst (Eds.), *Theories in intercultural communication* (pp. 229–321). Newbury Park, CA: Sage.

Kirkwood, W. G. (1983). Storytelling and self-confrontation: Parables as communication strategies. *Quarterly Journal of Speech, 69,* 59–74.

Labov, W. (1972). *Language in the inner city: Studies in Black English Vernacular.* Philadelphia: University of Pennsylvania.

Labov, W., & Waletsky, J. (1967). Narrative analysis: Oral versions of personal experiences. In J. Helms (Ed.), *Essays in the verbal and visual arts* (pp. 12–44). Seattle: University of Washington.

Langellier, K. M. (1989). Personal narratives: Perspective on theory and research. *Text and Performance Quarterly, 9,* 243–273.

Lionnet, F. (1989). *Autobiographical voices: Race, gender, self-portraiture.* Ithaca, NY: Cornell.

McGoldrick, M. (1993). Ethnicity, cultural diversity and normality. In F. Walsh (Ed.), *Normal family processes* (2nd ed., pp. 331–336). New York: Guilford.

Mncwabe, M. P. (1988). *Teacher neutrality and education in crisis: The Black teacher's dilemma in South Africa.* Johannesburg South Africa: Skotaville.

Owens, L. H. (1981). The Black family. In J. H. Cary & J. Weinberg (Eds.), *The social fabric: American life from 1607 to the Civil War* (3rd ed., pp. 231–245). Boston: Little, Brown.

Putnam, L. L., & Stohl, C. (1990). Bona fide groups: A reconceptualization of groups in context. *Communication Studies, 41,* 248–265.

Ricoeur, P. (1992). *Oneself as another* (K. Blamey, Trans.). Chicago: University of Chicago.

Ruesch, J., & Bateson, G. (1987). *Communication: The social matrix of psychiatry.* New York: Norton.

Rushton, W. F. (1990). *The Cajuns: From Acadia to Louisiana.* New York: Noonday.

Socha, T. J. (in press). Communication in family units: Studying the first "group." In L. Frey (Ed.), *Handbook of group communication.* Beverly Hills, CA: Sage.

Socha, T. J., Sanchez-Hucles, J., Bromley, J., & Kelly, B. (1995). Invisible parents and children: Exploring African-American parent–child communication. In T. J. Socha & G. H. Stamp (Eds.), *Parents, children and communication: Frontiers of theory and research* (pp. 127–146). Hillsdale, NJ: Lawrence Erlbaum Associates.

Spradely, J. P. (1979). *The ethnographic interview.* New York: Holt, Rinehart & Winston.

Stewart, J., & Logan, C. (1993). *Together: Communicating interpersonally.* New York: McGraw-Hill.

Taylor, S. J., & Bogdan, R. (1984). *Introduction to qualitative research methods: The search for meanings* (2nd ed.). New York: John Wiley.

van Manen, M. (1990). *Researching lived experience: Human science for an action sensitive pedagogy.* London, Ontario, Canada: State University of New York.

Whitchurch, G. G., & Dickson, F. C. (1999). Family communication. In M. B. Sussman, S. K. Steinmetz, & G. W. Peterson (Eds.), *Handbook of marriage and the family* (2nd ed., pp. 687–704). New York: Plenum.

Wood, J. T. (1982). Communication and relational culture: Basis for the study of human relationships. *Communication Quarterly, 30,* 75–84.

Wood, J. T. (1995). *Relational communication: Continuity and change in personal relationships.* Belmont, CA: Wadsworth.

❦ 10 ❦

Toward Improving Life at the Crossroads: Family Communication Education and Multicultural Competence

Thomas J. Socha
Old Dominion University

Jennifer Beigle
University of North Carolina, Greensboro

A common theme of the chapters in this volume is that problems concerning race relations in the United States take root at home. It is through family communication that we develop initial formulations of ethnic identity and orientations toward ethnic culture, our own and others (Allen, 1981; Boykin & Toms, 1985; Clark, 1992; Daniel & Daniel, chap. 2, this volume; Socha & Diggs, chap. 1, this volume). Further, ethnic identity and cultural orientation affect intraethnic and interethnic communication (Hecht, Collier, & Ribeau, 1993; Taylor, 1981) including how these skills develop (Daniel & Daniel, chap. 2, this volume; Socha, Sanchez-Hucles, Bromley, & Kelly, 1995).

Socha and Diggs (chap. 1, this volume) offer three conceptual frameworks for approaching the study of communication, race, and family: Afrocentric, cultural variability, and transformation. In particular, the transformation perspective assumes that communication in everyday family life is a primary context in which family members experience race and communicate about race and that communication in families (among other contexts) can facilitate or inhibit the development of multicultural values, intercultural sensitivity (Bennett, 1986),

209

and intercultural communication competence. Given this, in order to begin to improve the quality of interracial interactions now and in the future, families need to be educated about ways of communicating among themselves that can facilitate the development of multicultural values, intercultural sensitivity, and intercultural communication. Specifically, it is our contention that courses in family communication, particularly those offered in higher education, as well as parent-education programs, are optimally suited to the task of providing instruction to reach these aims. Thus, family communication courses can potentially make an important contribution toward improving race relations in the United States by teaching about how family interaction at home can facilitate the development of values and communication practices that can improve relationships across the racial divide outside the home.

Unfortunately, to date, ethnic culture has been generally neglected in family communication research (e.g., see Socha et al., 1995) and has received limited coverage in at least two family communication textbooks (i.e., Galvin & Brommel, 1996; Turner & West, 1998). For example, issues, such as racism, are mentioned in these two family communication texts, but how families use communication to avoid creating racist environments and also manage the damaging effects of racism needs more in-depth coverage. *Racism* is defined here as a belief in White supremacy, or as "prejudice plus power" (Katz, 1978, p. 51) Overall, more attention is needed for ethnic culture, especially in the family communication classroom (see Whitchurch, 1992, for a review). This general inattention can be attributed, in part, to family communication scholars' and educators' viewing their work from a Eurocentric perspective, which, similar to Eurocentrism in everyday life (Ellison, 1952; Katz, 1978), leads to a general neglect of ethnic culture by assuming that all families are similar to those of the dominant group (i.e., European Americans)and/or minimizing those who are different from the dominant group. The emphasis on Eurocentric values is not surprising, however, because in our experience (supported by survey results to be reviewed later), family communication scholars are mostly White, teach mostly White students, and conduct research at universities with mostly White populations.

Educators, including family communication educators, are counted among society's gatekeepers. That is, educators affect the flow of information to students, in this case, information that is relevant to the development of a more global understanding of family communication as it is viewed through the kaleidoscopic lenses of the world's ethnic cultures.

Given this backdrop, the two goals of this chapter are to (1) provide an assessment of the current state of knowledge, attitudes, and course practices of family communication educators with respect to African-American culture and, based on these results, (2) begin to lay a foundation upon which to build strategies to increase family communication educators' competence in providing communication instruction both within and across the racial divide. In particular, we report the results of a survey of family communication educators' knowledge, attitudes, and course practices concerning aspects of African-American culture and family life. Then, we use the results of the survey to lay a foundation upon which to build future instructional strategies and research. More specifically, we offer a selected primer of readings concerning African-American culture and African-American family life of relevance to the study of family communication.

Examining family communication through the kaleidoscopic lens of ethnic culture certainly poses new challenges to family communication researchers and educators. But, in doing so, we open up new opportunities to see more complex and interesting pictures of family communication in the tapestry of everyday family life and begin to provide instruction that truly speaks to all of our students.

A SURVEY OF FAMILY COMMUNICATION EDUCATORS ABOUT AFRICAN-AMERICAN CULTURE

The general purpose of the survey was to gather information about family communication educators' understandings about African-American culture. Specifically, we gathered information from family communication educators about (a) the ethnic and gender composition of students taking their family communication courses; (b) their attitudes concerning African-American culture and its portrayal in family communication textbooks; (c) their knowledgeability about aspects of African-American culture, African-American family life, and African-American family communication; (d) their attitudes toward communicating instructional information about races other than their own, and (e) information about their gender, culture, and education.

Sample

A total of 89 surveys were distributed in two ways. First, 39 surveys were distributed directly to those individuals who attended the 1997 business meeting of the Family Communication Division of the National Communication Association. Later, another 50 surveys were mailed to randomly selected universities listed in the National Communication Association directory who had members listed on the roster of the Family Communication Division. All completed surveys were returned in sealed envelops by U.S. mail.

A total of 36 surveys (40%) were returned of which 31 contained usable data (35%). The 5 respondents that returned questionnaires that did not contain usable data reported that they did not teach a course in family communication.

Demographically, the 31 family communication educators who responded to the survey were White (81%), female (74%), and held a Ph.D. (84%). They had been teaching for an average of 17 years ($SD = 8.87$) and teaching family communication courses for approximately 7 years ($SD = 4.53$).

Survey Items and Results

Ethnic Composition in Family Communication Classes.   The family communication educators were asked to estimate the ethnic composition of students enrolling in their family communication course(s). Overall, they estimated that African Americans comprised about 9% (SD = 8.58) of family communication students (3% reported that 40% of their class were African Americans and 6% reported no African Americans). For most respondents (88%), African Americans comprised no more than 10% of students in their classes, whereas European-American students comprised 71% of their classes (SD = 3.9).

Perceptions of Instructional Materials.   Five Likert-type items (anchors of 5, *strongly agree*; 1, *strongly disagree*) asked instructors to rate their perceptions of the representation of ethnic culture in the textbooks and supplemental readings they used. Most reported that family communication textbooks did not adequately represent a diverse range of cultures (M = 2.13, SD = 1.08), or present "enough" information about non-White cultures (M = 2.13, SD = .99). However, respondents did not perceive family communication textbooks to be "racist" (M = 2.10, SD = .79).

Two additional items asked for ratings about the practices of using supplemental readings about non-White cultures and classroom exercises about non-White cultures. The results paint a divided picture. About one half of the educators reported that they did assign such readings and did use such classroom exercises, whereas the other half did not (M = 3.13, SD = 1.52, for supplemental readings; M = 2.65, SD = 1.36, for classroom exercises).

Knowledgeability About Aspects of African-American Culture.   Table 10.1 lists 19 aspects of African-American culture, family life, and the effects of racism. We asked family communication educators to rate their knowledgeability of each of these 19 aspects using a 5-point scale (5, *expert*; 4, *very knowledgeable*; 3, *moderately knowledgeable*; 2, *slightly knowledgeable*; 1, *not at all knowledgeable*).

Reviewing the table, we find that across all 19 aspects family communication educators' rated themselves "slightly knowledgeable" to "moderately knowledgeable." Because the sample consisted of mostly Whites, it was not surprising to find that their knowledgeability about African-American family communication (M = 2.61, SD = .67) was lower then their knowledgeability about White family communication (M = 4.32, SD = .70). Also, their ratings for their knowledgeability of African-American family communication (M = 2.61, SD = .67) were generally consistent with their ratings of knowledgeability about other minority groups, such as, Asian American family communication (M = 2.48, SD = .96), Hispanic-American family communication (M = 2.42, SD =

.89), but higher than Native American family communication ($M = 1.9, SD = 1.01$). The topic that received the lowest average knowledgeability rating was the Black diaspora ($M = 1.52, SD = .81$), which refers to the global community of Africans dispersed throughout the world primarily because of slavery. The Black diaspora is relevant to understanding African-Americans' family communication because generations of African-American family stories and rituals are historically rooted in ancestral African homes. Many of these stories were lost or underwent significant transformation due to slavery. Yet, preserving such stories is important so that future generations might have a sense of their own history and learn about commonalities among African people of the world.

TABLE 10.1
Results of Family Communication Educators' Self-Rated Knowledgeability of Aspects of African-American Culture, Family Life, and Effects of Racism

Aspect	Mean	(SD)
Approaches to eliminating racism	2.84	(1.07)
Effects of racism on white people	2.74	(1.09)
African-American family communication	2.61	(.67)
African-American communication (general)	2.60	(.86)
Inter-racial family communication	2.58	(1.03)
African-American family communication and TV	2.52	(.77)
Institutional racism against African Americans	2.48	(1.03)
Symbolic racism against African Americans	2.48	(1.03)
Black History	2.45	(.77)
African-American values (cultural/religious)	2.45	(.77)
African-American cultural holidays	2.42	(.96)
African-American parent-child communication	2.42	(.81)
Films by and/or about African Americans	2.39	(.95)
Public policy issues and African-American families	2.29	(.90)
African-American identify issues	2.29	(.90)
Theory of Afrocentrism	2.03	(.95)
Black English (Ebonics)	1.90	(.87)
African-American children's literature	1.87	(.81)
Communication and the Black Diaspora	1.52	(.81)

Note. Scale items were: 5, *Expert*; 4, *Very Knowledgeable*; 3, *Moderately Knowledgeable*; 2, *Slightly Knowledgeable*; 1, *Not at all Knowledgeable*. Topics are arranged from those rated most knowledgeable to those rated least knowledgeable.

Instructional Values and Presenting Culture.   Respondents agreed that family communication educators should have experiences in interacting with people of diverse cultures (M = 3.87, SD = 1.34), should be knowledgeable about family communication in cultures other than their own (M = 4.10, SD = .83), and should make culture an integral component in family communication courses (M = 3.87, SD = 1.09). However, they were divided about whether family communication courses were a mechanism for the elimination of racism (M = 3.35, SD = 1.11).

Contrary to our original assumptions, most respondents disagreed that they were uncomfortable talking about race (M = 1.87, SD = 1.15) or talking about cultures other than their own (M = 1.81, SD = 1.01) in their family communication classes. Although most respondents reportedly felt comfortable when talking about race and cultures other than their own in the classroom, the responses varied somewhat. In addition, respondents agreed with the statement "I consider myself to be a competent communicator in multicultural contexts (M = 3.61, SD = .92), but, given the variability, some recognized room for improvement."

Future Directions.   Finally, we asked for feedback about four initiatives that we thought might be useful in moving family communication further in the area of ethnic culture. The respondents agreed that family communication textbooks should focus more on culture (M = 3.94, SD = .77) and that the National Communication Association should sponsor short courses (M = 4.06, SD = .81) and panels (M = 4.13, SD = .85) about family communication and culture at its meetings. Respondents also agreed that there is a need for a journal that focuses on family communication, in which a special issue might be devoted to culture (M = 4.19, SD = .95).

Discussion

The results of the survey paint a portrait of the current state of family communication education that resonates with our experiences: mostly White educators, teaching mostly White students, using instructional materials that are perceived to not adequately present a culturally diverse picture of communication in families. However, these family communication educators did acknowledge a need to improve their knowledge about communication in non-White families, in particular African-American families, and recognized that they need help in doing this. In response to this need, the next section provides a selected primer of readings about African-American family life directed toward family communication educators.

BUILDING A FOUNDATION FOR CHANGE

Because the survey demonstrated a need to enhance family communication educators' base of knowledge about African-American families, we decided to develop a primer of readings that educators, researchers, and students could consult about aspects of African-American family life. We modeled our primer after Bochner's (1976) primer of readings about the field of "family studies," which he developed in the early years of the field of family communication. In addition, we also added readings about racial awareness development and combating racism to the primer. These added readings introduce family communication educators to various classroom exercises and activities related to increasing racial awareness and combating racism. The foundational readings tend to be located in books and book chapters, but some pivotal journal articles are included.

Given the rather large literature about African-American families, it is surprising how little has made its way into widely read family communication literature. For example, Allen's (1986) annotated bibliography featured 1,153 articles about Black families published in 175 journals between 1965 and 1984. Numerous anthologies have also focused entirely on Black families (Hill, 1993) or aspects of Black family life: African-American children and childrearing (H. McAdoo & McAdoo, 1985); African-American men (Gary, 1981), African-American women (Williams, 1978); and African-American child and family psychology (Burlew, Banks, McAdoo, & Azibo, 1992). Also, there are numerous government-sponsored reports, such as the 608-page study published by the National Research Council's Committee on the Status of Black Americans (1989), which includes extensive coverage of Black children and their families. Of course, not all of the information contained in these publications is directly relevant to the study of communication in families; however, much of it is relevant and, collectively, provides a fuller understanding of the context in which African-American families interact.

Given the size of this literature and the goals of this chapter, we narrowed the focus to those areas of Black family life that we perceive to be of relevance to understanding family communication. Table 10.2 lists these readings, which are arranged according to the following topics: Black culture, Black families, Black children, Black male–female relationships, Black parent–child relationships, and cultural awareness and racism. The readings included for any given topic are far from exhaustive but rather are intended to provide an introduction to a given topic area as well as acquaint readers with prominent Black scholars who have studied Black family life. We devote the remainder of the chapter to providing an overview of these readings for each of these general topics.

African-American Culture

How to conceptualize African-American culture and approach the study of African Americans (e.g., Asante, 1990) and in our case, African American families (e.g., Hill, 1993), African American male–female relationships (e.g., Asante, 1981) and African American communication (Asante, 1993; Hecht et al., 1993) is problematic for scholars and families alike (see Socha & Diggs,

TABLE 10.2
A Primer of Selected Readings About Black Family Life
With an Emphasis on Communication

Topic	Selected Readings (in Chronological Order)
Black Culture:	Asante (1980); Baldwin (1985); Baldwin & Bell (1990); Anderson (1990); Asante (1990); Baldwin (1990); Covin (1990); Hecht, Collier, & Ribeau (1993).
Black Families:	Willie (1976); Shimkin, Shimkin & Frate,(1978); Sudarkasa (1980); H. McAdoo (1981); Nobles & Goddard, (1984); H. McAdoo (1992); Wilson (1992); Hill (1993); Littlejohn-Blake & Anderson-Darling (1993).
Black Children:	Holliday (1985); H. McAdoo & J. McAdoo (1985); Boykin & Toms (1985); Clark (1992); Belgrave, Johnson, & Carey (1992); Holmes (1995); Daniel & Daniel (1998).
Black Male–Female Relationships:	Asante (1981); Braithwaite (1981); Staples (1981); Aldridge (1989); Aldridge (1990); Bell, Bouie, & Baldwin, (1990), Aldridge (1991); Dickson (1993); Rosenblatt, Karis, & Powell (1995).
Black Parent–Child Relationships:	Allen (1981); Asante (1981); Braithwaite (1981); Staples (1981); Franklin & Boyd-Franklin (1985); J. McAdoo (1981); Wilson (1982), Socha et al. (1995); Daniel & Effinger (1996).
Racial Awareness/ Racism:	Hamersma, Paige, & Jordan (1973); Katz (1978); Kivel (1996); Richard (1996); Alicea & Kessel (1997).

chap. 1, this volume). For example, African-American parents are confronted daily not only with the problem of defining what African-American culture means to them and how they will pass their understandings of African-American culture along to their children (Boykin & Toms, 1985; Daniel & Daniel, chap. 2, this volume) but also how to teach their children how to interact with White people and members of other minority groups. Similarly, European-American children are socialized not only for participation in European-American culture but also for interaction with African Americans and members of other minority groups. The role of family communication in socializing children about how to interact with other cultures is an important topic that, to date, has been neglected in the family communication literature (see Davilla, chap. 5, this volume; Ferguson, chap. 3, this volume; Socha et al., 1995).

Boykin and Toms (1985, p. 34) framed this slippery problem of defining the nature of Black culture for African-American children by asking a series of questions:

We must ask ourselves what does it mean for a Black person to become an 'adequate' adult? What is the society of which he or she is a member? ... When we speak of the imposition of social order, is it not necessary to distinguish between the dictates of the larger society versus those of one's more immediate ecological circumstances? More-over, to what extent might the more proximal socialization messages be incompatible with distal socialization messages [i.e., messages from white society]? (p. 34)

These questions frame the complexities and contradictions outlined by Daniel and Daniel (chap. 2, this volume) inherent in raising Black children in a predominantly White society. Daniel and Daniel pointed out that many adults in minority cultures, particularly the African-American culture, teach their children how to function simultaneously in multiple and often contradictory cultural frameworks and racist environments. Dubois vividly described this process, which he labeled "bi-socialization" (i.e., socialization into Black and White cultures), in his now famous quote: "Two souls; two thoughts, two unreconciled strivings; two warring ideals in one dark body, whose dogged strength alone keeps it from being torn asunder" (1903/1969, p. 16).

Boykin and Toms (1985) argued that socialization of African-American children goes beyond Dubois' notion of bisocialization and that many African-American children are at least trisocialized for participation in at least three cultures:

the mainstream of American society [read White society], socialization informed by oppressed minority status, and socialization linked to a proximal Black cultural context that is largely non-commensurate with the social dictates of mainstream American life. (p. 46)

These three domains highlight the complexities of discussing the conceptualization of culture with respect to African-American family life. Because the literature about the domains of Black culture and oppressed minority status have received less attention in family communication literature and much has been said and written about White families, we focus on these two areas next.

Black Culture.   According to Boykin and Toms (1985), there is evidence that some African-American family behavioral patterns and values are consistent with West African traditions. In particular, Boykin and Toms (1985) specified nine defining dimensions of African culture that find expression among African Americans:

Spirituality—conducting one's life as though its essences were vitalistic rather then mechanistic and as though transcending forces significantly govern the lives of people;

Harmony—placing a premium on versatility and placing an emphasis on wholeness rather than discreetness;

Movement—approaching life rhythmically, particularly as expressed through the patterned interwoven mosaic of music, movement, and percussiveness;

Verve—psychological affinity for variability and intensity of stimulation emanating from the movement mosaic complex;

Affect—a premium placed on emotional sensibilities and expressiveness;

Communalism—sensitivity to the interdependence of people and the notion that group concerns transcend individual strivings;

Expressive individualism—a premium attached to the cultivation of distinctiveness, spontaneity, and uniqueness of self-expression;

Orality—a special emphasis on oral and aural modes of communication especially the use of the spoken work to convey deep contextual meanings not possible through the written word; and

Social time perspective—a commitment to time as a social phenomenon much more than a concoction objectively drawn through clocks, calendars, and other inanimate markers. (Boykin & Toms, 1985, p. 41)

Similar lists of Black cultural dimensions have also been developed; however, the items that are included in any given list and how these items are labeled vary (see Socha & Diggs, chap. 1, this volume). For example, Hecht et al. (1993, p. 96) included "core symbols of sharing, uniqueness, positivity, realism, assertiveness" in their framing of African-American culture, and Asante (1990) framed his discussion of the principle issues in Afrocentric inquiry in terms of African cosmology, epistemology, axiology, and esthetics.

When offered lists of cultural qualities, there might be a tendency to assume that these dimensions are exhaustive and uniformly held by members of the Black culture. However, it must be remembered that "There is no monolithic Black experience. There is no singular socialization pathway. Indeed, there is a tapestry of variegated socialization possibilities" (Boykin & Toms, 1985, p. 47). Lists of cultural values, however, can serve pedagogically as partial mappings of some of the unique aspects of Black cultural experiences and can draw attention to how orienting to different dimensions in different ways can affect how families communicate among themselves and with others (see Socha & Diggs, chap. 1, this volume, for a discussion of the cultural variability perspective). For example, the African cultural value of communalism, discussed by Socha and Diggs (chap. 1, this volume), affects to whom family members might turn for support, how that support is requested, and the manner in which support will be provided, if at all.

An Oppressed Minority.   There is no shortage of data arguing that African Americans occupy the status of an oppressed people. According to the National Research Council (1989):

The great gulf that existed between black and white Americans in 1939 has only been narrowed; it has not closed. Even more blacks live in households with incomes below the poverty line. Even more blacks live in areas where ineffective schools, high rates of dependence on public assistance, severe problems of crime and drug use, and low and declining employment prevail. (p. 3)

Based on an extensive study, the National Research Council (1989) compiled a thorough and detailed portrait of the current position of African Americans. We do not attempt to summarize the volumes of data they and others (e.g., Edelman, 1985) have put forth. We simply restate three of the National Research Council's (1989) predictions concerning African Americans:

Approximately one-third of the black population will continue to be poor, and the relative employment and earnings status of black men is likely to deteriorate further ... High rates of residential segregation between blacks and whites will continue. (p. 4)

It is surprising that, in spite of what is perceived to be greater opportunities for interracial interaction, the last prediction forecasts a reduced likelihood of Whites and Blacks interacting in more proximal ways, such as being neighbors. If voluntary residential segregation continues, then schools and media as well as families will continue to be especially key contexts for developing children's cultural understandings and increasing their intercultural competence.

It is important that discussions about race (ours included) not be conflated with discussions about economic class, that is, race and class are not the same even though they are often considered in the same context. A quote from one of the people Cose (1993) interviewed for his book highlights racism as it intermingles with economic mobility among middle-class Blacks:

I have done everything I was supposed to do. I have stayed out of trouble with the law, gone to the right schools, and worked myself nearly to death. What more do they want? Why in God's name won't they accept me as a full human being? Why am I pigeonholed in a 'Black job'? ... Why, when I most want to be seen, I am suddenly rendered invisible? (p. 1)

Episodes of overt racism may be fewer, but for Cose (1993) and others the face of contemporary racism, "prejudice plus power" (Katz, 1978, p. 51), still shows itself in more subtle ways, such as through the creation of glass ceilings that middle-class Blacks (as well as women and other minorities) can peer through to see advancement opportunities but which prevent them from attaining those opportunities. Such experiences can undoubtedly affect how African-American families communicate among themselves (e.g., by emphasizing intraethnic solidarity) as well as with others (especially Whites) and should become the focus of more family communication research.

African-American Families

Hill (1993) and his project team adopted a holistic approach (similar to the systems approach) and examined internal and external factors that influence African-American families. Applicable to family communication are their discussions of internal factors such as family structure, the African concept of family, and individual factors. We discuss each of these next.

African-American Family Structures.   Hill (1993) cited the work of Billingsley (1968) who developed a category scheme that resulted in identifying 32 types of Black family structures. There are three primary types: (a) nuclear, (b) extended (at least one related child/adult living with family), and (c) augmented (at least one unrelated child/adult living with family). Each primary type is subdivided further using three subtypes (a) incipient (married couples with no children of their own), (b) simple (married couples with their own children), and (c) attenuated (single parents with own children). This scheme reveals the complex ways that families can be structured, for example, the attenuated-extended-augmented family (i.e., a family that contains a single parent, one or more biological or stepchildren, at least one member who is from the extended family but not of the nuclear family, and at least one member who is not related either by birth or marriage). Hill pointed out (1993, p. 102) that Billingsley's classification is incomplete because it left out "children living in households headed by single relatives such as grandmothers and aunts."

Statistical data show that an " ... estimated 86 percent of black children and 42% of white children will spend some time in a mother-only or single-parent household" (National Research Council, 1989, p. 512). Further, "Between 1960 and 1985 the percentages of families that were headed by a black woman increased from 22 to 44 percent among blacks" (p. 512). However, Hill also asserted that, when drawing a structural picture of the African-American family, the concept of the extended family figures prominently. "The overwhelming majority of black Americans live in close proximity to kin ... 85% of all blacks have relatives that live in the same city but in separate households" (Hill, 1993, p. 105). "The Afro-American family tends to follow the pattern of African extended families and include all of the relatives, both legal and biological" (King, 1976, p. 154). Of relevance to family communication, family structure is, of course, intertwined with who talks with whom, who influences whom, and how family decisions are made. Given the emphasis on defining family in terms of the extended structure, African-American systems would seem to be likely to display communication patterns that are qualitatively different (e.g., involve more people, more discussion, and take longer) from European-American families' patterns (Diggs, 1995).

African-American Concept of Family.   In addition to conceptualizing the African-American family as an extended kin network (rather than in terms of the European nuclear family standard; see Shimkin, Shimkin, & Frate, 1978), Hill (1993) added that these families are child-centered, flexible, religious, and subculturally diverse.

Hill (1993, p. 108) cited various trends that speak to the "child-centeredness" of African-American families including reluctance of Black women to have abortions, success at finding informal adoptions for 90% of the one million children living without parents, and disproportionately lower rates of child abuse among Black families relative to Whites within a given socioeconomic strata. Further, "deeply rooted in … African heritage and philosophical orientation which … places a special value on children because they represent the continuity of life" (Nobles, 1974, p. 15).

According to Hill, flexibility and elasticity of African-American families are particularly evident in the sharing and exchanging of roles, for example, in the shifting of parental duties to older women, in women being primary breadwinners in some families, and in "black men are more likely than white men to perform household chores" (Hill, 1993, p. 112). Hill later reminded the reader of the variability of many of these findings among the 14 Black ethnic subcultures he identified (p. 115).

Finally, one prominent quality of African culture (mentioned in virtually all of the typologies) is African-American families' spirituality/religiosity (see also Dainton, chap. 7, this volume). "There appears to be much consensus that, if there is any area in which African cultural continuities are manifested by Black Americans, it is regarding religious beliefs and behavior" (Hill, 1993, p. 112). Hill (1993, pp. 112–115) also provided a brief overview with respect to family communication of various issues and trends concerning religious expression that is worth reading.

African-American Children

According to H. McAdoo and J. McAdoo (1985), "All children … regardless of race, ethnicity, social class or gender, must complete similar developmental tasks if they are to become competent adults … however, these developmental tasks are uniquely experienced in the environments of children's growth and development" (p. 9). Thus, in order to better understand African-American children's communication in their families, information is needed about the environments that African-American children experience and how these experiences affect their communication.

H. McAdoo and J. McAdoo (1985) focused on Black children in an edited volume that considers theoretical, socioeconomic, and educational issues as well as parental and familial environments. The volume contains many foundational chapters, in particular, the chapter by Boykin and Toms (1985, chap. 2) that reported their model of the socialization of African-American children (discussed earlier) and Holliday's (1985) study of the learning environments of African-American children that emphasized the breadth and flexibility of African-American children in response to what are, at times, harsh learning environments.

The important issue of self-esteem in the lives of African-American children is addressed by Diggs (chap. 6, this volume). Additional readings of relevance to communication are Belgrave, Johnson, and Carey (1992) who take an attribution approach to the study of self-esteem, and Clark (1992) who reviewed the literature about racial esteem. Also related to children's racial esteem are studies of Black children's race dissonance or Black children's White preference behaviors (Spencer, 1982, 1983, 1984). Spencer (1988) summarized the results of his research and concluded that across his studies "the failure of Black parents to reinforce ethnic consciousness and to deal explicitly with ethnic issues and institutionalized racial oppression may be a factor in Black children's White preference behaviors" (p. 107). This line of research emphasizes the role of Black parental communication in forming Black children's ethnic identity and in managing their esteem, which in turn, link to how Black children interact with White children (Holmes, 1995).

African-American Male–Female Family Relationships

Aldridge (1989, 1990, 1991) framed the study of African-American male–female relationships using the institutions of capitalism, racism, sexism, and the Judeo-Christian ethic, which places White males in superior positions over others. Her work examined interpersonal issues in the context of these four institutions and focused on differential socialization, game-playing, myths and stereotypes as well as producing a chapter on "Strategies for building healthy relationships." Various sections from Aldridge (1991) would make interesting additions for a readings packet in a family communication course. In particular, the sections in which she discussed "ideal forms of relating" as well as cultural differences in perceptions about male–female relationships as related to the sharing of feelings would be relevant to family communication.

Other foundational readings about Black male–female relationships help round out the picture: an Afrocentric view of male–female relationships (Asante, 1981); economic inequities confronting Black male–female relationships (Staples, 1981); and a chapter about the role of African-American males' verbal facility and initial impression management in male–female relationships (Braithwaite, 1981; and also see Kochman, 1981).

African-American Parent–Child Relationships

Black parent–child communication is discussed at length by Daniel and Daniel (chap. 2, this volume) and Ferguson (chap. 3, this volume) and is mentioned in most of the other chapters in this volume. We encourage examination of those chapters and offer a few additional citations that either were not covered in another chapter in this volume or we found especially useful in developing an understanding of Black parent–child communication.

Franklin and Boyd-Franklin (1985) discussed the historical and social contexts in which African-American parent–child relationships are built and how these contexts affect Black children's emotional and cognitive development. Race issues that occur in contemporary society are likely to affect how race is viewed at that moment, but there are also generational differences in how race is perceived that are also likely to affect Black family communication about race.

Socha et al. (1995) reviewed communication and related literatures, developed a preliminary conceptual model of cultural parent–child communication, and reported a descriptive and cultural comparative study of African-American discipline message tendencies, which found that African-American parents used intense forms of discipline messages. This chapter is also a useful resource as it provides an exhaustive bibliography of articles published in communication journals about Black families.

The final three citations complete the introduction and focus on perceptions of Black mothers, Black fathers, and Black grandmothers of parenting (Wilson, 1992); the socialization of Black male children (Allen, 1981); and a study of Black father–child verbal and nonverbal interaction (J. McAdoo, 1981).

Raising Racial Awareness and Combating Racism

It is necessary that family communication educators provide communication instruction that speaks to all families. However, because African-American students did not exceed 15% of any class and because family communication textbooks were perceived to focus mostly on White families, providing instruction about communication in Black families in particular presented many difficulties. Among them are (a) reliance primarily on an outsider's perspective in lectures and discussion, (b) a limited (sometime negative) pool of students' interracial experiences from which to draw examples, (c) difficulty in identifying quality readings about Black families, when such information is not provided in textbooks, and (d) inadequate background knowledge of Black culture in framing family communication issues and problems. However, if family communication educators are to provide instruction that speaks to all families, in addition to having more African-American family communication professors on faculties, all family communication professors should be educated about African-American culture and be able to present information about African-American family communication in culturally enlightened and culturally sensitive ways. Katz (1978) made this point in more general, but emphatic terms:

> The race problem in America is essentially a White problem in that it is Whites who developed it, perpetuate it, and have the power to resolve it … It seems ironic that so much of the research focuses on the oppressed instead of the oppressors. Racism has taken its toll on White people as well. (p. 10)

The readings offered in this section highlight various strategies that can be used in family communication classrooms to enhance the value of ethnic diversity for families and increase families' awareness and appreciation of cultures other than their own. The volume by Katz (1978) contains literally hundreds of exercises that are a part of an antiracism training program. The program is divided into six stages and begins by (a) an examination of societal inconsistencies, followed by (b) confronting the realities of racism, (c) dealing with feelings, (d) exploring cultural differences, (e) understanding whiteness, and concludes with (f) developing action strategies. Although the program is not specifically geared to families, many exercises can easily be adapted. For example, Exercise 35 (p. 142) asks Whites to reflect on what it means to be White in the United States and how this differs from what it means to be Black in the United States. This could easily be adapted to a family dinner conversation exercise. Exercise 37 (p. 146) offers a provocative read-aloud story about a Black child who is invited to the home of a White boy for dinner. The story highlights both subtle and glaring examples of racist messages communicated by a mother to her son's friend in the presence of her son.

Another excellent resource is Kivel (1996), whose very readable volume examines ways to combat racism at work and home. Kivel specifically included a chapter about combating racism in home and family. The chapter recommends first assessing the home for cultural diversity by examining "books, posters, cookbooks, calendars, paintings, magazines, newspapers, videos, games, computer games, toys, art materials, religious articles, sports paraphernalia and music" (pp. 222–223). After this is done, he suggested ways to open a home to more cultural diversity.

We round out these readings by including a scale that measures racial attitudes (Hamersma, Paige, & Jordan, 1973), which could be used in the family communication classroom; a classroom exercise that explores students' use of racial labels, which could be applied to families (Alicea & Kessel, 1997); and some guidance about how to teach the concept of *racial identity* to classes of predominantly White students using film (Richard, 1996). In particular, Richard (1996) teaches about Helms' (1990) stages of Black identity development using films. For example, *Do the Right Thing* (Lee, 1990) is used to show Helms' (1990) "encounter stage" where, for a Black person, he or she begins a process of questioning self and others about racial issues. This can lead to movement toward developing a positive, realistic Black identity or continue to fuel ambivalence about whether it is better to continue to define one's self in White cultural terms.

CONCLUSION

Problems with race begin at home. Family communication educators are in an especially good position to begin to give guidance and contribute solutions to these problems through increased research as well as by including the stories of African-American families in their classrooms. Future research should examine family communication education using the wide lens of culture. Specifically, family communication researchers should report demographic information about their samples (especially for biracial families), analyze their data for results attributable to culture, and report any significant, culture-specific findings. The Family Communication Division of the National Communication Association should consider ways to attract more African-American faculty and students. Family communication textbook writers should draw upon the existing literature about Black families as well as any culture-specific findings and work to present this information in ways that are culturally sensitive as well as in ways that help to combat racism. This would not necessarily involve developing separate chapters in family communication texts about culture (although it could), but more so using the strands of understanding of the world's many cultures to weave a tapestry that shows a topic's complexity from many different vantage points. In general, this study can be used as a first step toward a trend of continuous self-assessment in the area of ethnic culture for family communication.

In short, we aspire to teach students about family communication in ways that not only speak directly to them and their experiences but also teach them about the role that communication in their families plays in teaching and learning about how to communicate with the world's many others.

REFERENCES

Aldridge, D. P. (1989). *Sourcebook on Black male–female relationships*. Dubuque, IA: Kendall/Hunt.

Aldridge, D. P. (1990). Toward an understanding of Black male/female relationships. In T. Anderson (Ed.), *Black studies: Theory, method, cultural perspective* (pp. 89–97). Pullman: Washington State University Press.

Aldridge, D. P. (1991). *Focusing: Black male–female relationships*. Chicago: Third World.

Alicea, M., & Kessel, B. (1997). The socially awkward question: A simulation exercise for exploring ethnic and racial labels. *Teaching Sociology, 25*, 65–71.

Allen, W. R. (1981). Moms, dads, and boys: Race and sex differences in the socialization of male children. In L. Gary (Ed.), *Black men* (pp. 99–114). Beverly Hills, CA: Sage.

Allen, W. R. (Ed.). (1986). *Black American families, 1965–1984: A classified, selectively annotated bibliography*. New York: Greenwood.

Anderson, T. (1990). Black studies: Overview and theoretical perspectives. In T. Anderson (Ed.), *Black studies: Theory, method, and cultural perspective* (pp. 1–10). Pullman: Washington State University Press.

Asante, M. K. (1980). *Afrocentricity: The theory of social change*. Buffalo, NY: Amulefi.

Asante, M. K. (1981). Black male and female relationships: An Afrocentric context. In L. Gary (Ed.), *Black men* (pp. 75–82). Beverly Hills, CA: Sage.

Asante, M. K. (1990). *Kemet, Afrocentricity and knowledge*. Trenton, NJ: African World.

Asante, M. K. (1993). *Malcolm X as cultural hero and other Afrocentric essays*. Trenton, NJ: African World.

Baldwin, J. A. (1985). *African (Black) personality: From an Africentric framework*. Chicago: Third World.

Baldwin, J. A. (1990). Notes on an Africentric theory of Black personality. In T. Anderson (Ed.), *Black studies: Theory, method, and cultural perspective* (pp. 133–141). Pullman: Washington State University Press.

Baldwin, J. A., & Bell, Y. R. (1990). The African self-consciousness scale: An Africentric personality questionnaire. In T. Anderson (Ed.), *Black studies: Theory, method, and cultural perspective* (pp. 142–150). Pullman: Washington State University Press.

Belgrave, F., Johnson, R., & Carey, C. (1992). Attributional style and its relationship to self-esteem and academic performance of Black students. In A. Burlew, W. Banks, H. McAdoo, & D. Azibo (Eds.), *African American psychology* (pp. 173–182). Newbury Park, CA: Sage.

Bell, Y., Bouie, C. L., & Baldwin, J. A. (1990). Afrocentric cultural consciousness and African-American male–female relationships. *Journal of Black Studies, 21*, 162

Bennett, M. J. (1986). Towards ethnorelativism: A developmental model of intercultural sensitivity. In R. M. Paige (Ed.), *Cross-cultural orientation: New conceptualizations and applications* (pp. 26–51). New York: University Press of America.

Billingsley, A. (1968). *Black families in White America.* Englewood Cliffs, NJ: Prentice-Hall.

Bochner, A. P. (1976). Conceptual frontiers in the study of communication in families: An introduction to the literature. *Human Communication Research, 2,* 381–397.

Boykin, A. W. (1983). The academic performance of Afro-American children. In J. Spense (Ed.), *Achievement and achievement motives.* San Francisco: Freeman.

Boykin, A. W., & Toms, F. D. (1985). Black child socialization: A conceptual framework. In H. McAdoo & J. McAdoo (Eds.), *Black children: Social, educational, and parental environments* (pp. 33–51). Beverly Hills, CA: Sage.

Braithwaite, R. L. (1981). Interpersonal relations between Black males and Black females. In L. Gary (Ed.), *Black men* (pp. 83–97). Beverly Hills, CA: Sage.

Burlew, A. K., Banks, W. C., McAdoo, H. P., & Azibo, D. A. (Eds.). (1992). *African American psychology.* Newbury Park, CA: Sage.

Clark, M. L. (1992). Racial group concept and self-esteem and the academic performance of Black students. In A. Burlew, W. Banks, H. McAdoo, & D. Azibo (Eds.), *African American psychology* (pp. 159–172). Newbury Park, CA: Sage.

Cose, E. (1993). *The rage of a privileged class: Why are middle class Blacks angry? Why should America care?* New York: HarperCollins.

Covin, D. (1990). Afrocentricity in O Movimento Negro Unificado. *Journal of Black Studies, 21,* 126–144.

Daniel, J. E., & Daniel, J. L. (1998). Preschool children's responses to race-related personal names. *Journal of Black Studies, 28,* 471–490.

Daniel, J. L., & Effinger, M. J. (1996). Bosom buddies: A study of intergenerational communication. *Journal of Black Studies, 27,* 183–200.

Dickson, L. (1993). The future of marriage and family in Black America. *Journal of Black Studies, 23,* 472–491.

Diggs, R. C. (1995, June). *Black family communication: A course proposal.* A paper presented at the Speech Communication Association Black Caucus Summer Conference, Frankfort, KY.

Dubois, W. E. B. (1903/1969). *The souls of Black folks.* New York: New American Library.

Edelman, M. W. (1985). The sea is so wide and my boat is so small: Problems facing Black children today. In H. P. McAdoo & J. McAdoo (Eds.), *Black children* (pp. 72–82). Beverly Hills, CA: Sage.

Ellison, R. (1952). *The invisible man.* New York: Random House.

Franklin, A. J., & Boyd-Franklin, N. (1985). A psycho educational perspective on Black parenting. In H. McAdoo & J. McAdoo (Eds.), *Black children: Social, educational, and parental environments* (pp.194–210). Beverly Hills, CA: Sage.

Galvin, K., & Brommel, B. (1996). *Family communication: Cohesion and change* (4th ed.). New York: HarperCollins.

Gary, L. E. (Ed.). (1981). *Black men.* Beverly Hills, CA: Sage.

Hamersma, R. J., Paige, J., & Jordan, J. E. (1973). Construction of a Guttman facet designed cross-cultural attitude-behavior scale toward racial interaction. *Educational and Psychological Measurement, 33,* 565–576.

Hecht, M. L., Collier, M. J., & Ribeau, S. A. (1993). *African American communication: Ethnic identity and cultural interpretation.* Newbury Park, CA: Sage.

Helms, J. (1990). Toward a model of White identity development. In J. Helms (Ed.), *Black and White racial identity* (pp. 49–66). New York: Greenwood Press.

Hill, R. B. (1993). *Research on the African-American family: A holistic perspective.* Westport, CT: Auburn House.

Holliday, B. G. (1985). Developmental imperatives of social ecologies: Lessons learned from Black children. In H. McAdoo, & J. McAdoo (Eds.), *Black children: Social, educational, and parental environments* (pp. 53–69). Beverly Hills, CA: Sage.

Holmes, R. M. (1995). *How young children perceive race.* Thousand Oaks, CA: Sage.

Katz, J. H. (1978). *White awareness: A handbook for anti-racism training.* Norman: University of Oklahoma Press.

King, J. R. (1976). African survivals in the Black American family: Key factors in stability. *Journal of Afro-American Issues, 4,* 153–167.

Kivel, P. (1996). *Uprooting racism: How White people can work for racial justice*. Philadelphia: New Society.

Kochman, T. (1981). *Black and White styles in conflict*. Chicago: University of Chicago Press.

Lee, S. (Producer, Writer, Director). (1990). *Do the right thing* [film]. (Available from MCA Home Video).

Littlejohn-Blake, S. M., & Anderson-Darling, C. (1993). Understanding the strengths of African American families. *Journal of Black Studies, 23*, 460–471.

McAdoo, H. P. (Ed.). (1981). *Black families*. Beverly Hills, CA: Sage.

McAdoo, H. P. (1992). Upward mobility and parenting in middle-income Black families. In A. Burlew, W. Banks, H. McAdoo, & D. Azibo (Eds.), *African American psychology: Theory, research, and practice* (pp. 63–86). Newbury Park, CA: Sage.

McAdoo, H. P., & McAdoo, J. L. (Eds.). (1985). *Black children: Social, educational, and parental environments*. Beverly Hills, CA: Sage.

McAdoo, J. L. (1981). Black father and child interactions. In L. Gary (Ed.), *Black men* (pp. 115–130). Beverly Hills, CA: Sage.

National Research Council. (1989). *A common destiny: Blacks and American society*. Washington, D.C.: National Academy Press.

Nobles, W. (1974). Africanity: Its role in Black families. *The Black scholar, 5*, 10–17.

Nobles, W., & Goddard, L. L. (1984). *Understanding the Black family: A guide for scholarship and research*. Oakland, CA: Institute of Black Family Life and Culture.

Richard, H. W. (1996). Filmed in Black and White: Teaching the concept of racial identity at a predominantly White university. *Teaching Psychology, 23*, 159–161.

Rosenblatt, P. C., Karis, T. A., & Powell, R. D. (1995). *Multiracial couples: Black and White voices*. Thousand Oaks, CA: Sage.

Shimkin, D., Shimkin, E. M., & Frate, D. A. (Eds.). (1987). *The extended family in Black society*. Hague, Netherlands: Mouton.

Socha, T. J., Sanchez-Hucles, J., Bromley, J., & Kelly, B. (1995). Invisible parents and children: African American parent–child communication. In T. Socha & G. Stamp (Eds.), *Parents, children, and communication: Frontiers of theory and research* (pp. 127–145). Hillsdale, NJ: Lawrence Erlbaum Associates.

Spencer, M. (1982). Personal and group identity of Black children: An alternative synthesis. *Genetic Psychology Monographs, 103*, 59–84.

Spencer, M. (1983). Children's cultural values and parental childrearing strategies. *Developmental Review, 3*, 351–379.

Spencer, M. (1984). Black children's race awareness, racial attitudes, and self-concept: An interpretation. *Journal of Clinical Psychology and Psychiatry, 25*, 433–441.

Spencer, M. (1988). Self-concept development. In D. Slaughter (Ed.), *Black children and poverty: A developmental perspective* (pp. 104–123). San Francisco: Jossey-Bass.

Staples, R. (1981). *The world of Black singles: Changing patterns in male–female relations*. Westport, CT: Greenwood.

Sudarkasa, N. (1980). African and Afro-American family structure: A comparison. *The Black Scholar, 11*, 37–60.

Taylor, R. L. (1981). Psychological modes of adaptation. In L. Gary (Ed.), *Black men* (pp. 141–158). Beverly Hills, CA: Sage.

Turner, L. H., & West, R. (1998). *Perspectives on family communication*. Mountain View, CA: Mayfield.

Williams, O. (1978). *American Black women in the arts and social sciences: A bibliographic survey*. Metuchen, NJ: Scarecrow.

Willie, C. V. (1976). *A new look at Black families*. Bayside, NY: General Hall.

Wilson, M. N. (1992). Perceived parental activity of mothers, fathers, and grandmothers in three-generational Black families. In A. Burlew, W. Banks, H. McAdoo, & D. Azibo (Eds.), *African American psychology: Theory, research, and practice* (pp. 87–104). Newbury Park, CA: Sage.

Whitchurch, G. (1992). Communication in marriage and the family: A review essay of family communication textbooks. *Communication Education, 41*, 337–343.

Epilogue: Illuminating and Evoking Issues of Race and Family Communication

Kathleen Galvin
Northwestern University

Communication, Race, and Family: Exploring Communication in Black, White, and Biracial Families stands as a groundbreaking and evocative work that scholars and students alike will find compelling and insightful. The editors and contributors tackle tough and uneasy questions in a straightforward manner, illuminating scholarly concerns and modeling research agendas before only imagined by family communication scholars. A decade from now, these chapters will be seen as making a seminal contribution to significant research and thinking regarding the constitutive and reflective nature of communication about race within families. The authors' multimethodological contributions certainly will inspire young scholars to forge their own paths in related areas and their personal reflections will haunt readers' minds long after the last page has been turned.

Consideration of family ethnicity is significant to communication scholars because, contrary to popular myth, Americans have not become homogenized in a "melting pot." McGoldrick (1993) argued that ethnic values and identification are retained for many generations after immigration and play a significant role in family life and personal development throughout the life cycle, and Billingsley (1992) stressed the powerful role of African heritage in current African-American families. Cultural heritage affects family communication patterns across generations (McGoldrick & Gerson, 1985).

My reading of *Communication, Race, and Family* reveals issues of themes, future directions, and personal impact. The themes of communication competence, dialectical tensions, and contextual factors emerge as unifying forces. Multiple authors identify unique competencies for discussing and confronting racial concerns within the family. Socha and Diggs (chap. 1) establish the groundwork by identifying family as the context for constructing and managing an individual's ethnic/racial identity. Daniel and Daniel (chap. 2) provide compelling descriptions of parental racial socialization processes in response to the "hot stove" of racism, and articulate the necessity of developing the imperative communication mode to ensure a child's physical and psychological survival. Such an emphasis extends earlier findings on parenting minority children in the United States (Julian, McKenry, & McKelvey, 1994). Ferguson (chap. 3) continues this theme with her examination of derogation, powerful in its physical or psychological danger, thus necessitating parental instruction for responding to racial insults. Parents, quite literally, become communication educators as they teach children to select and implement self-protective strategies. Diggs (chap. 6) contributes the importance of positive parent messages regarding self, such as reinforcing the unique and social self. From a different perspective, Davilla (chap. 5) highlights the paucity of meaningful language for engaging in communication about race, especially for young people growing up in families in homogeneous White communities. Whereas most African-American family members develop communication competencies to socialize children against racism and derogation as well as to build self-esteem, such competencies remain invisible to European-American family members, many of whom have limited competence to discuss race.

Communication, Race, and Family foregrounds issues of struggle as Socha and Diggs cite the dialectics of integration–segregation and understanding–bigotry as tensions inherent in diverse, multicultural societies. In addition, the text raises other, related dialectical struggles including similarity–difference and protection–risk taking. Alexander and LeBlanc (chap. 9) discuss experiences of shared regional upbringing and a sense of shared "otherness or unity in opposition," reminding readers of the similarities that are frequently forgotten amidst the polarities. Orbe (chap. 8) depicts the multiethnic family as both a site of potential coming together and a place of identity struggle. As she addresses symbolic exchange between married couples, Dainton reports a similarity of marital experience for African-American and European-American couples, while speculating that biracial couples reflect a unique culture that may represent cultural transformation.

The protection–risk taking dialectic illuminates related tensions. The issues of protection receive significant attention; the simultaneous counterpart of risking or reaching out remains less developed. Orbe's (chap. 8) description of four orientations of interracial families communicating about race captures the struggle inherent in making sense of the needs for child protection, ties to kinship networks, and connections across boundaries. This extends the work of Rosenblatt, Karis, and Powell (1995) who discuss the pressure on biracial children to decide if they are Black or White, describing the protectiveness of some Black parents who exhibit concern about a White spouse's competence to socialize their child to live in a racist society. While Orbe (chap. 8) reflects on his life in a biracial family, Alexander and LeBlanc (chap. 9) model the outcome of engaging in cultural dialogue through the construction of Black–White narratives; each piece underscores risk taking as well as protection.

Contextual factors, especially the media, serve to remind readers of the many ways racial messages impact family understanding of race. Parks (chap. 4) demonstrates the extent to which racial socialization occurs through media choices, while Davilla (chap. 5) addresses the potentially powerful media influence on racial discussion in all White communities. Diggs (chap. 6) identifies the peer community as contextual factor, suggesting the important self-esteem messages arising from this source.

Future scholarly directions will involve attention to more subtle shadings of race-oriented family communication. For example, the concept of family will be considered more fully in terms of structure, socioeconomic status, and ethnicity. Family structure needs further delineation because there is considerable difference in family structure by race and strong variations across cultures on familial issues such as age at first marriage, single parenthood, divorce, older marriages, remarriage, and male and female roles (Dilworth-Anderson & Burton, 1996; Heaton & Jacobson, 1994). Even the definition of the concept family differs across ethnic groups; whereas the majority "White Anglo-Saxon" definition focuses on the intact nuclear unit, African-American families focus on a wide kinship network. The communication dynamics of single-parent families, with or without an extended kin community, needs attention because there is a higher proportion of births to unmarried Black women (70%) than to unmarried White women (25%; Blau, Ferber, & Winkler, 1997). Socioeconomic status will receive attention because African-American or Hispanic-American families are more likely to be poor (Zill & Nord, 1994), a factor which creates racial isolation and exacerbates stresses that impact family interaction. Parks (chap. 4) foreshadows this issue suggesting Black middle- and lower-class families receive more similar media choices than their White counterparts. Orbe (chap. 8) forecasts research that examines factors including socioeconomic status and gender.

The predicted increase in American interracial families should herald more interracial family research; Black–White ties, however, are expected to remain limited. According to Lind (1998), 1 in 25 American married couples today are interracial, but "although black-out marriage rates have risen, they remain much lower than out-marriage rates for Hispanics, Asians, and American Indians" (p. 38). Similar findings for interracial adoption, international and national, indicate interracial boundary crossing is less likely to involve Black children (Lewin, 1998). Clearly communication and boundary issues will remain part of the research agenda for the foreseeable future.

Finally, *Communication, Race, and Family* will impact family communication, education, and related instructional materials. This text will be cited in numerous textbooks, classroom discussions, and scholarly papers and serve as the impetus to develop units and courses in communication in Black, White, and biracial families. In addition, it provides family communication teachers and scholars with an incredible wealth of bibliographic resources (e.g., see Socha and Beigle's primer of readings, chap. 10). Hopefully it will influence marital and family enrichment programs offered by religious and civic organizations.

The impact of *Communication, Race, and Family* goes beyond the academic. After reading the opening chapters, I found myself reflecting on a turning point in my family life as the White mother of an Asian daughter who began to encounter her sense of otherness as a toddler. The following recreates her verbal attempt to make sense of her reality: "Mommy, you have blue eyes. Daddy has blue eyes. Matthew has blue eyes. Katie has blue eyes. Mommy, I have brown eyes." Thus began an ongoing dialogue which, although representing a biracial Asian/White family interaction, raised issues of difference and racial socialization, imperatives for handling derogation, as well as sibling strategies of explanation and defense. There are significant communication experiences contained within these chapters.

This work serves as a testimonial to the efforts of Black and White colleagues to write together on difficult issues as well as efforts by Black and White scholars to risk joining a dialogue of immense importance to our field. Now that the silence has been broken more voices must join the conversation.

REFERENCES

Billingsley, A., (1992). *Climbing Jacob's ladder—The enduring legacy of African-American families.* New York: Simon & Schuster.

Blau, F. D., Ferber, M. A., & Winkler, A. E. (1997). *The economics of women, men and work* (3rd ed.). Upper Saddle River, NJ: Prentice-Hall.

Dilworth-Anderson, P., & Burton, L. M. (1996). Rethinking family development: Critical conceptual issues in the study of diverse groups. *Journal of Social and Personal Relationships, 13,* 325–334.

Heaton, T. B., & Jacobson, C. K. (1994). Race differences in changing family demographics in the 1980's. *Journal of Family Issues, 15,* 290–308.

Julien, T. W., McKenry, P. C., & McKelvey, M. W. (1994). Cultural variations in parenting perception of Caucasian, African-American, Hispanic, and Asian-American parents. *Family Relations, 43,* 30–37.

Lewin, T. (1998, October 27). New families redraw racial boundaries. *New York Times,* pp. A1, A18.

Lind, M. (1998, August 15). The beige and the black. *The New York Times Magazine,* pp. 38–39.

McGoldrick, M. (1993). Ethnicity, cultural and diversity and normality. In F. Walsh (Ed.) *Normal family processes* (2nd ed.), (pp. 331–336). New York: Guilford Press.

McGoldrick, M., & Gerson, R. (1985). *Genograms in family assessment.* New York: W. W. Norton.

Rosenblatt, P. C., Karis, T. A., & Powell, R. D. (1995). *Multiracial couples—Black & White voices.* Thousand Oaks, CA: Sage.

Zill, N., & Nord, C. W. (1994). *Running in place: How American families are faring in a changing economy and an individualistic society.* Washington, DC: Child Trends.

About the Contributors

EDITORS

Thomas J. Socha (PhD, University of Iowa) is University Professor and Associate Professor of Communication at Old Dominion University in Norfolk, Virginia. His primary areas of teaching and research are family communication, group communication, children's communication, and research methods. Dr. Socha has published various articles and chapters in these areas as well as a coedited book, *Parents, Children and Communication: Frontiers of Theory and Research* (with Dr. Glen Stamp; 1995, Lawrence Erlbaum Associates). He has been quoted in newspapers and magazines including *TV GUIDE*, *Redbook*, *Chicago Tribune*, and the *Orlando Sentinel* among others about family communication and children's communication. Dr. Socha was named editor of the *Journal of Family Communication* (Lawrence Erlbaum Associates). In 1999, he serves as the Chair of the Family Communication Division of the National Communication Association and Chair of the Interpersonal Division of the Southern States Communication Association.

Rhunette C. Diggs (PhD, Ohio State University) is Assistant Professor of Communication at the University of Louisville in Louisville, Kentucky. Her primary areas of teaching and research are family communication and interpersonal communication, as well as teaching courses in small group communication, communication research methods, and communication theory. Dr. Diggs' research focuses on family communication and self-esteem, particularly that of adolescents'. She is both a consultant and communication trainer for various family and children's agencies.

CONTRIBUTORS

Bryant K. Alexander (PhD, Southern Illinois University at Carbonbdale) is Assistant Professor in the Department of Communication Studies at California State University, Los Angeles. His research interests include cultural identity and critical pedagogy in performing culture in the classroom.

Molefi Asante is Professor and Chair, Department of African American Studies at Temple University. Dr. Asante has published 38 books and more than 200 articles and is the founder of the theory of Afrocentricity. Dr. Asante's work is cited widely and includes consultancies for numerous school districts (e.g., New York, Detroit) concerning rewriting curricula.

Jennifer Beigle is a graduate student at the University of North Carolina at Greensboro. Ms. Beigle is a former president of Old Dominion University's chapter of the Lambda Pi Eta, the National Communication Honor Society and a former Undergraduate Teaching Assistant in Communication. She is interested in group communication and has presented her work at the Undergraduate Honors Conference of the Southern States Communication Association.

Marianne Dainton is Assistant Professor of Communication at Lasalle University in Philadelphia. Her publications have appeared in *Journal of Social and Personal Relationships* and *Family Relations*. She has prepared various chapters as well. Her focus is on everyday and routine communication that shapes and characterizes everyday relationships.

Jack L. Daniel is Associate Professor and Vice Provost for Academic Affairs, University of Pittsburgh. One of the founders of the National Communication Association's Black Caucus and an active researcher of African American communication, he is examining intergenerational communication as well as writing a psychological novel, *We Fish,* which addresses African-American father–son relationships.

Jerlean E. Daniel is Assistant Professor, Program in Child Development and Child Care, School of Social Work, University of Pittsburgh. She is President of the National Association for the Education of Young Children.

Roberta A. Davilla (PhD, Ohio University) is an Assistant Professor of Communication Studies at the University of Northern Iowa. Her research interests include parent–child communication, parent–adolescent communication, and instructional development.

Isabel B. Ferguson is an attorney (JD, University of Pennsylvania Law School) and communication researcher (MA, Annenberg School of Communication, University of Pennsylvania) who collaborates on communication projects examining the evaluation of child development and educational programs, legal argumentation, as well as parent–child communication.

Kathleen Galvin is Professor of Communication and Associate Dean of the School of Communication, Northwestern University. Dr. Galvin published the first and highly successful family communication textbook in the field of communication as well other books, articles, and chapters about family communication, interpersonal communication, and communication education. Dr. Galvin is also a family therapist.

H. Paul LeBlanc, III is a doctoral student in Interpersonal Communication in the Department of Speech Communication at Southern Illinois University at Carbondale. His research interests include family interaction and negotiation of rules, roles, and relationships. He is particularly interested in multimethod inquiry of family communication.

Mark P. Orbe (PhD, Ohio University) is an Assistant Professor of Speech Communication at Western Michigan University (recent update). Dr. Orbe's research interests focus on the effects of culture on communication in various contexts including interpersonal and family systems. His research has appeared in journals (e.g., *Howard Journal of Communication, Communication Quarterly, Communication Studies*) as well as in several edited volumes. He is completing a book-length manuscript that explores the relationship between communication, culture, and power.

Sheri L. Parks (PhD, University of Massachusetts) is Associate Professor of American Studies and Associate Dean of Undergraduate Studies at the University of Maryland in College Park, Maryland. Her primary interests involve public aesthetics, family, and culture. Active in public discussions of media texts and the role of media in lives of families, she has been quoted by the *Washington Post, Los Angeles Times, Parenting Magazine, The New York Times,* and *The Baltimore Sun,* and has appeared on *The NBC Evening News with Tom Brockaw.* She is completing a book on the Black mother and popular culture.

Author Index

A

Abernathy, T. J., 153, 154, *164*
Aboud, F. E., 4, *21*
Abramowitz, R., 70, *88*
Adams, G. R., 105, 106, 137, *143*
Adams, J. H., 30, *41*
Adelmann, P. K., 148, 149, 154, *164*
Adler, P. S., 19, *21*, 100, 103
Aldridge, D. P., 170, *178*, 216, 222, 225
Alejandro-Wright, M. N., 29, *41*
Alexander, A., 69, *88*
Alicea, M., 216, 224, *225*
Allen, B. A., 52, 66
Allen, W. R., 11, *22*, 29, *43*, 46, 67, 107, *143*,
    209, 215, 216, 223, *225*
Ancelet, B. J., 184, *206*
Anderson, E., 8, *22*
Anderson-Darling, C., 216, *227*
Anderson, T., 216, *225*
Andreasen, M. S., 69, 70, *88*
Applegate, J. L., 31, *42*, 142, *143*
Aronson, E., 48, 54, 66
Asante, M. K., 3, 11, 12, 13, *21*, *22*, 106, 107,
    109, 121, 140, 141, 142, *143*, 148,
    164, 215, 216, 218, 222, *225*
Azibo, D. A., 215, *226*

B

Baerger, D. R., 148, 149, 154, *164*
Baldwin, J. A., 13, 14, *22*, 28, *41*,163, *164*, 216,
    225
Baldwin, J. D., 108, 109, 110, *143*
Bandura, A., 108, 109, 110, *143*
Banks, W. C., 215, *226*

Bantz, C. R., 20, *22*
Bates, K. G., 140, *143*
Bateson, G., 201, *207*
Bauman, R., 198, *206*
Baumrind, D., 77, 79, 85, *88*
Baxter, L. A., 201, *207*
Beals, G., 167, *179*
Beebe, S. A., 127, *143*
Beebe, S. J., 127, *143*
Belgrave, F., 216, 221, *225*
Bell, Y. R., 13, 14, *22*, 163, *164*, 216, *225*
Bender, L., 3, 5, *22*
Bennett, M. J., 4, 17, 19, *22*, 209, *226*
Bernstein, B., 30, *42*
Billingsley, A., 220, *226*, 229, *232*
Bingham, S. G., 51, 66
Blaine, B., 108, 109, 115, 119, 127, 129, *143*
Blau, F. D., 231, *232*
Blumer, H., 121, 123, 124, 137, *143*, 147, *164*
Blyth, D. A., 111, *145*
Bobo, L., 150, *164*
Bochner, A. P., 215, *226*
Bogart, L., 47, 66
Bogdan, R., 185, *207*
Boscolo, L., 74, *89*
Bouie, C. L., 163, *164*, 216, *225*
Bower, R. T., 72, *88*
Boyd-Franklin, N., 29, *42*, 52, 66, 216, 222, *226*
Boykin, A. W., 5, *22*, 51, 52, 66, 209, 216, 217,
    221, *226*
Bradford, L., 110, 112, 115, 136, 145, 161, *164*
Braithwaite, R. L., 216, 222, *226*
Brasseaux, C. A., 182, 184, *207*
Braxton, G., 71, *88*
Broadnax, S., 108, 109, 115, 119, 127, 129, *143*
Brody, G. H., 149, *164*
Broman, C. L., 149, *164*

Subject Index

243